Branding With Brains

In an increasingly competitive world, we believe it's quality of thinking that gives you the edge – an idea that opens new doors, a technique that solves a problem, or an insight that simply makes sense of it all. The more you know, the smarter and faster you can go.

That's why we work with the best minds in the business and finance to bring cutting-edge thinking and best learning practice to a global market.

Under a range of leading imprints, including *Financial Times Prentice Hall*, we create world-class print publications and electronic products bringing our readers knowledge, skills and understanding, which can be applied whether studying or at work.

To find out more about Pearson Education publications, or tell us about the books you'd like to find, you can visit us at **www.pearsoned.co.uk**

Branding With Brains

The science of getting customers to choose your company

Tjaco Walvis

Financial Times Prentice Hall is an imprint of

Harlow, England • London • New York • Boston • San Francisco • Toronto • Sydney • Singapore • Hong Kong
Tokyo • Seoul • Taipei • New Delhi • Cape Town • Madrid • Mexico City • Amsterdam • Munich • Paris • Milan

PEARSON EDUCATION LIMITED

Edinburgh Gate
Harlow CM20 2JE
Tel: +44 (0)1279 623623
Fax: +44 (0)1279 431059
Website: www.pearsoned.co.uk

First published in Great Britain in 2010

ISBN: 978-0-273-71995-3

British Library Cataloguing-in-Publication Data
A catalogue record for this book is available from the British Library

Library of Congress Cataloging-in-Publication Data
A catalog record for this book is available from the Library of Congress

10 9 8 7 6 5 4 3 2 1
14 13 12 11 10

Designed by Sue Lamble
Typeset in 9.5pt Melior by 30
Printed and bound by Ashford Colour Press, Gosport

The publisher's policy is to use paper manufactured from sustainable forests.

Contents

Word of gratitude / vii
Publisher's acknowledgements / viii
Introduction / ix
How a disturbing compliment gave rise to a book

1 Where branding gets it wrong / 3
Branding suffers from a flawed model of how customers decide and misconceptions about how strong brands are built

2 Persuading subconscious minds / 21
Customers make brand choices using a subconscious but stable algorithm that favours brands built according to three laws: relevance, coherence and participation

3 Law No.1: Relevance / 47
Brands built to be distinctively relevant are more likely to be chosen by the brain

4 Making your brand uniquely rewarding / 65
Know your customers' subconscious cocktails of goals and be radical in how your brand delivers upon them

5 Law No.2: Coherence / 85
Brands built to be coherent through time and space are picked by the brain's algorithm

6 Aligning the business with the brand strategy / 113

Integrate everything you do by working from a specific but flexible brand concept that is meaningful for everyone, from customers to the CEO

7 Law No.3: Participation / 139

Brands that are open and participatory are favoured by the brand-choice algorithm

8 Getting your audience to enter the game / 165

Make participation immediately rewarding and rethink every medium to be more engaging

9 Is this book morally wrong? / 191

Users – and not ideas – carry ethical responsibilities, so it all comes down to you

10 Come again? / 209

Can you please repeat what you just said?

Notes / 221

Index / 237

Word of gratitude

To Roland van der Vorst, Kim Dingler, Sander Bakker, Patrick van der Gronde, Zwier Veldhoen, Ruben Esser, Boris Nihom and everyone at THEY for your help and enormous support.

To Professor Dr Wiep van Bunge, Dr Andreas Kaufmann, Erik van der Meijden, Huib Morelisse, Liz Gooster, Rupert Morris, Professor Dr Jack Vroomen and Professor Dr Fred van Raaij for your time and invaluable comments and suggestions.

To Harjo, Dieneke and Tjeerd Walvis, Sven van der Steen and Alfred van Bunge for encouraging me to push boundaries.

To Jolene, Maudy, Mare and Jette for being the most important, heartening, encouraging and lovely women in my life.

To everyone who helped me along the way, thank you all!

Publisher's acknowledgements

We are grateful to the following for permission to reproduce copyright material:

Screenshots
Screenshot on page 176 from Contest dates for preliminaries, http://edition.cnn.com/ELECTION/2008/primaries/results/scorecard/, Courtesy CNN

The Financial Times
Graphic on page 116 from Starbucks article, Dec 12th 2008, www.ft.com, Financial Times

The publisher would like to thank the following for their kind permission to reproduce their photographs:

(Key: b-bottom; c-centre; l-left; r-right; t-top)

Architectural Association Photo Library: Suzanne Schmelcher 157; **Corbis:** CNRI / Med Net 212cl, Images.com 212cr; **DK Images:** 20-21; **Getty Images:** AFP 101, 124, 147, 169, AFP 101, 124, 147, 169, Alan Thornton 64-65, Junko Kimura 201, Nicolette Wells 164–165, Smari 84-85, Time & Life Pictures 39, 55, 138-139; **GNU Free Documentation license:** 2-3, 179cl, 190-191 ; **Pearson Education Royalty-Free / Commissioned:** Medio Images 31, Photodisc 37, Photodisc / Photolink / S. Meltzer 208-209; **Press Association Images:** Matt Slocum 112–113; **Ruflanz Advertising Agency:** Ruf Lanz, Markus Ruf, Danielle Lanz 88; **The Advertising Archives:** 94, 106, 122, 123, 152; **The Coffee Company:** 179c; **THEY:** Lies Musch @Witman Kleipool 97

All other images © Pearson Education

Every effort has been made to trace the copyright holders and we apologise in advance for any unintentional omissions. We would be pleased to insert the appropriate acknowledgement in any subsequent edition of this publication.

Introduction

'You know, I really admire you guys', a client told us after our final presentation to the board he chaired. 'It is an achievement how you make such a vague subject like branding this concrete.' It was a nice enough compliment, but it worried me. It was the fact that he so casually and confidently described our discipline as 'vague'!

Not everyone is as candid, of course, but this executive is by no means the only decision maker who sees branding this way. Indeed, in my experience, the higher you go up the hierarchy the more likely you are to meet people who see branding as an intuitive and rather unprofessional field, driven by fads, jargon, unsupported assumptions, an uncomfortable reliance on popular culture and an unclear relationship with the bottom line. It is not that these executives do not understand the value of brands. They see that some brands influence the choices of customers and stakeholders. Many know that strong brands can be worth up to 75 per cent of the entire market value of listed companies. But, in their thinking, those are the brands of others. And many executives assume (incorrectly) that they are consumer brands that invest huge sums in advertising. In short, there is a big gap between the economic value of brands and the professionalism and image of the discipline that builds them. The point is that in many boardrooms all over the world, there is no common framework for clear and intelligent discussions about how brand strategy contributes to growth. And marketers have found it very hard to change this.

Let me go straight to one of the root causes of this problem, and the core subject of this book, by asking you a question. When you last bought a soft drink, a car, a pair of jeans, a copier, corporate banking services, or any other branded product or service, did you know why you chose that particular brand? Think about it for a moment. Do we have any idea why, out of the dozens of possible brands we know, we select a particular one? Although we can rationalise it afterwards, the honest answer is no. Our brain selects it for us, largely below our awareness. Neuroscientific studies make it increasingly clear that our brain makes the majority of our choices almost entirely subconsciously and only the outcome of that process gains access to our conscious mind. Consequently, we simply have little clue about how and why we buy.

But if we ourselves have no clue, how can branding play its role in matching supply and demand in an increasingly complex, abundant and globalised world? What can marketers, who make their living trying to persuade us to buy their brand, hope to do? It is literally a billion-dollar question. And our inability so far to provide concrete answers to this question is the main cause of the fuzziness of branding as a profession and the uncertainty about its effectiveness. So how do the billions of human brains in the world go about making brand choices? And how can you make sure your brand influences those choices in your favour when clients decide which brand to buy?

The answer presented in this book is as simple as it is intriguing. The brain makes brand choices in much the same way as Google selects websites: it follows something we can call a subconscious algorithm and this algorithm is highly stable. This algorithm favours brands built according to three principles that I call the three 'laws' of branding: relevance, coherence and participation. Brands built according to these three laws emerge from our subconscious brain and have the highest chance of being chosen. This simple finding has enormous consequences for branding professionals. It provides deep insight into how we make choices ourselves as customers and into the way marketers try to influence us. In fact, it has vast implications for everyone trying to influence and persuade others consistently, over longer periods of time. It does not matter whether you are a company selling branded products and services in global or local markets, a city seeking to host the Olympic Games or a world fair, or a government seeking to rescue the environment. In all cases you need to change people's long-term attitudes and behaviours in your favour to succeed. The principles discussed in this book will guide you in this quest. Web marketers play on Google's algorithm to make sure their site appears as high up the search list as possible. Similarly, marketers should play on the brain's algorithm to make sure their brand is chosen out of the thousands of brands stored in our long-term memory. So what does the algorithm look like and how can you tailor your brand strategies to it? That is what this book is about. Reading it will help you build stronger brands more effectively and confidently. It will give you a framework for more professional strategic branding discussions in your organisation, stimulating you to reflect on what is wise and what is unwise in branding. It will give you a profound insight into the way brands persuade you as a customer. And finally, it will help make branding less vague and more concrete!

When the world zigs, zag

This line is the motto of a great advertising agency.[1] I mention it because it is insightful, but also because in a way it sums up the nature of this book. Writings on branding often validate the prejudice against the industry that my client voiced, that there is more form than substance to it. Marketing books and speeches often favour hyperboles above intellectual rigour, for obvious reasons of self-promotion. Some would say that there are few fields that can match us in our fondness for fuzz. My goal here is to find out what makes branding effective. Instead of just adding another book to the pile, I take a fundamental, no-nonsense look at branding and ask: what is the bottom line in branding? What is the essence? What are the goals we must aim for? These questions have been asked before. But my approach to answering them is new. I will show you how brands built in the right way can create the physical changes in our brain that shape our behaviour. Now that is quite a 'zag'.

This book is based on a comprehensive scientific review of fundamental neuroscientific research. Over a two-year period, I analysed hundreds of research projects – including Nobel Prize-winning work – aimed at understanding the functioning of the smallest elements of our brain: neurons, or brain cells (Walvis,

Tjaco H. (2008) Three Laws of Branding: Neuroscientific Foundations of Effective Brand Building, *Journal of Brand Management*). That study and this book are the first in the world to apply findings from this 'micro' level of the brain to branding, in a systematic way. (Most other books rely only on functional magnetic resonance imaging (fMRI) scanner studies that look at the brain as a whole and hence draw conclusions that are more general and less suitable for actioning.) This book presents the practical consequences of these insights for executives, marketers and branding professionals, arising out of more than a decade of experience that I have gained in brand consultancy and advertising.

There is enormous practical and scientific interest in the convergence of marketing and economics on the one hand and neuroscience on the other. A new field called 'neuromarketing' studies how marketing works or fails to work in our brain and how products or advertising campaigns could be improved. Thus far, it has only reported rather fragmentary findings and does not yet provide a new, practical model for brand strategy that marketers can use to build brands more effectively.

I believe we need to go one level deeper and take a perspective on branding that goes more in the direction of 'neuroeconomics': a new field that studies choice behaviour by combining neuroscientific data with established economic theory.[2] It is a much bigger and more rigorous field that is richer in scientific data and more advanced in the theory of how we make choices. My focus, however, will be on explaining a practical framework. I am less concerned with scientific details – although I provide references for those who are interested. The result is that this book gives you a new appreciation of how our brains choose brands. It also provides a reliable and practical framework for building the kinds of brands that draw our brains to them.

The principles I will explain have been shaped and applied in the branding practice at THEY, and before that when I acted as a private consultant and researcher. My current work as a partner at THEY is focused on positioning, brand architecture and concept development, in a wide range of industries including fashion, fast-moving consumer goods, financial services, government, media and publishing, pharmaceuticals, private banking, postal services, retail, regional and city branding, telecommunications and world expositions. I have worked closely with and learned from outstanding colleagues, large and small national and international clients, media companies and research agencies, as well as creatives, designers, architects, management consultants, retail specialists, internet marketers, brand activation specialists, academics and other professionals. This book presents a synthesis of this experience. However, not only the smart and intelligent lessons are included. I also present examples of what I call 'brainless branding', because failures can be at least as instructive as successes. As a result, this book allows you to separate the wheat from the chaff in branding. It will help you build stronger brands faster, more reliably and at lower cost by helping you to concentrate on what matters most.

Are we irrational?

Some of my findings are quite shocking. Ever since the concept of the subconscious began to influence the thinking of business leaders in the 1920s, it has been pitched against the idea of rational behaviour. That is, we are either acting out our erratic, subconscious drives or we are rational. Some people, notably American commentator Walter Lipman, went so far as to argue that if it is true that people are driven by subconscious and thus irrational forces, then we need to rethink mass democracy.[3] We have long been afraid of the subconscious. But is this justified? And what does subconscious choice mean for branding?

I believe that equating the subconscious with irrationality is simplistic and wrong. The dichotomy between being rationally driven and subconsciously driven is a false one. Instead, we will combine both sides of the debate, based on scientific evidence, to suggest that our brain behaves rationally, but in a subconscious way. That is, the brain's subconscious brand choices are strongly biased towards optimising reward, based on our personal goals. Studies show that this goes not only for humans but also for animals (for example, birds and monkeys), indicating that this feature is not a uniquely human characteristic but the result of an evolutionary struggle for survival.[4] In some cases our brain aims to balance risks or costs with rewards (weighing the costs of World Cup tickets against the chances of watching a good game, for example). In other cases it aims to experience certain mental and emotional states (for instance, by selecting ClubMed for a family holiday). In yet other situations the goal is to influence how others see us (such as by buying a Patek Philippe watch). I will argue that in all these cases, our brain's 'search engine' pulls out from our vast memory the brand that can best and most reliably satisfy our 'cocktail of goals' in the given situation. This cocktail of goals is highly situation- and category-specific and can change from moment to moment. But the end result is that the brain generally behaves in a way that is rational and goal-optimising. And this starting point offers an exciting new way of thinking about customer behaviour and brand strategy that we will explore in the chapters that follow.

Reading guide

Chapter 1 analyses the problematic state of branding and outlines the book's new approach to building brands more effectively and reliably. How can we build stronger brands faster, and more quickly and cheaply? The framework outlined in this chapter is an answer to this question. Chapter 2 shows that our choice processes take place almost entirely subconsciously. It introduces a new paradigm for understanding brand choice. Does subconscious choice mean we are irrational? Is branding always manipulation because it is aimed at influencing the subconscious? This chapter deals with these controversial issues, among others.

Chapter 3 takes up the idea that three laws determine the likelihood that a brand is chosen by the brain's brand-choice algorithm. The first one is the law of relevance. But what does it mean and why is it a true 'law'? In this chapter, Leica is an important case study. Chapter 4 presents tools for implementing the law of relevance. What are the consequences of the first law and what must you do to put it into action?

Chapter 5 discusses the law of coherence. What is this law and why does it work? What are the consequences of ignoring it and how can chief executive officers (CEOs) work with it? Chapter 6 describes ways in which this second law can be implemented. In these chapters we look at McKinsey & Company, Volkswagen and Starbucks among other cases.

Chapter 7 describes the third and final law, that of participation. What is participation and why does it work? In Chapter 8 we ask how brands can engage their audience. What are the drivers of participation? Some of the cases discussed are Nike Plus, Barack Obama's presidential election campaign and *The Dark Knight*.

The key question in Chapter 9 is, can we apply medical neuroscientific knowledge and use it to sell more branded products and services? Is this book ethically wrong? It discusses these moral issues by applying three widely accepted moral theories (those of Immanuel Kant, Aristotle and John Stuart Mill) to the book itself. It provides executives with arguments to make their case against allegations about doubtful morality in connection with this new approach.

Chapter 10 summarises the main actions for implementation gleaned from this book. If you are not interested in the 'what' and the 'why' but just want to know what you must do, you could go straight to this chapter, or refer back to it as you read through the earlier part of the book.

Chapter 1

Where branding gets it wrong

For many companies around the world, their brand is their single most valuable asset. Coca-Cola, Microsoft, IBM, GE, Intel, Nokia, Toyota and Disney – some of the world's most powerful brands – have brand values of between $25 and $70 billion. Brands account for more than a quarter of these companies' market capitalisation (the number of outstanding shares multiplied by the share price). Meanwhile, companies from some of the world's most rapidly expanding markets, like Lenovo from China, Tata from India and Havaianas from Brazil, are acutely aware of the value of their brands. Bangalore-based GMR recently announced that it conducted a brand valuation project.

The shares of strong brand companies consistently outperform the general stock market index and are less risky investments (see Figure 1.1). Why? Because strong brands, more so than weak

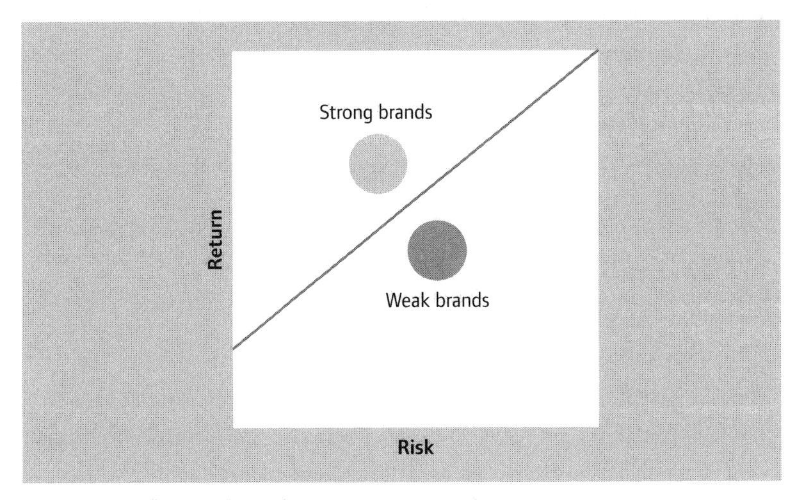

FIGURE 1.1 Strong brands are more attractive investments

brands, boost sales, improve margins and reduce cash flow volatility for their owners. Branding is therefore a powerful risk management tool for firms, their chief financial officers (CFOs), and private equity and other investors. In the face of an economic downturn, brands can provide a cushion against revenue decline, as people are more loyal to strong brands than to weak ones. One study showed that if you had invested $1,000 in a portfolio of companies with strong brands, your investment would have been worth $4,525 six years later versus $3,195 if you had put it in the general stock market. The difference of $1,330 is attributable to better branding. And this phenomenon is seen not only in consumer segments driven by advertising but also in business-to-business sectors.[1]

But where does this added value come from? It comes from a brand's meaning. For *executives*, a brand's specific meaning can provide a clearer direction for strategic and operational decision making, significantly improving top management performance. But the ultimate power of brands lies in the fact that for millions of us as *customers*, brands have acquired meaning which we always carry with us deep within our minds. A Harley-Davidson executive once famously said that the company does not sell motorcycles but something much more significant. 'What we sell,' he said, 'is the ability for a 43-year-old accountant to dress in black leather, ride through small towns and have people be afraid of him.'[2] Such rich meanings are stored in our long-term memory and drive our decisions when we make a buying choice, an employment choice, a voting choice, an investment choice, and so on. In other words, brands generate stable cash flows, higher margins, bigger market shares by their power to influence the choices of the brains they are stored in. This brain-view of choice is so intriguing that a field called 'neuroeconomics' now studies economic choice behaviour with the use of techniques from neuroscience. Similarly, 'neuromarketing' has made global headlines and stirred controversy, as we shall see.

So far so good: brands are meaningful to customers and important business assets in the process of value creation. But problems begin to arise when we shift our focus from brands to branding – the process of building them. Many decision makers perceive branding as a lot of hot air. They see it as being guided largely by intuition, rules of thumb, creativity, fads, buzz words, and the impression of being in sync with what is hot and happening. As one top executive at Shell once lamented, 'If we invest €300 million in a new plant, I get a pile of reports on my desk that is two fists high. But when I invest €300 million in a global branding effort, there are two sheets of A4 on my desk to support the proposed campaign and media mix. How do I know we are making the right investments?' This book starts from the acknowledgement that such views merit attention and that indeed there is too big a gap between the economic significance of brands and the professionalism of the field that creates them. In many cases, therefore, branding adds less meaning to the lives of customers and to the value of companies than is actually possible.

The gap is perpetuated in the endless stream of books on the topic.[3] Many of them provide practical insights and models you can use the next day. But surprisingly few dig deep enough to help you develop yourself into a more effective branding professional for the rest of your career. As a result, we constantly run the risk of embracing new fads without really getting better at what we do. Too little effort is invested in creating an objective and reliable foundation for branding, by rigorously analysing the fundamentals – the key factors you must aim for when building stronger brands. This omission leads to at least four widespread misconceptions that this book will help you remedy.

- **From conscious to subconscious choice**. Almost our entire field works on the assumption that customers make choices consciously and deliberately. Most of our models and research techniques are based upon that. Yet when we look deeper, we see that in reality all customer choices are made almost entirely subconsciously, making many of our current views on customers unreliable and in need of serious updating. We will have to get our heads around this astonishing finding, and this book will help in that.

> Customer choices are made almost entirely subconsciously

- **From irrational to goal-driven clients.** Many of us feel that customers often act irrationally, making decisions based purely on 'emotions' or an altogether lack of sense. Some of us conclude from this that we must simply try to exploit our customers' irrationality, for instance by infusing more emotion into our advertising campaigns. This is a seriously misleading view that puts customers out of reach and marketers out of touch. Customers instead are very goal-driven and emotions are actually indicators of relevance. In principle, the brain chooses rationally, but in a subconscious way. This demands a new understanding and new approaches to what customers find important, as we shall see.
- **From sloppy to consistent branding.** We often think we can get away with inconsistent product launches, conflicting marketing messages, service levels that do not match the promises we make in advertising, and so on. Elementary neuroscientific research suggests, however, that such acts induce brand memory loss – our brand is slowly erased from our customer's memory – putting our entire historical investment in the brand in jeopardy. Inconsistent brands are dying brands, and we will find out exactly why this is so.
- **From access to engagement.** There is a widespread misunderstanding about customer participation, identifying it simply with the use of social media, user-generated content, word-of-mouth, etc. Again, basic neuroscience shows that meaningful interaction with our environment has a strong and beneficial impact on our memory and the very structure of our brain. This finding requires us to put much more energy into understanding why customers would *want* to make the effort and interact with our brand in the first place. It also requires us to look differently at the participatory power of traditional media, instead of simply labelling these as 'old-fashioned' branding vehicles. The game is no longer about reaching people with your message. It is all about fostering engagement through relevant creative content, no matter through which media. This book will help you go from push to pull communication.

These issues are difficult to tackle because there have never previously been any impartial and verified branding principles.

Branding often remains a matter of personal opinion and individual taste. This undermines the credibility and contribution of individual marketers and of the marketing function as a whole. This must change. Consider one illuminating example from our practice that underlines why.

Several years ago, we created a new positioning concept for a company that consistently ranked in the global top five of best-performing companies in its industry. The campaign we created from the positioning energised the firm and aligned people from sales throughout the company, to marketing to the management board and the operational personnel. It tested well in customer research and was launched with a splash. But after a few months of success, the client telephoned. 'The supervisory board wants a presentation of the campaign,' our client said. 'Can you give it?' During the meeting, board members ordered the campaign to be stopped, on the grounds that they thought it too frivolous. No business arguments were given, no branding logic was put forward, no customer considerations supported the verdict. It was just a matter of personal taste. The whole initiative was cancelled by 'the powers that be' and from the marketing point of view the firm was cast into disarray for years.

Events like these happen every day. Yet the economic and personal consequences of such brainless branding are increasingly worrying. With the marketing landscape changing so rapidly, we have to bring more objectivity to the table. Mounting competition from developing countries, market fragmentation, the explosion of the media landscape, the growing importance of word-of-mouth, and the rise of consumer control are all making marketing increasingly complex and the value of strong brands ever more explicit. A recent McKinsey study showed that even the most seasoned marketers feel challenged by these developments.[4] The pressure on chief marketing officers (CMOs) is also growing from *within* companies, as CEOs and boards demand that marketing departments improve their relevance, accountability and performance.[5] In 2007, CMOs in American consumer branded companies lasted a mere 26.8 months in their jobs, compared with 99.6 months for CEOs in American firms.[6]

From brainless branding to branding with brains

The answer is *not* to make marketing just quantitative and scientific. That could ruin creativity, which is essential to branding. But we can make branding more *objective*, based on the advances made in neuroscience over recent decades. We need to guide creativity, without interfering with it. That requires a common frame of reference more reliable than anything available before now. With such a frame of reference, the branding discussions about business in your organisation and the branding decisions can become more focused and fruitful. A more objective, reliable and effective branding framework benefits everyone, at all organisational levels.

> we need to guide creativity, without interfering with it

A more brainy view of brand choice

This book is based on the idea that our brains make the majority of brand choices in much the same way as Google selects websites: by following a stable, subconscious algorithm.[7] To put it another way, the brain uses a fixed set of rules or criteria to decide which brand best satisfies its needs in a given time, place and context. For this task it integrates a wide range of available information, both from our long-term memory and from our senses. This process is the same regardless of whether we are talking about Ben & Jerry's customers buying ice cream, BMW drivers buying new cars, Nokia users wanting new phones, FedEx users in need of freight services, PwC clients seeking help with improving regulatory compliance, and so on.

This process is set in motion by the rise of a subconscious goal or need: e.g. thirst or hunger, or the need to dress, shave, send a package, issue a financial report, buy a home, honour a loved one. *The brain's algorithm is designed to select the brand that seems best to fit this purpose.* This selection process itself also takes place almost entirely subconsciously. Only the end result – the optimal brand – is able to get access to our consciousness. Brands, we might say, fight out a 'battle for awareness' under the rules of the algorithm.

This deceptively simple yet radical model has enormous consequences for branding. For one thing, it makes the task of marketing extremely clear. Web marketers play on Google's algorithm to make sure their site appears as high up the search list as possible. Similarly, brand marketers in any industry should play on the brain's algorithm to make sure their brand is at the top of their customers' minds at the moment they choose which brand to buy. To succeed, marketers must know what the algorithm looks like and tailor their branding approach so as to meet the brain's choice specifications. This book helps you do that.

The brand-choice algorithm

The brain's brand-choice algorithm is of course a metaphor. We do not have a 'rule' programmed somewhere in our mind. But if we look at how the brain goes about making brand choices, we could formulate its algorithm as follows: Select the brand

1. that best fits our present purpose;
2. that has signalled this to us most frequently in the past; and
3. that we have interacted with most intensely.

The algorithm can be seen as a marketing-oriented summary of findings from fundamental neuroscientific research into the structure of our brain, as the following chapters will show in much more detail. The algorithm does not change from situation to situation or from person to person – all brains are unique in their details but alike in their workings. It is the product of our millennia-long evolution as a species. Therefore, a key point of this book is that marketers *cannot influence the algorithm* but must accept it as a given. What marketers *can* (and must) do, then, is to use the algorithm to structure all their branding efforts so as to maximise the chance that their brand is chosen.

To help, the book translates these neuroscientific laws in terms that marketers know and understand, and then outlines their consequences for your daily practice. The result is what can be called the three laws of branding:

- *Law No.1: Relevance.* The first law states that the more uniquely relevant your branding efforts, the higher the chances are that your brand will be chosen by the algorithm. Relevant brands are better linked to the dopamine or reward system in the brain, which strongly influences our behaviour. Brands that are not distinctive tend to repress each other in the battle for awareness, so that uniquely relevant ones become favoured. This law is discussed in Chapters 3 and 4.
- *Law No.2: Coherence.* The second law says that the more your branding efforts are coordinated across time and space, the higher the chance your brand will be chosen. Coherent branding means repetition of a similar message through the years and across all touch points. When brain cells repeatedly communicate with each other, this communication becomes more efficient. As a result, coherence makes it easier for the brain to retrieve the brand and thus more likely that it will win the awareness battle. This law is discussed in Chapters 5 and 6.
- *Law No.3: Participation.* The third law says that the more interactive the branding environment that you create for customers, the more likely it is that the brand will be selected by the brain's algorithm. The brain forms numerous new cell connections in response to interactive environments, improving the memorability of a participatory brand and the chances that it will win the awareness battle. This law is discussed in Chapters 7 and 8.

The branding triangle

These three laws maximise the chance that your brand is selected by the brain's algorithm. Moreover, the laws interact and reinforce each other to form a branding triangle (see Figure. 1.2). They should be applied in combination, as the strongest brands are built when you implement all three. Adidas, for example, followed all three laws as part of its long-running *Impossible Is Nothing* campaign when it invited athletes like David Beckham and Jonah Lomu to make drawings about great adversities in their careers and how they overcame them.

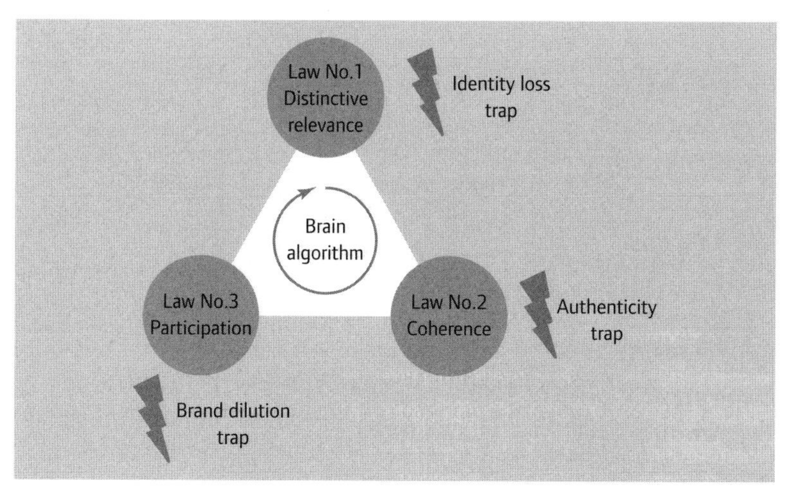

FIGURE 1.2 The branding triangle

The campaign was linked to drivers like perseverance and coping with life's difficulties. It thus associated itself with themes of deep personal significance for many people in a way that is different from Nike's more glamorous and adrenaline-driven approach (Law No.1). Moreover, the campaign was in line with the *Impossible Is Nothing* concept, thus sticking to its red thread (Law No.2). Finally, the drawings were put on show and people could engage via a website that helped them to visualise how to take on their own challenges in life (Law No.3).

Adidas created a good balance within the triangle, but with other brands we sometimes see that one law is strongly over-emphasised (which is still better than not following the laws at all). In that case, the laws can become contradictory as each also holds a trap (see Figure 1.2). When exaggerating distinctive relevance, for example, brands could become trend chasers just to be in tune with customer needs. They then risk losing their own identity, becoming fickle, launching ill-conceived products and becoming less interesting to participate in. It is even possible that the brand becomes so distinctive that it loses its relevance. The small-car brand Smart, for example, created innovative cars that were so different from the typical car that customers had difficulty in perceiving them as suitable alternatives.[8]

A brand focusing on coherence, on the other hand, could fall into the authenticity trap. Such brands try to stay true to their own identity, but risk losing touch with what customers find relevant and allow no customer participation. Levi's may have suffered this problem. On the other hand, when you bet everything on participation, your brand could hand over so much control that it becomes unrecognisable and loses its edge and relevance. Wikipedia would lose its strength as a brand very quickly if there were no screening of articles by devoted brand loyalists, thus preventing an 'anything goes' mentality. As with so much in life, therefore, implementing the three laws of branding is a matter of balance.

Newton's apples

Neuroscientific research shows that these three laws must be the focal points of all your branding efforts. That is, *everything* you do (not just your advertising) should strengthen your brand's distinctive relevance, make it more coherent and induce more people to participate in the brand. If not, your actions may not strengthen your brand.

When Isaac Newton published his laws of gravity and motion in 1687, people already knew, of course, that apples fall to the ground. But his theorems enabled more precise and reliable explanations and predictions of natural phenomena. In our more modest case, the effects are similar. Learning more about the brain's subconscious decision processes and about the *why* and *how* of these objective laws should allow you to improve your effectiveness as a professional. (Especially useful if your competitors read this book too!)

Brands that are built according to the three laws have a higher chance of being chosen. Marketers should work with them in the same way as engineers work with the laws of gravity. If you invest €1,000 in a sports brand such as Adidas that follows these laws, your return will be higher than if you invest this sum in a sports brand that does not follow them – other factors being equal. If you include these principles in your branding strategy more consistently, diligently and passionately than your competitors, you will eventually beat them in the battle for brand preference. Your customers will forget your competitors.

Brands built in line with the brain's brand-choice algorithm are chosen consistently, with the result that they enjoy a sustainable competitive advantage. They produce higher returns (larger market share, sales growth, price premium, distribution margin) at lower risk (lower customer churn rates, more stable repeat sales), resulting in superior performance. The chapters that follow are therefore devoted to a detailed explanation of these laws, their neuroscientific underpinnings and the tools to implement them.

A more valuable approach to brand building

There are several myths and misunderstandings about branding that stand in the way of implementing the more productive approach explained in this book. To make branding more valuable and less 'vague' for companies and more meaningful for customers, organisations need to change a number of things. Experience shows that the following actions can boost the branding effectiveness of your organisation and the ability to implement the three laws.

Step 1: Accept that branding is not the same as advertising

Google and Apple have built immensely valuable brands with relatively small advertising budgets. Google's and Apple's advertising expenditures are both around 1.5 per cent of net sales while Procter & Gamble, for example, invests around 10 per cent of net sales in advertising.[9] Yet there is a widespread misconception that branding and advertising are the same thing. As Huib Morelisse, CEO in the Netherlands for one of Europe's largest energy companies, RWE, says: 'Our brand in the business-to-business market is stronger than in the business-to-consumer market. Yet we invested hardly anything in b-to-b advertising. We built our brand by investing in a responsive sales and service model.'[10] Equating branding with advertising is one reason why responsibility for managing the brand is often delegated to the communications department so that the board can concentrate on 'more important matters'. Thus, management teams cut themselves off from the nurturing of one of their most valuable assets.

branding is *not* the same as advertising

Management teams must understand that advertising is what you say, while branding is what a company says *and does* as perceived by customers and stakeholders. As the three laws will show, branding encompasses everything that influences the impression people get from your brand – so not just your marketing communications. The buying process, the product experience, other products you offer under the brand name, packaging, the friendliness of your service desk, press coverage, stories told by peers, forum discussions, etc. are all part of the process by which the brains of customers construct your 'brand'. All these things send signals to the brains of your customers. This means that the entire business strategy must be developed with the brand in mind – and this can only be done at the most senior level in organisations.

If you just focus on advertising and fail to develop a business strategy that integrates all these factors, you do not engage in branding and leave your fate largely to others. You then risk investing your marketing money below the fair rate of return you ought to expect. To build a brand, your mantra should be that brand strategy *is* business strategy and, vice versa, business strategy *is* brand strategy. This book explains principles that help you implement this idea.

Step 2: Link executive remuneration to branding success

The second misconception is that the communications department rather than the board is responsible for branding. Given the value of brands and their dependence on a strong business strategy, branding is a CEO issue. Moreover, implementing the three branding laws requires a cross-divisional approach and long-term perspective that only the management of an organisation can guide.

Executives should therefore be rewarded for branding success. They should have a personal incentive to provide the vision, the support, the management systems and so on that are needed to create a *branding-law-oriented organisation*. It would be wise for investors, boards and remuneration committees to link executive compensation in part to the long-term appreciation of brand value. According to Mercer, a global HR consulting firm specialising in executive compensation, some companies with strong brands already include measures related to sustained brand value growth in their short-term and long-term incentive plans.[11] This is not yet a common practice, but it should become so in firms that take branding seriously. Top management commitment to branding tends to make organisations more brand-oriented which, studies show, means they can enjoy profit margins nearly twice their industry average.[12]

Step 3: Learn to judge creativity more objectively

The third misconception is that there can be no common standards for evaluating the fruits of creativity in advertising and branding. Many marketers and executives lack a solid frame of reference by which they can judge creative proposals. This should be no surprise, as it is not their primary profession. But the problem is that without a proper frame of reference people often fall back on personal taste instead of using objective success factors. Moreover, by making branding issues personal, most people turn defensive when challenged. This ruins the possibility of having professional discussions that lead to a good decision.

What this book tells you is that every branding and business initiative can be judged against criteria that the laws provide:

- Is it relevant to the target group and distinct from competitors?
- Is it coherent and credible given the history of the brand?
- Is it conveyed in the most participatory way possible?

Of course, in some situations additional criteria (awareness, for example) are needed. But these three criteria should drive branding discussions and executives should use them to structure decisions. By thus focusing on output quality, they can leave the creative process itself to creative experts. There is no need to prescribe the colour combinations of a corporate identity, the music for a commercial, the tone of a campaign – that is the job of creatives. What counts is whether the overall effect created meets the three laws. Thus, we liberate creativity from the grip of bureaucracy and profit more from the intuitive brilliance of experienced creatives. And we no longer engage in discussions that are essentially about personal taste.

Step 4: Prioritise your research programme

The fourth misconception is that traditional branding research is a reliable source of information for making branding decisions. But few research tools measure how relevant, coherent and participatory the brand is. Moreover, most research tools are still based on the mistaken idea that customers make branding decisions consciously and deliberately. Existing quantitative techniques are inadequate and require adaptation (see Chapter 4). For instance, quantitative brand tracking research often measures a range of variables (such as awareness, image, consideration, preference, advertising recall and recognition, advertising likeability) of which the relative importance is unclear.

Many marketing managers become lost in quantitative tracking data. This is because many 'intermediate' factors are also reported, without indicating whether they are really correlated to preference and sales. Intermediate factors are such things as advertising awareness, recall, likeability, impact, reach, wear-out and stopping power. These factors can be useful, but are less important in charting brand success than 'end measures' like awareness and preference. The three laws help to prioritise tracking data, by explaining which factors measure the chance that the brand is chosen. By using the three branding laws to structure your research programme, you gain a serious advantage in the quality of your marketing intelligence. This helps to make your branding efforts more effective.

Conclusion

This book states that a more reliable approach to branding is needed because the gap between the value of brands and the reliability of the branding profession is no longer sustainable. The approach presented in the following pages is aimed at making branding more effective, dependable and objective. It presents a model of brand choice based on neuroscience that does justice to the role of the subconscious and proposes three branding laws that, when implemented, maximise the chances that a brand is chosen. This perspective provides three main benefits:

- It makes creativity more productive.
- It makes branding discussions more focused.
- It makes branding decisions more solid.

It is an approach that helps to focus creativity on clear targets, thus freeing it from the grip of tunnel vision, short-termism, personal taste and cluttered research.

Most of the rest of this book is devoted to explaining how your customers' subconscious algorithm selects which brands to buy and how the three branding laws can work to maximise the chance of your brand being chosen.

TIM RICE'S
DISNEY'S
BEAUTY AND THE BEAST
DEBORAH COX IS AIDA
STARRING MUSIC SENSATION
DEBORAH COX AS AIDA
INFORMATION CENTER

Chapter 2

Persuading subconscious minds

Branding could enhance the lives of customers and the value of companies far more than it does. To do that, we need a more objective and reliable approach to branding, based on insights from neuroscience. We have already discussed how the brain makes brand choices in much the same way as Google selects websites: it follows a fixed algorithm to select from our memory (index) the brand (site) that best fits our purpose. This process takes place outside our conscious awareness and is fast, automatic and effortless. It is underpinned by three branding laws (relevance, coherence and participation) which maximise the chance of your brand being selected by the brain's subconscious algorithm.

This approach – which we will explore in the chapters that follow – represents a radical break with conventional wisdom about how customers make choices. It requires us to let go of some of our most cherished views about ourselves and how we make decisions. Also, we will have to manoeuvre through the most controversial terrain in the marketing field: that of subconscious influence and manipulation. We turn to this first.

The limits of consciousness

The branding industry has long been clinging to an archaic view of how customers make brand choices: the idea that people decide *consciously and deliberately*. Not only is this view wrong; as we will see, it is debilitating. For instance, many people are experiencing an increasing 'choice overload' in both their work and their private life.[1] Our time pressures and hectic lifestyles deplete our capacity to deliberate consciously all our decisions, leaving marketers who stick to this model increasingly powerless.

Distortions of an outdated view

The conscious-choice model is embedded in the practices of all the industry's major players: brand owners, creative agencies, consultancies, media companies, research agencies and marketing faculties. It is a systemic problem. Most importantly, it has been part of our general view of human nature since the seventeenth century, when French philosopher René Descartes formulated his famous dictum, *Cogito ergo sum* (I think, therefore I am). Since then, the idea that we are conscious and deliberate beings has become ever more deeply ingrained in the stories we tell ourselves about what it is to be human.

In marketing, the concept of deliberate choice is known the world over by the acronym AIDA, which stands for: attract *attention*, attain *interest*, create *desire*, get *action*. We have all had to learn it on our marketing courses. AIDA is the poster child of conscious-choice models in marketing. It was formulated by E. St Elmo Lewis as early as 1898 and popularised by sales expert Edward Strong in 1925, who explained that it identifies 'four states of consciousness which must pass through the mind of the prospect before he will buy'.[2] The fact that the AIDA theory originated between the death of Wild West legend Jesse James in 1882 and the start of the First World War in 1914 does not necessarily invalidate it. But it does mean that it dates from an entirely different era in marketing, before many of the commercial inventions and scientific discoveries that have changed the way we look at ourselves and our world.

The AIDA model has been endlessly revised since then, but it has never changed fundamentally. The best-known version of it is called the 'marketing funnel' which is used in most advertising agencies, consumer research companies and management consulting firms to analyse the decision process (see Figure 2.1).[3] One reason for the funnel's popularity is that it has a foundation in behavioural science and is measurable. Indeed, in its best form the marketing funnel is a wonderfully clear, smart and systematic tool. It is little wonder that marketers have grown quite attached to it. So when analysts at Forrester Research – a global leader in market intelligence – sought to rethink the marketing funnel in 2007, they could not bring themselves to declare it dead. However, while their new version of the funnel rightly embraces the influence of social media, it still makes no reference to the role of subconscious processes.[4] And this is a general trend that illustrates how conventional the marketing industry can be. The result is that most marketers and agencies all over the world work with a limited – and distorted – view of how customers decide about brands.

Awareness	Familiarity	Consideration	Purchase	Loyalty
Do you know this brand?	Are you familiar with the performance and the models of this brand?	Did you consider this brand the last time you bought a car?	Did you buy this brand when you last bought a car?	Will you buy this brand again the next time you buy a car?

FIGURE 2.1 Example of the marketing funnel for a car brand

Conscious choice is an oxymoron

The problem then is not so much in AIDA itself. It is still a wonderfully simple and useful segmentation model. The problem is that the branding industry has used it as a model for how choice works, neglecting the mounting evidence of the large role of subconscious processes in the choices and decisions we daily make in all aspects of our lives. These subconscious processes have profound consequences for anyone involved in branding. Studies in psychology and neuroscience have shown that we are not the consciousness-driven beings that, for centuries, we thought we were. Much of this research builds upon work done in the 1980s by Benjamin Libet, an American psychologist and neurophysiologist.

Libet, in a famous experiment, asked people to perform a simple motor activity, like moving their finger, at a moment they could choose themselves. He used an electroencephalogram to measure their brain activity. What he found was that, on average, brain activity related to the finger movement occurred around 300 milliseconds before subjects reported awareness of their conscious will to move their finger. Libet concluded from this that conscious acts are initiated by subconscious processes – leaving little room for an autonomous conscious free will. Our conscious mind seems to have a veto that can block subconscious decisions only once they enter our awareness.[5] His findings have sparked controversy and heated debate. In fact, many psychologists, philosophers and even Libet himself at first sought to explain away the conclusions that his data suggested. Yet others have repeated his experiments and made similar findings.

For centuries, philosophers, poets, moralists and politicians have emphasised that our consciousness is what makes us distinctly human. We have become emotionally attached to 'consciousness'. But the view that has begun to emerge is that many if not all of our conscious decisions are subconsciously prepared, sometimes seconds before we think we consciously make them. Even decisions that we are sure we make deliberately and consciously are in reality preceded by subconscious brain activities.[6] As we are unaware of these subconscious processes, we only appear to ourselves to be acting from conscious will.

our conscious decisions are subconsciously prepared

Clearly, this view has serious consequences not only for marketers, but also for research agencies which rely on consciously reported buying intentions and preferences (to name a few dimensions) in their studies and reports. Consciousness plays a different role in our lives from what we have always thought. And brand choice is much more automatic than AIDA marketers think.[7]

EXAMPLE

Four insights into ourselves

There are at least four insights that help us understand the effect of subconscious processes on ourselves and our customers.

Insight No.1: We are gaining our subconscious. Many scientists estimate that only 5 per cent of our choices are based on conscious deliberation, so that 95 per cent of our decisions are made entirely subconsciously.[8] The role of consciousness is different from what we thought but *not* useless. So we are not giving up something that we love dearly, we are gaining awareness of the enormous power of our subconscious brain processes.

Insight No.2: We are brilliant without knowing it. Consciously, we can do only one thing at a time. But subconsciously, we are breathtaking multi-taskers. Some researchers estimate that the capacity of our subconscious brain is 200,000 times higher than that of the conscious mind. We simply could not survive using our conscious faculties only. As cognitive scientist Stephen Pinker has said, the problems that we humans solve subconsciously as we see and walk and plan and make it through the day are far more challenging than landing on the moon or sequencing the human genome.[9]

Insights No.3: We can control our emotions. The importance of subconscious processes does not make us pliable slaves or instant emotional response automatons. People can and do control their impulses, and it is associated with higher happiness. Neuroscientific research into meditation offers one interesting example, as studies indicate that regular meditation – a conscious activity – can significantly *reduce* emotional reactivity. This in turn is associated with better health and a higher sense of well-being.[10] We are more than a bag of disorderly passions camouflaged by a thin veil of consciousness.

Insight No.4: We are subconsciously rational. We do not optimise and coordinate all our choices throughout life so as to maximise our overall success and happiness, achieving 'maximum utility'. But our subconscious choices are goal-oriented and purposeful and anything but irrational. We can thus display what economists call 'bounded rationality' – rationality within certain limits. For example, receiving social recognition can be important for us, and our brain can learn to see owning a Rolex watch as a way to achieve this. There is nothing irrational about that, unless you think that a need for social recognition is silly. Of course, the need to satisfy certain goals can be so strong that it becomes self-destructive, as in the case of alcohol and drug abuse. In normal cases, however, studies show that subconscious processes can lead to even better, more satisfying purchase decisions than choices that are made analytically. This seems especially true when buying more complex products such as houses or cars.[11]

Subconscious rationality

So what does subconscious algorithmic choice mean for the practice of branding? The key consequence is that we must put the concept of subconscious rationality at the centre of our understanding. The brand-choice process takes place almost entirely below our awareness (subconsciously), yet selects the brand with the highest and most likely ability to satisfy our goals at that particular moment (rationally). In response to a customer goal, several brands that could fulfil it are activated. From these, our brain's choice algorithm selects the one most likely to meet our needs. I call this process subconsciously rational because it seeks to maximise our realised gain in that particular situation, but takes place outside our awareness. Which brand is selected? We have seen that our brain selects the one most consistently built according to the three branding laws. This brand is the first to be granted access to our conscious mind and will then be chosen – unless we veto it. This is the main idea of this book's brand-choice model. As the optimal, most preferred brand enters our conscious mind first, a brand's 'accessibility' is a key quantifiable measure of brand strength in our model. Accessibility is the ease or swiftness with which a brand comes to mind in response to the activation of a goal.

To illustrate, take the example of a young couple who have just had their first child. Their brains are undergoing massive adjustments. Their views on life change, their priorities shift, new relevancies arise (buying the right type of nappies, to breastfeed or not and for how long, and so on.) and existing ones are altered. Suppose that this couple come to the point where a new family car becomes an issue (which is quite likely). While a year ago a BMW Z4 might have looked an ideal car to them, a baby may make such a vehicle an impractical, even irresponsible, choice. So how do their brains tackle the issue of car brand selection? Figure 2.2 shows the brand-choice model this book proposes. It breaks this swift process down into four phases, so that we can watch what happens in slow motion.

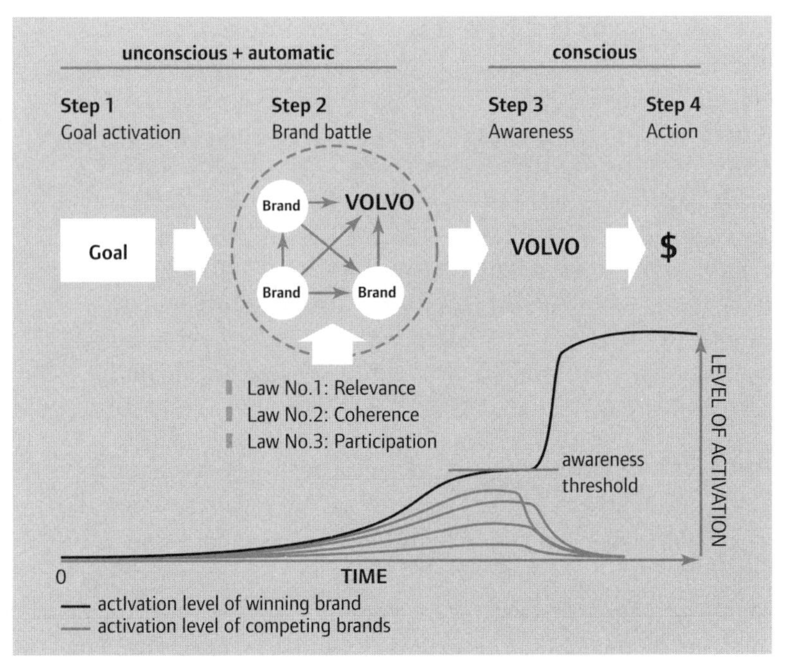

FIGURE 2.2 Brand choice is subconscious, fast, algorithmic and purposeful

Stage 1: Goal activation Brand choice starts with the emergence of a customer goal, in this case buying a new car. This goal can arise within our own mind or be triggered by something around us (for example, our couple noticing that the pushchair does not fit in their current car or an uncle telling them their car is not suitable for transporting a baby.). At this stage, our couple are not necessarily aware that this has become a goal in their brains.[12]

Immediately, a cluster of related relevancies becomes co-activated in connection with this goal. In their situation, concepts like 'high-speed safety', 'impact protection', being seen as 'successful and responsible young parents', 'feeling joyful and proud' could be evoked. As a result, a blend of goals and sub-goals around family safety becomes active, although we are not aware of this happening. That is, we cannot verbally report all these goals let alone state their relative importance. Note that this cocktail of goals is always specific to a certain product or service category (cars, mobile phones, banking services, etc.). Note also that in our model the desire to experience or express emotions (for example, joy, pride) can play an important role in brand choice and that it can be rational to fulfil such desires, even when we are unaware of them and they may not come to the surface in conventional focus group research. Emotions are often indicators of relevance, of things we value greatly.[13]

The goals and sub-goals then rapidly elicit from our long-term memory several brands that could satisfy them. These brands are activated through their association with our goals (a process sometimes called 'bottom-up' activation).[14] In the case of our couple, Volvo, BMW, Saab, Toyota and Ford may now be evoked.

Stage 2: Brand battle These brands subsequently engage in a battle for awareness. Neuroscientists have found that stimuli compete for access to our conscious minds. This holds not only for external information like visual data or sounds but also for internal cues like thoughts, actions, goals, meanings, memories and brands.[15] In the case of our young family, Volvo, BMW, Saab, Toyota and Ford now enter a competition for access to their awareness.

This competition is resolved rapidly, automatically and effortlessly based on what economics Nobel laureate Daniel Kahneman called 'automatic affective valuation' – reflexive judgements based on subconscious attitudes[16] – and the frequency and intensity of previous experiences with these brands. So which brand wins? This book argues that the battle for awareness is won by the brand built most systematically according to the three laws of relevance, coherence and participation. Why? Because this brand reaches the highest activation level and, when evoked vigorously enough, crosses the awareness threshold first and suppresses the other brands (Figure 2.1). It is the preferred brand, with the strongest behaviour-shaping associations, and thus has the highest chance of being chosen.[17]

As a result of all this, Volvo may win the awareness battle. Volvo may be most strongly and uniquely associated with our couple's top goal of 'family safety' (Law No.1). After all, Volvo has spent at least twenty years associating its brand name with this concept (Law No.2). Moreover, our couple may have had a Volvo before or experienced a Volvo as children when their own parents drove one (Law No.3).

Stage 3: Awareness The winner of the brand battle enters our consciousness first and we now begin to realise that a choice process is going on. In other words, a core property of our subconscious decision-making process is that only its outcome (the preferred brand) is admitted to our conscious mind (see Figure 2.3). So Volvo is the first brand name that pops up in the mind of our couple and when it does, it receives their conscious attention. This results in a further so-called top-down activation of the Volvo brand, quickly expanding it into a full-scale ignition of the neuron networks representing the brand. This activation happens at the cost of the other brands. In other words, conscious attention for Volvo suppresses the other contenders (Figure 2.2), creating a 'winner-takes-all effect'. Moreover, Volvo can now remain 'on line' in our couple's consciousness for a longer period.

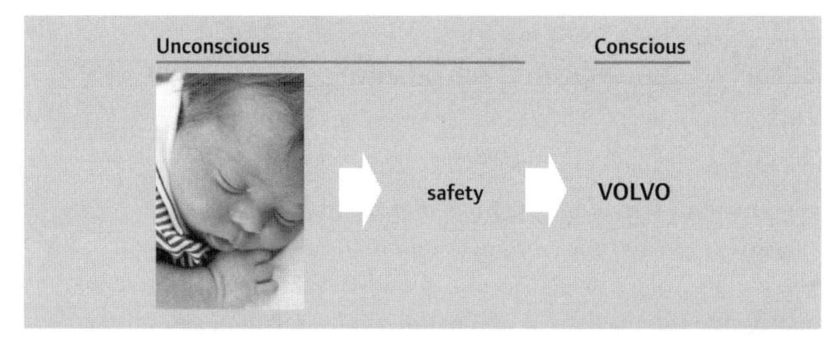

FIGURE 2.3 Simplified activation process for young parents' car choice

Stage 4: Action As the first brand (Volvo) is the preferred brand, it will actually be chosen (unless our conscious mind deliberates or vetoes our choice). It is the brand that our couple's brains have decided best and most reliably fits their cocktail of subconscious goals. It is deemed to have the highest probability of delivering the benefits sought. We now consciously think about the brand, and this means its activation can extend to other brain systems.[18] We can start to talk about it, think about it, actually buy it, or deliberate about the brand and veto it, as we will see in the next section. Sometimes it is only at this stage that we become aware of our goal. For example, it is entirely possible that we only realise we are thirsty when we notice we have begun looking around for a Coke vending machine.

These stages are the four phases in the brand-choice model this book proposes. To make sure your brand does well, you must implement the three laws with dedication.

Brand evaluation and conscious veto

We have seen that brand choice is a subconscious, fast, algorithmic and purposeful process. In some cases, however, we consciously veto the outcome of this selection process or deliberate it. If you still cannot let go of AIDA, you can think of this deliberation phase more or less in AIDA terms. For instance, we can consult our own knowledge, check information from websites, read a brochure, talk to a sales representative, ask knowledgeable friends or colleagues, visit a forum, etc. But when does this deliberation happen?

brand choice is a subconscious, fast, algorithmic and purposeful process

Conscious deliberation requires a certain maturity

Deliberating and vetoing subconscious choices and thus controlling one's behaviour in a goal-directed way requires effort and well-developed cognitive skills, absent in children. It happens only in mentally mature, motivated adults (leading some to question the ethics of advertising to children[19]).

Joint decisions lead to deliberation

Importantly, deliberation occurs when people take a decision jointly, as may be the case with the couple in our example, and in many families and businesses. Others may have a different preferred brand and thus we enter a discussion about the pros and cons of various brands.

High involvement favours deliberation

Table 2.1 lists four factors whose presence creates high involvement and hence the chance of conscious deliberation.[20]

TABLE 2.1 Four factors increasing the likelihood of conscious deliberation

Factor	Description	Typical examples
Functional risk	The importance of the product and the degree to which a bad purchase has functional consequences	Washing machine, vacuum cleaner, private banking services
Emotional risk	The degree to which a bad purchase has emotional consequences (e.g. embarrassment or frustration)	Clothing, car, TV set, hairdresser
The chance of making an error	The perceived probability that a bad purchase will be made	Used car, mortgage
Pleasure value	The amount of self-gratification and reward the product or service brings	Perfume, champagne

Deliberation usually takes place with products such as television sets or audio equipment, cars and cameras. But the level of involvement is situation-dependent. For example, in the case of cars – a classic high-involvement product – some people consider only one brand: the brand of their previous car.[21] This brand could have become so relevant to a customer (Law No.1) or the customer has interacted so heavily and satisfactorily with it (Law No.3) that no other brand is considered. In other cases, low-involvement products can suddenly become very important. For example, ice cream can become a high-involvement product when you serve it at Christmas or during a dinner with your boss in your home, creating high functional and emotional risks (spoiling the evening or appearing 'cheap'). Consequently, you may decide to buy Ben & Jerry's or Haägen-Dazs over a private-label product.

Yet even when the final choice stage is conscious and deliberate, the three laws can influence the decision. Two reasons for this are especially worth mentioning.

- *The three laws strongly determine the consideration set.* When we seek to buy a digital camera, for instance, we consciously compare only a limited number of brands in the 'consideration set'. On average, consideration sets contain one to five brands.[22] Brands built according to the three laws of branding have a higher probability of entering the consideration set and hence of being deliberately chosen than brands that are not.

- *The three laws influence conscious evaluations.* Evaluation is based not only on external information but also on brand information stored in long-term memory. Brands built according to the three laws can have an edge in this process, as their brand information is more 'accessible'. Some time ago, Sony created impressive 60-second commercials for its Bravia flat-screen television set, associating it with image vividness – one of the most relevant aspects of flat screens. This information can shape our subconscious attitudes but also be easily retrieved from memory, thus giving Sony an edge when a customer consciously ponders the relative performance of various brands. Moreover, our subconscious brand attitudes – which are strong and positive for brands built according to the three laws – are difficult to control.[23]

Google and the brain's search engine

We can now see why brands are chosen in our brain in much the same way as the Google search engine selects websites (although our brain's algorithm existed first, of course). Table 2.2 illustrates this.

TABLE 2.2 A comparison of how the brain and Google make choices

	Brand choice by the brain	**Site selection by Google**
Step 1: Goal	An unconscious goal arises in our brain	We type a search string in the Google bar
Step 2: Competition	Brands enter into a battle for access to our awareness, based on their compliance with the three laws	Websites in Google's index compete for access to our computer screen, based on their compliance with the PageRank™ algorithm
Step 3: Awareness	The brand that best fits that algorithm enters our awareness first and gets our attention	The site that performs best against the PageRank™ algorithm is placed at the top of the results page
Step 4: Action	We choose the first brand as our preferred option, unless we consciously decide otherwise	We click (most likely) the site at the top of the list, unless we consciously skip it

Google's PageRank™ algorithm is the equivalent of the three laws of branding, which govern the competition between brands for entry into our awareness. Google's algorithm is a secret, but the brain's algorithm is not. In the chapters that follow, we will discuss the laws and their practical implications in detail.

Rational brand choice

The brand-choice algorithm is an subconscious mechanism for making what we can call 'rational' or optimal brand choices. The idea that customers are rational may strike you as surprising. Of course, we are not always making the best possible choices. In fact, there are many known biases in the way our brains work (such as over-optimism, loss aversion) that lead us to make sub-optimal decisions in some situations.[24] But studies show that humans and animals (e.g. lions, monkeys, ducks) make many important decisions almost exactly as the mathematical models that calculate the most rational course of action would predict.[25] Evolutionary forces have made many species goal-optimising. And of these, man is the only truly consciousness kind. It seems consciousness is not needed for making complex decisions in the best possible way. Now there's a thought.

Truth and lies about neuromarketing

The finding that our brand choices emanate from subconscious processes leads to a conclusion of the highest importance for brand owners: branding must be aimed at influencing customers' subconscious minds. Even conscious deliberation and brand vetoing – acts we perform in full awareness – are subconsciously prepared. Hence, the whole business of branding must be aimed at influencing the subconscious processes that underlie our brand choices.

> branding must be aimed at influencing customers' subconscious minds

Swaying the subconscious

Now we enter the most contentious terrain in modern marketing. For many people, the idea that marketers are targeting our subconscious minds evokes thoughts of Orwell's Big Brother, Huxley's *Brave New World* or Spielberg's film *Minority Report*. Critics have contended that it could present a regression in man's long struggle towards becoming a rational and self-guided being.[26] Some neuromarketing advocates have amplified these fears by claiming that their techniques provide such unprecedented insight into our minds that marketers can now get customers 'to behave the way marketers want them to behave'.[27]

Indeed, the fears run deep. Commercial Alert – an American consumer organisation run by Ralph Nader – asked the US Senate Commerce Committee to investigate neuromarketing. Why? Because this organisation foresees a near future in which marketers and politicians can literally peer inside our brains and modify neural activities so as to influence our behaviour to serve their own ends. Commercial Alert fears that this would undermine democracy and is therefore against using medical techniques for anything other than to cure people. Some neuroscientists are also sceptical about the intentions of corporations experimenting with neuromarketing.[28]

So what are we to make of this? The truth may be more intriguing for marketers and less frightful for consumer activists. Consider the following two statements as a concise, no-nonsense briefing on the subject.

Statement 1: Brain scanning techniques invade the marketing field but provide no brand strategy breakthroughs

Brain-scanning techniques like electroencephalography (EEG), fMRI (mentioned earlier) and magnetoencephalography (MEG), (which allow scientists to look inside the living human brain), are increasingly being used to study subjects relevant to marketers.

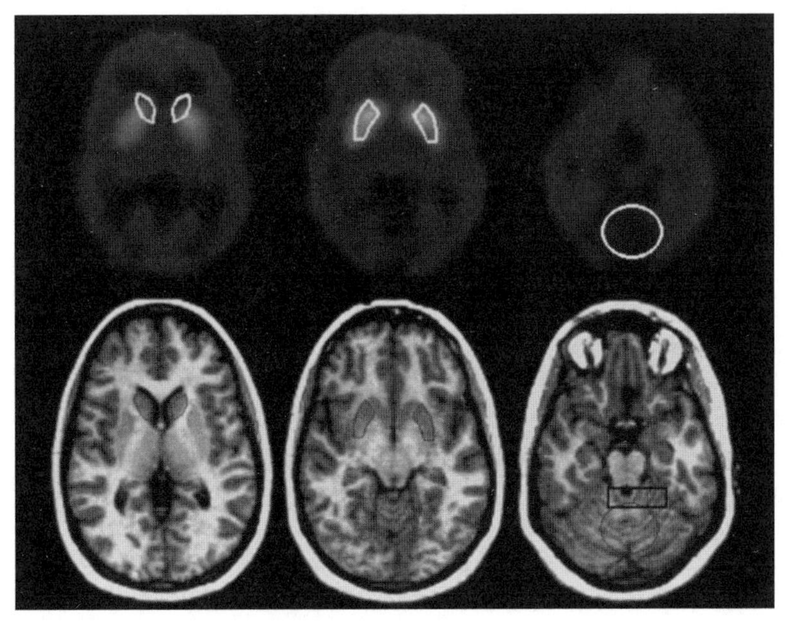

Brain scans showing neural activity

These technologies – often leased from hospitals – have been used to monitor a taste test of Coca-Cola v. Pepsi, pre-test a Jack Daniel's campaign, contrast the responses of Democratic and Republican US voters to war images, post-test the $85,000-per-second adverts aired during the Super Bowl, fine-tune the interior of a Mercedes, optimise film trailers and investigate the role of price in product choice – to name but a few.

Myth: *Marketers will find a buy button in our brain that they can switch on or off.* The greatest fear of critics is that through such studies, marketers will ultimately find a 'buy button' in the brain circuitry responsible for choice that marketers can manipulate at will. Certainly there are highly specific areas in the brain that are critical for our ability to make choices – especially a region at the front of the brain called the orbitofrontal cortex, damage to which can cripple our ability to make decisions.[29] But the idea that these brain areas can be micro-managed from the outside by inserting a marketing message is neuro-nonsense. There are no magic messages to which all customer brains always and automatically respond by buying the product pitched. It would be like an amoeba commanding a whale. The human brain is too complex and robust for that.

Mythbuster: *Brain scans tell marketers which brain areas are active.* Brain-scanning technologies register which brain areas are active. So scientists can see what happens when people taste Coke and Pepsi, see a Jack Daniel's advert, look at war imagery, watch Super Bowl adverts, interact with a car interior, watch a film trailer or rate various product–price offers. What most scanning studies do is classify brain activities – this or that area is active. Researchers can then roughly infer what this means, based on a 'map' that neuroscientists have created of the brain's functions (for instance, the amygdala is active, which means the brain is responding with fear, emotion or aggression). Many books on neuromarketing present such a map and explain the role of the various brain areas, although this map is far from complete, as neuroscientists do not know the exact function of each area. Moreover, scanning techniques generally identify activity in too large a section in the brain to support more than loose correlations. It is a rather blunt instrument, with a relatively low resolution.[30]

However, the most important limitation is not technical but conceptual. It is not clear, for example, how Pepsi marketers must change their branding strategies when they know, as one study showed, that Coke produces a much higher blood flow in the prefrontal cortex and the hippocampus – regions implicated in planning, decision making, personality expression and memory, among others.[31] In some cases, neuroimaging techniques can help marketers create better adverts or products by telling us more reliably what is going on in people's subconscious minds than they can reveal to us when asking them. But my point is that most neuromarketing studies do not provide a basis for action if your goal is to build a stronger brand. They can tell us more about the *brand*, but not much about *branding*. Moreover, some studies use what we know about brands to learn more about the brain instead of the other way around. That is why I propose a different approach in this book, one that relies more on fundamental neuroscientific research and less on inferences from brain scans of marketing-related tasks.

Statement 2: Most advertising works 'subliminally' but building a true brand still takes time

Most advertisements that we see do not receive our conscious attention. Recent estimates about the daily number of commercial messages we encounter vary between 500 and 5,000, or between 0.5 and 5 per minute all day, every day.[32] Whatever the exact figure, it is clear that we see more adverts than we process consciously. However, we do process them *subconsciously* and they do have an effect on us.[33] Surprising as this may seem, advertising has *always* worked like that, as 'clutter' is not a new phenomenon. In 1759, Samuel Johnson complained about newspapers crammed with adverts.[34] So the reality is that *most* adverts in the media fail to win the battle for awareness and thus work subliminally (i.e. below the threshold of consciousness). Advertising largely boils down to subconscious persuasion. Research shows that adverts can change our subconscious attitudes without changing our conscious attitudes – influencing our purchase behaviour without our knowing it.[35]

Myth: *Subliminal advertising effects do not turn us into mindless buying robots*

With neuromarketing, history repeats itself. The public anxiety about subconscious persuasion goes back to Vance Packard's 1957 book *The Hidden Persuaders*. Packard warned that advertisers used 'motivational research' to make appeals to us based on deep psychological studies, often presenting them to us outside our awareness. James Vicary, a market researcher at that time, reported that he boosted sales of Coca-Cola and popcorn by hiding adverts that flashed for .03 seconds in a film. He later confessed it was a hoax.[36] Subconscious persuasion does work, however, especially when the unnoticed message is *relevant* to the customer – in line with our first law of branding. For example, flashing 'Drink Liptonice' – known as a thirst quencher – increases the chance that *thirsty* individuals will choose and drink Liptonice when given the choice.[37] Yet a casual confrontation with a roadside hoarding does not create a desire so complusive that we are willing to throw everything but the kitchen sink at it just to get our hands on a Liptonice, or a new lingerie set, or a car-insurance policy.

> subconscious persuasion *does* work – when the message is relevant

Mythbuster: *Serious influence still requires a systematic and long-term approach* Neuromarketing does not turn customers into programmable machines. Positive results accrue only from prolonged and regular repetition, conforming with the second branding law. But the idea of connecting products to hidden wants was already being pioneered in the 1920s. A fascinating BBC documentary called *The Century of the Self* portrayed Sigmund Freud's American nephew, Edward Bernays, as the originator of the concept of linking products and services to our hidden and private desires.[38] Bernays opened a 'counsel on public relations' in New York in 1919 and made a fortune by applying Freud's theories on the subconscious to selling products, as he worked for companies such as the American Tobacco Company, Best Foods, CBS, Cartier, General Electric, Procter & Gamble, and others.

It seems, however, that marketers have forgotten about the overriding importance of the subconscious and have zeroed in on the AIDA-type conscious-choice models discussed above. Why marketers went astray is another matter, but neuroscience is surely putting us back on that old track. By refocusing on the subconscious, however, we must not make the mistake of thinking that it can provide sensational quick wins. That itself would be an act of brainless branding. The result of an effective subliminal message is measurable.[39] But one message does not build a brand that enjoys enduring subconscious preference. If that is what you want (and I contend that, given the value of strong brands, that is what marketers *ought* to want), a more systematic approach is needed that is spelled out by the three laws.

Our subconscious algorithm selects brands based on our implicit attitudes (Law No.1) and the frequency (Law No.2) and intensity (Law No.3) of previous experiences with these brands. Such characteristics are not instilled in an instant but usually require months or even years of regular contact with a brand. The human mind is not so easily fooled, as the algorithm has a built-in safeguard against mistakes: we learn from experience. It makes creating outstanding products an extremely effective form of branding. An advert engineered by neuromarketers may persuade us to buy a certain product. But if the product does not satisfy us, we are unlikely to fall for the subconscious lure again.

Branding as subconscious persuasion

Given what we now know about the brain, everything in branding must be aimed at persuading the subconscious. But this idea could hardly be further removed from marketing practice today, with its reliance on deliberate choice models. The following steps can help your organisation make the shift.

Step 1: Accept that brand choice is a subconscious phenomenon

The idea that we are driven by our conscious mind is an illusion. It arises because we are unaware of the subconscious processes that underlie and precede our conscious actions. Not only is choice a subconscious phenomenon, most of the impressions that build brand associations are registered and processed outside our conscious awareness as well. For example, most adverts in most media never catch the conscious attention of customers. They influence our subconscious attitudes without our even noticing them. In short, branding is a subconscious mind game to a much higher degree than we ever thought. We must substitute our deliberate-choice model with a more accurate one that includes the dominance of subconscious processes in brand choice. Unfortunately, the AIDA model is based on asking customers for conscious answers about processes they have not the slightest conscious clue about.

The dominance of the subconscious does not necessarily make us more pliable than we thought – although vetoing our subconscious choices does require motivation and effort. Nor does it make us plainly irrational. Indeed, we are subconsciously rational in the sense that the brain processes that guide our choices are purposeful and goal-oriented. We just do not know about them and may thus not understand our subconscious drives. It is also true that our hidden purposes sometimes contradict our conscious thoughts about ourselves and that they can conflict with other, more important goals we may have. Smoking, for example, can effectively fulfil the need to control our emotions, regain inner harmony, fend off stress and suppress unwanted feelings. In that sense, it is a purposeful and effective solution. Unfortunately, it is not only a short-lived solution – we quickly need another cigarette – it also undermines our more vital goal of maintaining our health.[40] We may display a subconscious form of what economists call 'bounded rationality'. A successful life may require us to stretch these bounds outwards, eliminating conflicting behaviour.

We may not always have logical explanations for what we do, because our subconscious motives are hidden and unknown to us. But we may assume that our behaviour is still a matter of cause and effect, so that if we did know our subconscious drives – and in many cases there are techniques by which we can – our behaviour would look understandable and logical, although maybe not always optimal.

The process described in Figure 2.2 takes place almost entirely subconsciously and automatically. And it delivers a preferred brand without our intervention – much like a vending machine producing a can in response to a coin. What marketers can do to improve the chances of their brand being chosen is influence the way their brand is encoded in their customers' brains, by following the three laws explored in Chapters 3 to 8.

Step 2: Start focusing on 'accessibility' as a key measure

The alternative view on brand choice presented here comes with a specific key indicator of brand strength: accessibility. We have seen that our brain selects the brand most consistently built according to the three branding laws. This brand is the first to gain access to our conscious mind and will then be chosen in response to a goal. Accessibility measures the ease or swiftness with which a brand comes to mind in response to the activation of a goal.

This means that the standard measure of top-of-mind awareness must be broadened and take prominence in quantitative brand research. What we should measure is which brands have the highest top-of-mind awareness in response to the subconscious purchase drivers in the category (using specific qualitative techniques). In the car example, this means you cue people with statements regarding status, safety, fuel consumption, interior design, price, etc. and register which of the category's brands comes to mind first in response to each statement. In Chapter 4, we will look at a tool that has been designed specifically for this purpose.

Step 3: Prepare yourself for suspicion and concerns

Neuromarketing is controversial and the idea that branding is primarily aimed at influencing the subconscious choice processes of customers may be even more so. People are understandably afraid of this. *Caveat emptor* (buyer beware) gains a new meaning in this context. But brand owners should be prepared for this so that they can respond wisely. In Chapter 9, we will consider whether using neuroscienctific knowledge in branding is morally acceptable. The chapter provides ethical perspectives and arguments of value to both marketers and consumer advocates.

Step 4: Understand the differences between the new approaches and traditional

Perhaps you are not interested in the why and how of brand choice and the three laws. Perhaps you are only interested in what you must start to do to implement the ideas in this book. While the chapters that follow answer this question in depth, Table 2.3 summarises some of the key differences between the traditional and this book's approaches.

TABLE 2.3 Traditional and *Branding with Brains* approaches compared

	Traditional approach	**Branding With Brains Approach**
Brand choice	Is conscious and deliberate	Is subconscious, fast and algorithmic
Qualitative research	Uses interview techniques (e.g. focus groups) that are biased towards cognitive, socially desirable answers	Uses motivational research designs (e.g. projective techniques) that explore subconscious choice drivers
Quantitative research	Measures the brand-to-associations relationship (e.g. Citibank is proactive in dealing with my problems)	Measures the associations -to-brand relationships (e.g. Proactive in dealing with my problems: which bank is the first that comes to mind?)
Brand positioning	Tracks performance on brand values. Analyses brand image	Tracks performance on a 'universe' of customer goals
Concept development	Creates a 'big idea' for advertising	Analyses brand association networks. Crafts a concept that is meaningful to customers and to the strategic and operational decisions of executives
Brand communication	Create adverts based on a key insight	Develops encompassing yet specific brand concepts based on needs cocktails
Brand management	Protects your brand against misuse	Opens up the brand and encourages brand participation

Conclusion

Brand choice is a predominantly subconscious, memory-based process that follows a fixed algorithm. This view represents a radical break with conventional wisdom.

The process is fast, largely automatic and purposeful. It is set in motion by the activation of a customer goal 'cocktail' which further activates brands in the memory that could fulfil this category-specific cluster of needs (goals specifically related to cars, or to insurance, or to parcel services, etc.). These brands enter a competition for awareness that is resolved quickly based on our brand-choice algorithm. The winning brand enters our awareness as the preferred option and will be adopted – unless our conscious mind deliberates or vetoes our choice. The preferred brand, the one that enters our mind *first*, is said to be the most 'accessible' brand. Accessibility is the end measure of the degree to which a brand has been built according to the three laws or, in other words, is favoured by the brain's algorithm.

Especially in categories in which brands strongly shape choice behaviour (for example, cars, beer, mobile phones, parcel services),[41] accessible brands are winning brands. This is not because people simply go with the first brand they can think of but because the first is the most suitable brand. The accessibility of your brand at the moment of choice is therefore all-important.[42]

The three laws of branding help maximise the chance of your brand being chosen. That is why the remainder of this book looks at them in detail.

Chapter 3

Law No.1: Relevance

Many decision makers see branding as an unruly, fluffy discipline that is hard to integrate into their business routines and strategic thinking. This attitude cuts them off from managing their most valuable asset. By contrast, this book offers executives and marketing professionals an objective, common framework for brand strategy based on neuroscientific insights gained over several decades. A cornerstone of the framework is that our brain makes brand choices using an unconscious algorithm, selecting brands that have been built according to the three laws of relevance, coherence and participation. In this chapter, we look at the first law of branding so that in the next chapter we can see how to put it into action in order to build stronger brands.

Why the brain picks relevant brands

Have you noticed that people with expert experience in a particular field can make complex decisions very quickly when under great time pressure? For example, surgeons, firefighters and police officers in the aftermath of natural catastrophes or attacks are often able to save many lives because they are able to act instantly, even in relatively new circumstances. Research shows that experienced decision makers rarely need to choose between options when facing deadlines, because only a single option comes to their mind. Which option? Only the most relevant course of action enters their conscious awareness. The rejected options are filtered out.[1]

Relevance and survival

In a similar way, we all make most of our brand choices quickly, largely automatically and purposefully. The brain quickly retrieves information it considers important to a certain task or situation and suppresses less relevant impressions. In some cases the brain selectively forgets certain information so as to make it easier to remember things that are more important.[2] Relevance is a key criterion by which the brain structures and restructures itself and stores and retrieves information. Therefore, it is of the utmost importance for brands.

> relevance is of the utmost importance for brands

Relevance is at the heart of the brand-choice process that is set in motion by the activation of a 'cocktail' of goals, which then activates brands in the memory that could fulfil those needs. In order to be chosen, the networks of neurons representing our brand must be connected with the networks of neurons representing the most important customer goals. Activation of the goal then leads to a quick and automatic activation of our brand, based on the brain's pre-set evaluations of the brand, or what are sometimes called 'heuristics' or 'affective tags'.[3] This, then, is a key task for brand strategy: we must position our brand in such a way that it satisfies the cocktail of goals of customers. The cocktail of goals the brand is linked to defines the meaning of the brand for customers. Therefore, we sometimes call the cocktail the *field of meaning* in which the brand is positioned.

The evolutionary logic of relevance is easy to see. Survival and reproductive chances increase when biologically significant information, for example about food or sex, is well stored in the memory and easily retrievable. But what does this mean for brands? Clearly, iPhones, televison sets or accounting services do not satisfy basic biological needs like nutrition and breeding. So how can brands become truly relevant, coveted and sometimes even craved?

Branding and social learning

Part of the answer is through a learning process that is part of what sociologists call 'socialisation'. Through socialisation we gain an understanding of our culture and find our way of living within it. We 'download cultural software', so to speak. We learn the skills, norms, habits, attitudes, values, social roles, language and symbols we need to participate within our society. And in this development we also learn the value and specific meaning of brands through our interactions with family, peer groups, teachers, colleagues, role models, advertising and the media. Social class, for example, with its normative rules about what is and what is not acceptable, can thus have a strong influence on our tastes, likes and interests – as French sociologist Pierre Bourdieu has famously observed:

> To the socially recognised hierachy of the arts, and within each of them, of genres, schools or periods, corresponds a social hierarchy of the consumers. *This predisposes tastes to function as markers of 'class'.*[4]

So while brands initially have little fundamental biological importance (compared with food, water, shelter, and so on), we learn to appreciate the abstract rewards of iPods, Nike running shoes, Diesel jeans, ING Direct accounts, McKinsey consulting services, etc. Previously irrelevant things can become powerful symbols of reward. The brain assigns them a high relative value and strongly activates our dopamine circuits when we think of them. The result is that through 'brand socialisation' we learn to value things we previously did not need. Although within an indigenous community our brands mean next to nothing, they gain enormous significance within our affluent societies, to the extent that some people tattoo brand logos on their skin. But how does this work? What happens inside our brain during this process?

Neuroscientists have found that the process of cultural learning is influenced by a brain function called the dopamine system, which plays a role in reward and motivation. Neurologically, what happens during brand socialisation is that abstract rewards rise to the same level of importance as food and sex. We learn to associate a Starbucks logo with the biological rewards of a warm, gratifying cup of coffee and a BMW with positive comments from friends and colleagues, for instance. Brands gradually become promises of reward, strongly guiding our thinking and action towards obtaining them. Through social learning we gradually assign brands a 'substituted' biological relevance. This learning process is so powerful that cults or fundamentalists can come to value an idea or ideology more highly than life itself and are prepared to die for it.[5]

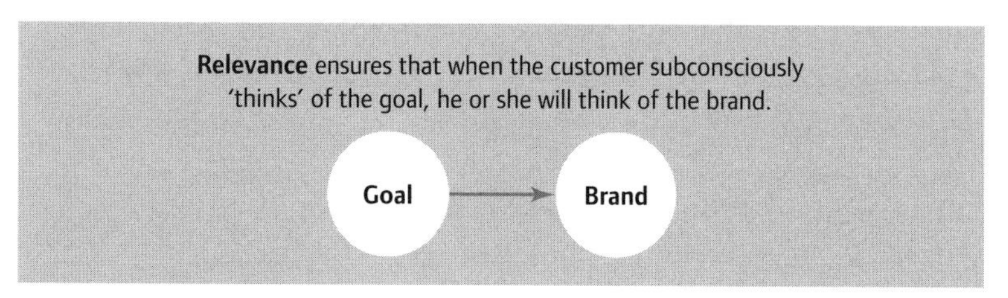

FIGURE 3.1 Law No.1: Relevance

So building a brand in the mind of customers is a learning process in which the brand – from the viewpoint of the marketer – must become linked to their subconscious goals and become highly valued by the brain. A brand must promise and prove to the brain that it delivers important rewards like nutrition, shelter, security, social contact and status. Through information and experience, the brain must create new physical connections between the circuits of neurons that represent brands, those that represent goals and those that record value and reward. So car brands become connected to safety and status, among other concepts. Private banks must link themselves to confidentiality and financial expertise. High-end camera brands must become associated with creative freedom and picture quality. Nappies must link themselves to dry babies and feelings of good parenthood. This process of brand socialisation happens less through explicit persuasion, such as 'Hilfiger Jeans are trendier because Brad Pitt wears them.' It happens mostly through implicit persuasion – imitation of examples, rejection by peers of people who use other brands, for instance. Our culture, then, is rich in symbolic meaning. And with the increasing intensity of communication and the global mixing of cultures, we live in a symbolic maze that marketers must understand at a deeper level than most traditional tools permit.

Emotions as indicators of relevance

In many cases, brands that have associated themselves with the things we find important generate stronger emotional responses. Emotions are a way in which the brain detects value. Sometimes we are aware of these emotions, sometimes we see them only in subtle bodily expressions, and sometimes they are registered only in brain scans. Some marketers conclude from this that all we have to do is associate positive emotions with our brand to make it strong and powerful. This is a mistake. In the context of brands, emotions that lead to choice and actual buying seem to flow from relevance, not the other way round. We are excited about a new iPhone *because* it is so uniquely relevant to us and satisfies our subconscious needs cocktail so well. Emotions let us know what is relevant and significant to us.[6]

So how do we come to associate our brands with customer goals? Advertising plays its part, especially for undifferentiated products. But making products and services that actually fulfil needs better and more distinctively than competitors is the most important precondition. For brand choice is not only determined by the expected reward, or brand promise. The brain also keeps track of errors in reward prediction, so that a brand that disappoints us is less likely to be chosen in similar circumstances in the future. Other influences are cost, effort, uncertainty and the potential value of delaying reward.[7] Choice is therefore situation- and category-specific and the learning process ensures that the brand's mental value is continually updated. A brand, therefore, is a constantly evolving mental asset, even if its marketer sits still and does nothing to change it.

Winning the awareness battle

It is clear, however, that the more rewarding (i.e. relevant) a brand seems to be, the more likely it will win the competition for awareness. Our brain is geared towards optimising our chances of survival and the brand with the highest 'substituted' biological relevance is most likely to be selected. The relevance of a brand depends on its association with the cocktail of customer goals activated in a certain situation. But how does the brain choose between several relevant brands? BMW, Volvo, Volkswagen, Audi are all great car brands, linked to important goals such as safety and status. So which one is selected?

The simple answer is that your brain selects the brand with the highest overall relevance to you. It must either be linked to goals which other brands are less associated with (for example, a Volvo is less strongly associated with upper-class sophistication than is a Jaguar); or be more rewarding by better fulfiling the customer goals (for example Ben & Jerry's ice cream provides more indulgence than a supermarket's own-label brand). Brands that are associated with the same goals and have equal potential for fulfilling them then engage in a more vigorous battle for awareness. Identical brands can repress each other, giving a distinctively relevant brand a better chance of entering our awareness and receiving our attention.[8] Brands lacking distinctiveness will lose the awareness battle.

Choice, therefore, takes place largely based on relevance or the expected value of a brand. This expected value can be thought of as an unconscious attitude that allows us to make fast and reflexive judgments.[9] Again, this attitude can express itself in the form of an emotional response to a brand of which we may or may not be aware.

Leica and the art of photography

One brand that has been particularly good at implementing the first law is Leica, the German optics company. Leica produces a range of products of which its digital and analogue cameras and lenses are the best known. The company's first camera was introduced in 1925 at a trade fair, and Leica has been at the forefront of technical perfection ever since.

The anatomy of brand love

Traditionally, Leica was the brand used by the world's most famous professional photographers and photo journalists – people like Henri Cartier-Bresson, Robert Capa, Alfred Eisenstadt, James Nachtwey and Anton Corbijn. As a result, many of the world's most memorable images have been shot with Leicas.

Photographs, as American essayist Susan Sontag observed, help shape the visual frame of reference by which we interpret what we see, decide what is worth looking at and what we morally have the right to look at.[10] Thus, Leica probably has had more influence on our collective visual education than any other photography brand. This, along with Leica's unrelenting pursuit of technical perfection, its beautiful designs and its exclusivity, has given the brand a cult status among professionals and passionate amateurs alike. It has become intimately connected with the needs cocktail and valuation centres in the brains of potential clients, so much so that it generates strong emotional responses that resemble those of a love affair. In 2006, eBay and *Stuff* magazine in the UK named the Leica M3 the 'top gadget of all time', ahead of the the iPod, the Walkman and the Game Boy.[11] Cartier-Bresson once said that the Leica felt like 'a big warm kiss, like a shot from a revolver, and like the psychoanalyst's couch'.[12] Few brands get such deeply personal praise from their professional clients. In the words of Leica's CEO Andreas Kaufmann:

> Leica has always been a brand that you simply want to have. And that is what we want it to be. For example, not so long ago a famous photographer called me and said: 'Can you give me an M8 in return for some PR I will do for you?' So I gave him the M8. Then a week later he forwarded me an email from his agent who reminded him that he had a sponsor contract with another camera brand. So he, somewhat disappointed, gave me back the M8. Then two months later, his wife called me. And she said: 'You know, he really wants the M8. Can't we arrange something so that I can give it for his birthday?' So now he finally has an M8.[13]

In short, Leica is connected with the needs cocktail of a highly demanding group of people – professionals and amateurs – for whom a camera is not a toy, but a tool with which to create art.

Boosting relevance

It is easy to idolise Leica. But it is much more interesting to see how Leica is dealing with the adversity it met several years ago (see Figure. 3.2). In the early 2000s, Leica lost ground to digital cameras. In response, it introduced high-quality digital cameras for everyday use, sold its lenses to Panasonic and presented a more professional digital camera called the M8. These moves brought the company stability and provided a new foundation on which to rebuild its brand.

Leica is currently redefining itself to boost the relevance of its brand to today's demanding customers. It has introduced a new digital camera system, the Leica S2, which is a medium-format range with autofocus. By introducing its first automatic focusing system, Leica closes the perceived digital gap with other leading brands and regains relevance within a larger group of professional photographers.

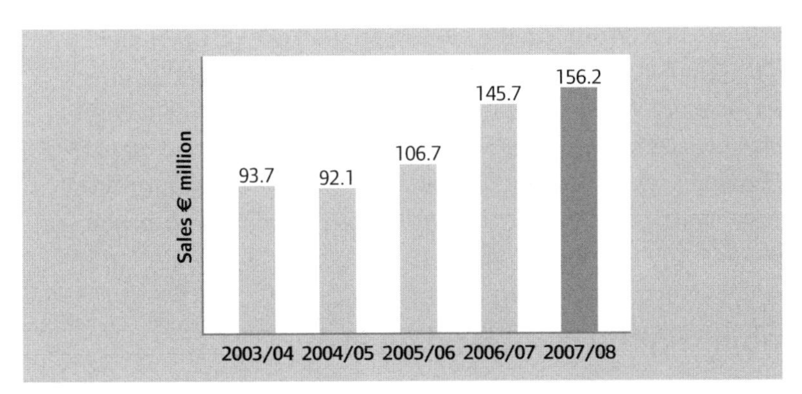

FIGURE 3.2 Leica is on its way back

Source: Leica Camera Group *Annual Report 2007–2008*

Analysing Leica's response

We can use the branding triangle to analyse these moves more closely. Leica certainly did not fall into the identity-loss trap (Figure 1.2). It did not, for instance, recklessly bring out cheap digital cameras as soon as the technology became available. Such an attempt to keep up sales would have undermined its brand identity. It would have created low-quality associations in people's minds and threatened its legendary status. Some pundits say Leica did fall into the authenticity trap, in that it stuck too long to the technologies that defined its legacy: mechanical, analogue cameras. In part, this is the result of unfortunate communication management by the company. It presented its first digital camera in 1996 and earned a patent for autofocus in the 1970s. But in both cases, it decided not to switch to the new system. In the first instance it deemed digital quality not yet good enough; in the case of autofocus, its board at the time judged that its clients did not need it and handed the patent over to Panasonic.

What Leica chose to do, then, was to address its brand strategy problem not by launching an advertising campaign or a PR window-dressing operation. It chose instead to solve two product-related issues: boosting its digital prowess and bringing in autofocus. It did so in a way that could strengthen the brand's distinctive relevance among a younger generation of professional photographers and demanding amateurs. It launched a new professional flagship that could boost its position at the high end of the market. From there, it can work down to upgrade its entire product line, strengthening its relevance in keeping with the brand's history and core identity. This means Leica will strengthen its associations with classic customer goals like creative freedom, lens quality, technical excellence and quick shooting, while customers will connect its brand with new needs like digital picture quality.

Embracing the first branding law

Competitors in any industry fight out a battle for conscious awareness whenever customers are faced with choice. Companies compete in markets. But their brands compete in the brains of potential customers. Coke fights Pepsi, Nike runs against Adidas, Apple battles Sony and FedEx combats UPS in the subconscious minds of potential clients. The law of relevance is a key factor in winning the battle, and the following actions will help you to develop a brand strategy that embodies the first law.

Step 1: Be rigorous in implementing the first law

The brain's algorithm for selecting brands is strongly biased towards brands that are different in a relevant way. Our brains are hard-wired to seek reward from brands. In a sense, it is all that our brains want. Creating distinctive relevance is therefore the overriding criterion for any brand, in any situation, in any activity aimed at customers. Executives at any level should ask themselves: does this new product, service, experience or advertising campaign stand out from the competition in a way that satisfies the subconscious goals of my particular group of customers? In short, is it uniquely rewarding?

> our brains are hard-wired to seek reward from brands

Step 2: Apply it to all low-cost brands too

Relevant differentiation is a prerequisite for any brand, including low-cost players. AIDA and conventional wisdom never told us that relevant differentiation was an imperative for any brand in any industry. But it is, because relevance flows from the very structure of our brain. Being the low-cost brand in the market can be highly relevant to certain customers. Brands like the Aldi chain in retailing and easyJet in aviation cannot ignore relevant differentiation in their low-cost strategy if they want to be chosen by the brain's algorithm.

Step 3: Always start at the bottom

We have seen that our brains learn the value of brands through a process of cultural learning. In this process, the value our brains place on basic rewards (those provided by nutrition, shelter, mates, etc.) is extended to the more advanced rewards provided by cars, mobile phones, parcel services, machine tools, and so on, through what psychologists call 'operant conditioning'. This means that when building a strong brand, we must start by linking it to the most elementary needs of the category first before we can attach more 'emotional' values. We must start at the bottom.

For example, an insurance company selling pension services cannot start with promising a luxurious life in retirement (i.e. more abstract end values) before its potential customers have associated the brand firmly with basic, functional category values like being trustworthy, possessing the necessary financial expertise and making products that provide tangible benefits. The most successful 'thematic' advertising campaigns, therefore, are often the ones that show how the brand's mentality provides functional relevance. For instance, mobile operator Orange – owned by France Telecom – wanted to stand out by presenting itself as a sophisticated lifestyle brand in its advertising. Unless it made clear how this mentality simultaneously translated into better functional benefits (for example, better service, extended freedom in use, simpler billing.) it could never build a brand that its customers' brains would find strongly rewarding. Very often, this is where the problem lies. Many companies do not develop products and services with their brand in mind. They do not start at the bottom. Thus, they end up with a distinctive promise but a weakly relevant brand. Implementing the first law is often not so much a creative challenge, but a managerial and organisational one.

Brands are relevant to the degree that they trigger biological or psychological reward signals in our brains that activate the dopamine system. Applying the first law of branding, therefore, means educating customers' brains on the rewarding features of a brand, by associating the brand with existing needs and then gradually replacing them with more abstract needs and distinctive rewards. This means that we build brands by starting with instrumental associations before we can gradually add more emotional ones.

Step 4: Understand how customers learn and change

The fact that branding is a cultural learning process also means that the value customers place on particular brands can change. This has two important implications for marketers.

> marketers can influence the factors customers use to select brands

First, instead of taking customers' needs as a given, marketers can influence the factors customers use to select brands in their industry. In his book *A New Brand World*, Scott Bedbury, former marketing director at Nike, describes how Nike was able to transform the trainer category by consistently communicating a spirit of 'irreverence' (an emotional benefit). Today, such a mentality seems relevant for a broad group of consumers whereas in the 1980s all that counted to Nike's narrow client base was the ability to produce a lightweight professional running shoe (a functional attribute).[14]

Secondly, broad value shifts in society as a whole will sooner or later filter into the needs cocktails that customers use subconsciously to activate brands from memory. The challenges of sustainable development, for example, have become relevant to many people in the west. A McKinsey study conducted in 2008 found that 56 per cent of executives around the world said companies should balance profits with contributing to the public good because it was 'the right thing to do'.[15] Similarly, customer choices are increasingly influenced by the idea that, in the words of economist Jeffrey Sachs, we share a common fate on a crowded planet.[16] Sustainability and a whole cluster of related associations have infiltrated the needs cocktails of customers in all sorts of industries, from food and energy to cars and financial services, changing the dynamics of brain competition. The key for brands is to be the first to associate their brands with these new elements in their customers' needs cocktails. This creates a competition for associations, which we shall explore in the next chapter.

Conclusion

The principle of relevance is a key part of the brain's algorithm for making brand choices. The higher the relevant differentiation of a company's branding efforts, the higher the chance the brand will be chosen. This is the first law of branding.

Brands are in large part built through a socialisation process, in which the abstract rewards of brands rise to the same level of importance as food and sex. The brain assigns brands a 'substituted' biological relevance.

Distinctively relevant brands have a higher chance of being chosen – all other factors being equal – as the battle for awareness is biased towards valuable concepts that stand out. This provides a review criterion that you can use to assess all customer-facing initiatives: does this new product, service, experience or advertising campaign stand out from the competition in a way that satisfies the subconscious goals of my customers?

The first law is also crucial for low-cost brands. Moreover, to facilitate the emergence of brands with more abstract promises we must begin by associating them with the functional needs of the category. Finally, brands can influence the needs cocktails that customers use to evoke brands. Similarly, broad societal trends like sustainability can quickly infiltrate the needs cocktails of customers in diverse industries.

So how can you implement the first law to build a stronger brand? Chapter 4 will show you.

4 Chapter

Making your brand uniquely rewarding

The branding triangle helps you to tailor your brand strategy to the way our subconscious decides what we buy. The first law flows from the idea that the brain selects the brand it considers best able to satisfy our biological and cultural goals. We subconsciously select the brand that is the most uniquely rewarding, based on its associations with the brain's reward centres.

But too often the multifaceted cocktail of subconscious needs to which we must link our brand is almost entirely unknown to marketers. In most cases, insight into customer behaviour is narrow and superficial instead of rich and deep. Hence, the creative concepts used to position the brand are often only based on an analysis of brand image, the positioning of competitors' and customers' socially desirable answers about themselves. Given the major role of the subconscious in brand choice, we must adopt different tools to be effective. This chapter outlines some of the most important changes we must make.

Gathering 'thick' customer information

Social scientists sometimes distinguish between 'thin' and 'thick' information. The first refers to factual and objective data, such as the monthly number of units sold or the customer churn rate. Thick information is qualitative data that is rich in meaning, such as the insight that some working parents experience feelings of guilt towards their children. To associate our brand with the cocktail of subconscious goals, we must gather 'thick' and 'thin' customer information.

'Think different'

Most standard research methods do not help to identify subconscious customer goals, as they read only from customers' conscious minds. Typical focus groups, for example, ask people to answer questions about products, services, brands, advertising and other topics of interest to marketers. But have you ever seen a mother admitting before the whole group that she only buys Pampers because she feels guilty when spending less on private-label nappies? When we were creating a campaign for the introduction of Mars Delight, the women we were targeting did not tell us directly that they longed more for chocolate when they had struggles with their husbands or boyfriends. Do you remember the quote from the Harley-Davidson executive in Chapter 1? The chances are that no 43-year-old accountant has ever told the researcher in a focus group that he loves his Harley primarily because it allows him to have people fear him. We once did a test-drive study for Dodge using its biggest SUV. From the twinkle in peoples' eyes after they drove it, we could see they loved it. But nobody said explicitly they loved the feeling of power the car gave them. If we are to win the subconscious battle of brands, we must start to focus on the factors that determine our customers' choices below their own awareness.

Option 1: Start asking indirect questions

The first option is to use interpretative and sense-making research methods that elicit subconscious motives ('*Verstehen*'). Such methods do not ask direct questions but indirect ones. Common research questions like, 'Would you respond to this job advertisement, if you were looking for a new challenge?' are quite useless. Our actual behaviour is determined by subconscious thoughts and attitudes that are situation-specific and to which we have no direct access.[1] For this reason, tools like the Zaltman Metaphor Elicitation Technique (ZMET) have received more attention. Such techniques use images, metaphors, archetypes and storytelling to explore how customers think and feel about brands. They can be used to delve for insights, because they help us access the areas we cannot access consciously.[2] One funeral services company, for example, found that people often longed for more personal involvement with the ceremony but were afraid to say so because they were unsure about what was and was not appropriate. The company adjusted its positioning and propositions to help its clients in this area. Other techniques go even deeper and explore what, for example, energy means to people. Such techniques would find that energy is part of the deep biological need for shelter and the equivalent of what fire must have meant to our prehistoric ancestors. The results of such techniques are rich and meaningful clusters of goals that are useful for the development of brand concepts and communication campaigns.

Ethnographic, narrative and diary-reporting techniques are increasingly being used to gain a better understanding of true behaviour and its underlying causes. One company, for example, found out through narrative techniques that people who claimed to despise what they called 'manipulative' television shows like *Treasure Island* and *Big Brother* nonetheless tuned in to such shows because of their desire to unwind at the end of a working day. This is the sort of insight that conventional techniques are less likely to reveal. In online research, picture-sorting techniques are being used to gain quantitative insight in implicit associations.

One of the key points of these methods is that they avoid asking customers direct questions, because as human beings we are not well informed about the drivers of our own behaviour.[3] If an insurance company asks someone how likely he or she would be to choose that company when in need of a retirement scheme, the company will get an answer. But the answer is unreliable. It may not be a lie, but it is essentially devoid of meaning. We are asking customers to step outside their own experiences, to separate themselves from the context in which this choice would take place, and we assume they have accurate insight into the subconscious cocktail of goals and the insurance company's relationship with it that will influence their choice in that particular situation. In a way, the question is absurd.

Ernst Dichter, in his 1964 *Handbook of Consumer Motivations*, made a wonderful overview of motives and drivers behind a range of products and services, based on almost therapeutic interview methods.[4] This type of research has completely fallen out of fashion, despite the fact that insight into motives is crucial for implementing the first law. Sense-making research techniques will gain ground in the coming years.

Brain-scanning technologies like fMRI can also tell us what is going on inside our brains – things we ourselves do not know – as we mentioned in the Coca-Cola example in Chapter 2. Yet although brain imaging is a fascinating and very tangible application, most experts do not expect it to bring about a real revolution for branding soon. For one thing, most techniques are still expensive and inaccurate. Functional MRI, for example, takes images at intervals of generally 1–4 seconds and cannot currently take pictures of areas smaller than 1 millimetre – in which hundreds of thousands of neurons are located. Moreover, subjects must lie perfectly still, as movements greater than a few millimetres can result in unusable data. And a further problem is that when we are lying still for an hour or so in an fMRI machine in a laboratory, our brain functions may not be typical of the real-life situations we want to study.

> keep in touch with customers and listen well

Option 2: Learn to listen

The second option is simply to keep in touch with customers and to listen well. Nike does this. Even in smaller markets, it has dozens of people who do nothing but have conversations with customers. Their job is to get new products into the hands of customers and ask them what they think about them. They not only listen with a view to improving existing products; they also talk to clients about their lives in general, so that they can find ways in which the company can develop more accurately tailored products. Other teams are in constant contact with professional users, trying relentlessly to come up with designs that better fit their evolving demands. They use no focus groups, no standard research tools; instead, they simply maintain an open line to key customers 24 hours a day. McKinsey & Company, the management consulting firm, is another example. Its partners are on first-name terms with many CEOs from global top-1,000 corporations and often act as confidants. Often these relationships are decades old, and even if they are not necessarily billable they are nevertheless valuable to both parties. As a result, McKinsey has the reputation of being always within arm's reach, of knowing what is going on in boardrooms, and what its clients value when.

Ingredients in our needs cocktails

Not only must we change the way we delve for insights, we must also change what we look for. Traditionally, marketers look especially for the functional benefits sought by customers. Take the soup category. In most cases the focus is on taste varieties, saltiness, freshness of ingredients, convenience of packaging, and so on. There is nothing wrong with this. But Figure 4.1 shows that, in addition to the product, there are six other types of goals customers can use for activating brands.[5] If your brand is not connected to them while your competitors' brands are, your brand may not be found by the brain's subconscious search engine.

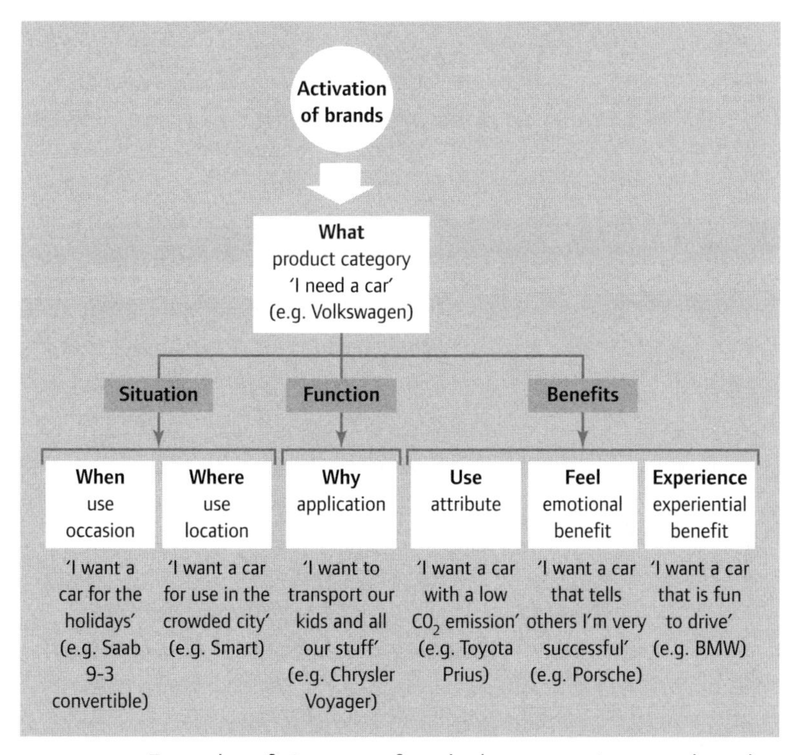

FIGURE 4.1 Examples of six types of goals that can activate car brands

Apart from guiding you on what to look for, Figure 4.1 can help you think of alternative ways to position your brand. For example, RVS, an insurance company that is part of the ING Group, created a 'moment' strategy, based on identifying the crucial life stages at which people's financial situation can change dramatically. By positioning itself as a financial guardian, it differentiated itself from competitors who were focusing on more instrumental benefits like transparency and reliability. The seven categories of goals represent the ingredients of our needs cocktail.

Product category – what

In almost all cases, the product category is part of the activated cocktail of goals. For instance, people want beer (Heineken), a mobile phone (Nokia) or a cup of coffee (Starbucks), and brands are activated based on the strength of their link with the category name. In fact, product category strongly determines the specific composition of the needs cocktail – which is why it is placed hierarchically above the other headings in Figure 4.1.[6] Product category will seldom be the only goal, unless a person is a new and inexperienced user in a category and has no specific associations with it.

Time of use – when

The time of use is the second ingredient of the cocktail of goals that determine the brands we activate. During the summer we look at certain apparel brands, food brands or holiday destination brands that we might not consider in winter. Similarly, whether we use a product or service in the morning or evening or for business or pleasure affects the brands we consider.

Place of use – where

The place where the product or service will be used is a third factor the customer's brain can use to activate and select brands. On the beach, customers are drawn towards different beverage brands from those they habitually use at home or in a hotel or in the car – if only because of availability or convenience.

Application – why

The role the customer seeks to give the product or service can influence the brands the brain evokes. For example, whether a customer takes photographs for a magazine or newspaper, for the family album or for sharing with friends by SMS will influence the brand of camera that will suggest itself.

Attributes – use

In most instances, we also look for specific functional features. A company may look for an accounting firm with global offices. An entrepreneur who just sold his company for several millions may look for a private bank with strong investment competences. A young family may want a contract with an energy company that is 'green'.

Emotional benefit – feel

In many situations, people also look for emotional benefits. We may want an MP3 player we like to be seen using, a bank that is socially responsible, or a watch that James Bond wears.

Experiential benefit – experience

Finally, customers are drawn to brands because they are looking for specific experiences. Experiences can be sought in order to attain a certain state of mind or simply in order to do particular things during a period of time. Customers may seek a romantic setting to spend a weekend in (Venice), or a car that is fun to drive (BMW).

Together, these elements comprise the needs cocktail that activates the brands that compete for choice. In the short term these dominant 'choice drivers' are a given for all brands. In the long run, however, they can change, often as a result of broad trends in society. Moreover, brands can influence the drivers customers use to select brands in their industry. In Chapter 3, we briefly discussed how Nike transformed the long-term choice drivers for trainers.

Getting thin customer information

Thin information is more quantitative in nature and is less dependent on context and interpretation. Most companies have lots of it. It can be very useful in building a more relevant brand. However, implementing the branding triangle requires that we change some of the ways in which we gather thin, factual information about the brand.

Repairing brand tracking tools

Most companies use quantitative research to track the status of their brand's image. In most cases the research designs do not reckon with subconscious brand choice. Brand image is usually measured haphazardly, and without relating it to customer behaviour. Here are three basic improvement options.

- *Formulate specific research statements.* In most cases the items measured are broad values (reliable, efficient, professional, etc.) or generic statements (e.g. offers good-quality service). It is often impossible to turn such general measurements into specific recommendations for action.
- *Use a complete set of items.* The statements should be collectively exhaustive. They should measure the whole cocktail of goals. In reality, however, they measure only two or three types of the goals mentioned in Figure 4.1, and may well omit certain crucial drivers.
- *Establish distinctive relevance.* Companies should determine (1) the relevance of each item, to find out which are choice drivers and which are accessories, and (2) the differences in how competitors score on them. In my experience, this is too often forgotten. Companies measure brand awareness and brand image using an incomplete set of badly formulated statements that reflect their core values. Yet image scores and overall awareness say nothing about the economic success of a brand.[7] Meaningful brand management is impossible without establishing the link between brand image and customer choice.

Taking these three measures will improve the value of current brand tracking studies, at little additional cost.

How well does your brand mix?

In the Volvo example in Chapter 2, our young couple sought to satisfy a blend of goals and sub-goals related to *family safety*. Volvo did well, because in the minds of these potential customers Volvo was strongly associated with this cocktail – as a result of their own experiences, stories told by others, years of advertising and seeing other people driving one. The cocktail is different for every category, however, so it would be extremely valuable if brand research could measure how well your brand is connected to the right elements of your customers' needs cocktail. This would provide invaluable information for focusing your brand strategy.

Classic brand research is not suited for this purpose because it measures brand image the wrong way round. It gives people a brand, say Volvo or Leica, and asks what associations they have with it (see right-hand side of Figure 4.2). Thus, we get an idea of how people perceive a brand. Volvo is safe, fuel-efficient, moderately expensive, and so on.

> classic brand research measures brand image the wrong way round

This is certainly useful. But it overlooks the fact that associations have two directions: from brands to needs and from needs to brands. And the most interesting direction is hardly ever measured. What we measure is: what do customers think of when they think of our brand? But does our brand come to their minds in the first place? Few brands know, because almost nobody measures this aspect! We measure evaluation but not activation. The question is: when customers subconsciously call to mind the needs they want to satisfy, are they drawn to our brand? If the answer is no, we are not even considered in the subconscious choice process. So we need to confront customers with questions such as: 'If I say "fuel-efficient in city traffic", which car brand is the first that comes to your mind?' We can thus establish the degree to which a brand is linked to the subconscious cocktail of goals.

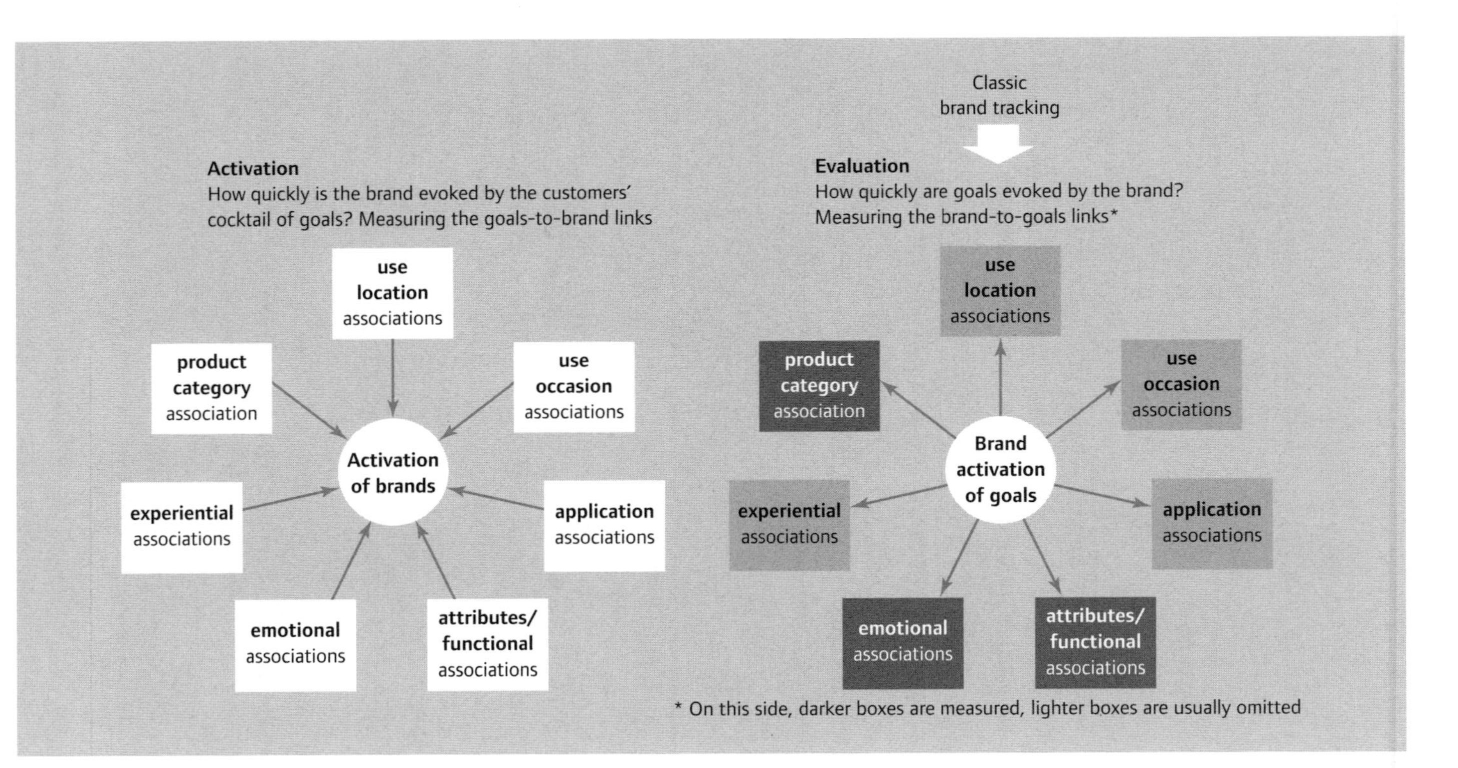

FIGURE 4.2 The two directions of brand associations

Because conventional tools do not measure this, we have created a research tool at our brand consultancy practice at THEY that does. It measures how well a brand and its competitors are linked to your customers' cocktail of subconscious needs. Figure 4.3 shows an example for interior decorating magazines, where the bars indicate the relevance of a range of customer goals and the lines show how well a leading magazine, Brand X, is associated with those goals (solid line) relative to the average of its competitors (broken line). The degree to which the brand is associated with relevant customer goals can then be expressed in a single figure: an index of brand strength. Brands strongly linked to the most relevant goals get a higher score than brands strongly associated with less relevant goals. It provides you with two things: (1) a figure with which to compare the strength of your brand's subconscious brain position with that of its competitors; and (2) visual insight into needs cocktails.

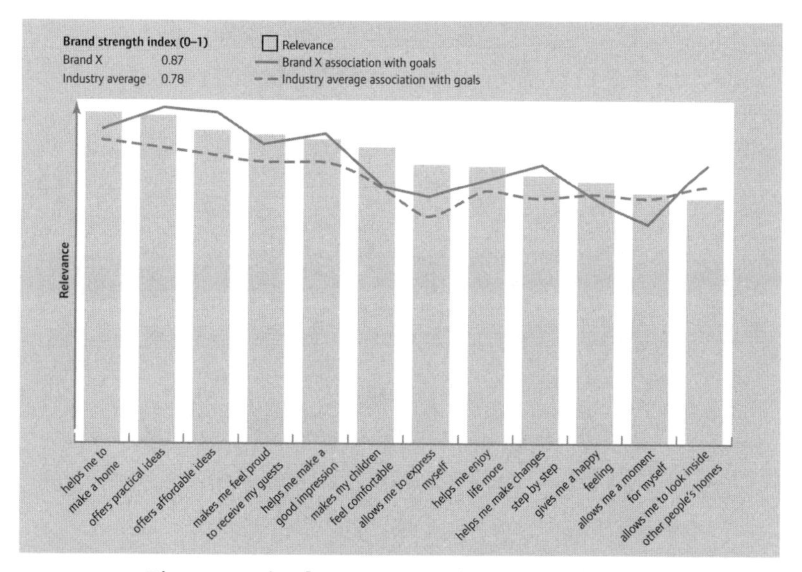

FIGURE 4.3 The strength of association of interior decorating magazines with relevant customer goals

Pondering needs cocktails

Through several analyses, the data gathered for the brand strength index can be turned into visual maps of needs cocktails. These can then be analysed for the purpose of positioning a brand and developing a creative brand concept.

Mapping cocktails of goals

Figure 4.4 shows a ficticious partial map of the needs cocktail for Leica, the camera brand discussed in Chapter 3. The figure shows three purchase goals: to demonstrate good taste, to experience creative freedom and to document family life. The size of the circle indicates the relevance of these goals, showing that creative freedom is the most important of the three to the target group. We do not determine this by asking people directly what they consider relevant – this would cause them to provide conscious, deliberate answers that are unreliable. We determine relevance by calculating correlations with market share, overall brand attitude, or other behavioural measures – thus avoiding asking people questions about their subconscious behaviour. This also allows us to calculate the value of creating stronger associations. In a study for Jeep, for example, we calculated the market share gain of a 1 per

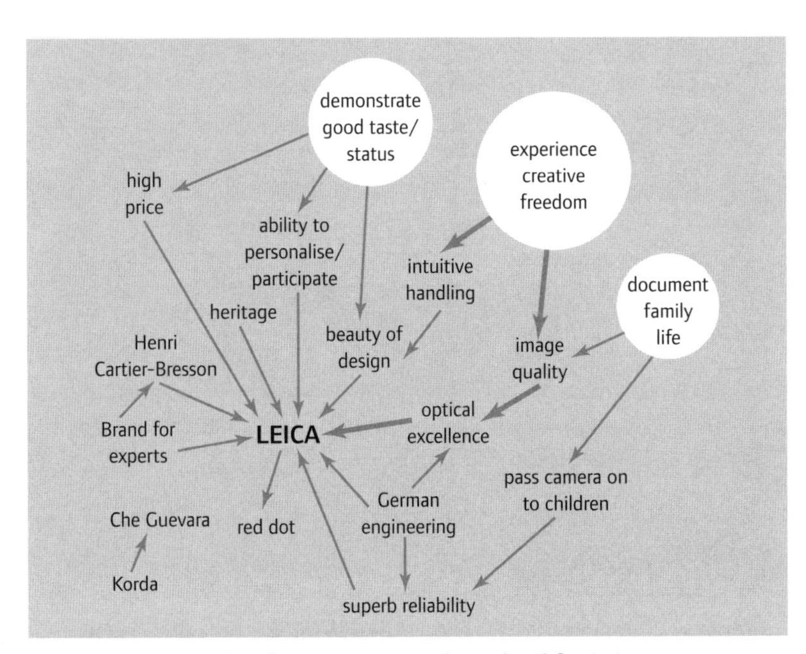

FIGURE 4.4 Example of mapping a needs cocktail for Leica

cent change in a brand driver and then calculated the extra profit for the company as a result of such a market share increase. This gave us a better insight into the balance between the branding investments and the extra profits resulting from them.

The thickness of the arrows in the figure indicates the degree to which Leica is associated with certain needs. Figure 4.4 shows that Leica could improve its relevance by strengthening its link with 'creative freedom' because this arrow is thin. The law of participation (Chapters 7 and 8) would allow a brand to create more and new connections with goals. Figure 4.4 indicates also that emphasising – in this fictional example – its German heritage is not very useful, as it is not a purchase driver. It only supports the notion of optical excellence, which is part of the broader concept of 'creative freedom'.

Charting a brand strategy

Most positioning studies analyse customer needs, the positioning strategies of competitors, developments in the market and the capabilities of the company itself. The needs cocktail can play a central role in such an analysis (see Figure 4.5). Different competitors can be plotted on the needs map and market analysis can be used to create scenarios about how the importance of some goals will change and which new ones will emerge. The current positionings of competing brands can be shown, indicating which associative links they are seeking to strengthen.

Instead of using only thin information about the market, the brand and the customer, we measure how well the brand is associated with the cocktail of subconscious needs that drives choice. A needs map allows us to analyse needs cocktails and brand-association networks, knowledge that will help us to develop much more effective creative brand concepts and brand strategies.

For instance, Figure 4.4 quickly highlights at least four plausible angles for creative concept development and positioning. We could position Leica on each of the three customer goals, or seek a more encompassing concept that integrates all three – we could position Leica as a fashion accessory, as a professional tool for creating artwork, as a valuable recorder of precious family history, or as a combination of the three.

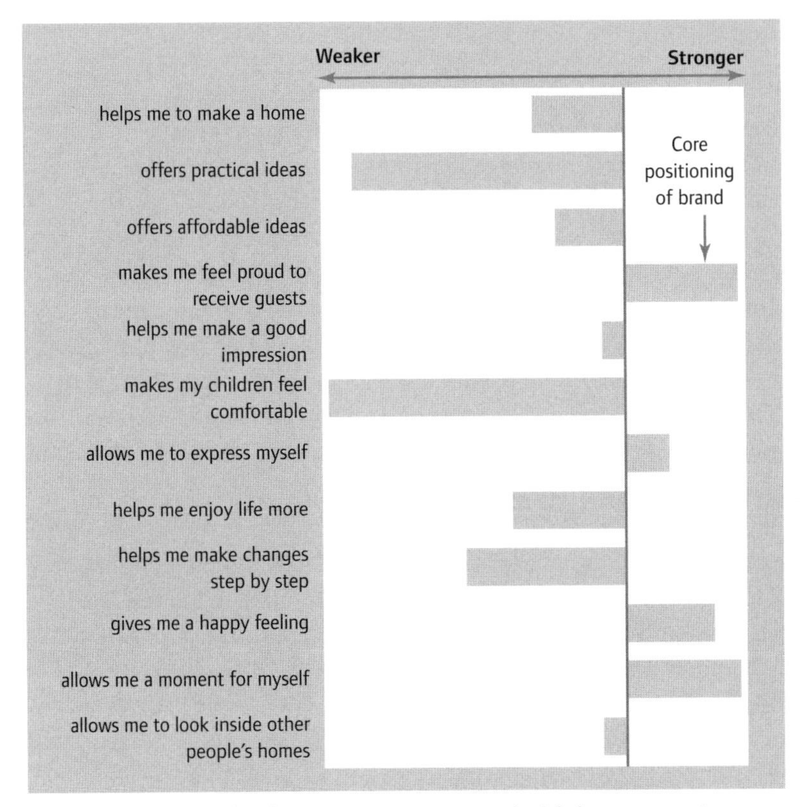

FIGURE 4.5 Strength of associations compared with key competitor

A brand concept should then be worked out and described in detail, so that it can guide communications, product development and strategic decisions. When positioning the brand as a tool for creating artwork, for instance, we may further emphasise that Leicas are being stripped down to their bare functionality or we may simplify the digital interface, in a way that makes a real difference.

Making your brand more distinctively relevant

To sum up, there are two actions you can take to implement distinctive relevance in your brand strategy.

Step 1: Research the subconscious

Ignorance of your distinctive relevance makes your brand vulnerable. Yet in many companies, there is no deep knowledge of the subconscious goals that explain customer behaviour and how well the brand fulfils them. Most research methods are not very helpful as they only read from customers' conscious minds. Successful branding depends on knowing your customers' subconscious goals.

> successful branding depends on knowing your customers' subconscious goals

But when do you know customers well? My rule of thumb is: when you can draw their goals and how your brand is associated with them (in a similar way to the Leica example in Figure 4.4). In other words: when you can confidently draw a map of your customers' needs cocktail.

To do this, you must gather both 'thick' and 'thin' information (i.e. qualitative and quantitative data) in a way that taps the subconscious. You may need to think about interpretative qualitative techniques that use storytelling, projection and metaphors as well as more ethnographic techniques like diary-keeping. Some successful brands rely on extensive personal contact with clients as their main source of 'thick' customer information. Figure 4.1 suggests seven categories of goals to identify. Together, these goals blend into the needs cocktail that activates the brands that compete for final selection by the brain's choice algorithm.

Figure 4.2 suggests that in quantitative research most marketers only measure whether customers associate a very limited set of goals and image aspects with their brand (brand-to-goal link). But you also need to measure how well customers' needs and goals activate your brand (goal-to-brand link). In this way, we measure a brand's accessibility – how well your brand is positioned to win the battle for choice (see Chapter 2). Next, you must determine the relative relevance of these goals and calculate the overall strength of your brand. We use the brand strength index for this purpose (see Figure 4.3). Relevance can shift rapidly, however, within specific categories and within society as a whole. This has happened with the sustainability trend that has become part of many people's needs cocktails in the food, energy and automotive industries. So we need to make regular assessments of the elements of the cocktail.

Step 2: Create brand concepts based on needs cocktails

Creating maps of needs cocktails is based on the diversity of goals in a certain category, the relative importance of those goals and the strength of the brand's associations with them. Such a map creates a visual impression of the neural networks that represent brands and customer goals.

Competing brands can also be plotted, to highlight the associative links they are seeking to strengthen through their brand strategies. Trend analysis can be used to predict shifts in the cocktail that can affect all brands in a category. Needs maps integrate a broad range of valuable data sources in a way that is directly relevant for creative development – which is almost unprecedented in brand strategy. Possessing this data is necessary but not sufficient. It is always about what you do with it and how well you are able to translate it into powerful creative brand concepts. This process cannot be codified but depends almost entirely on the quality and experience of the creative and strategic professionals involved in the process.

Conclusion

Under the influence of the dopamine system, our brains learn about brand rewards and guide our choices towards them. Distinctively relevant brands have a higher chance of being chosen – all other factors being equal – as the battle for awareness is biased towards uniquely relevant concepts. This is the first law of branding.

To implement this first law, we must keep our brand associated in a unique way with the evolving goals customers subconsciously use to activate brands from memory. Leica has been very good at associating itself with choice drivers and as a result of the digital revolution in photography is now establishing more powerful associations with these new customer goals.

The essence of Chapters 3 and 4 can be summarised in several key lessons marketers can use to benefit from the first law of branding.

- Understand how the brain's algorithm is biased toward relevant brands.
- Establish what customers subconsciously consider to be relevant.
- Understand how competing brands are associated with these drivers.
- Position yourself so that you associate your brand with these drivers.
- Use the law of relevance to assess the strength of your business strategy, brand strategy, campaign proposals, product development, etc.
- Understand how drivers can change and how this affects the unique relevance of your brand.

The first law must be applied not in isolation but in combination with the other two laws (see Figure 1.2). In the next two chapters, you will learn how to use the second component of the branding-with-brains framework when we discuss the law of coherence.

Chapter 5

Law No.2: Coherence

We have seen that our brain makes brand choices using a subconscious algorithm, selecting brands that were built according to the three laws of relevance, coherence and participation. The first law states that the brain selects the brand it considers best able to satisfy our biological and cultural goals, based upon its associations with our needs and reward centres. The second one states that the brain selects the brand that has reinforced these associations most frequently in the past. This is the law of coherence. In this chapter we seek to understand the second law so that in Chapter 6 we can see how to put it into action to build stronger brands.

McKinsey's logic of coherence

One company that has skilfully fulfilled the requirements of the second branding law is McKinsey & Company, the most influential consulting firm and one of the strongest business-to-business brands in the world. McKinsey solves senior management issues in the world's leading businesses, governments and institutions. It is the most prestigious firm in its industry and has ranked first or second most-desired employer for MBA graduates for more than a decade. Throughout its existence it has stuck to a simple and relevant business idea and has implemented it with distinctiveness and rigour.

Create your brand promise and stick with it

McKinsey sprang from the vision of Marvin Bower. Bower's idea was 'to provide advice on managing to top executives and to do it with the professional standards of a leading law firm'. McKinsey helps top managers to improve the performance of their organisation and their own credibility as leaders. Bower defined the 'what' (top management advice) and the 'how' (high professional standards) of his company and was disciplined in bringing everything it did in line with his beliefs. He was determined, even ruthless.[1] McKinsey's brand concept originated in the 1930s and the company has stuck with it throughout its history.

McKinsey recruits only the brightest students from any background from the best schools with the highest grades, trains them extensively both on and off the job and screens them using an 'up or out' system in which they either advance rapidly or are asked to leave. McKinsey rarely advertises, unless it wants to attract new recruits (the below advert is from a 2005 university poster campaign).

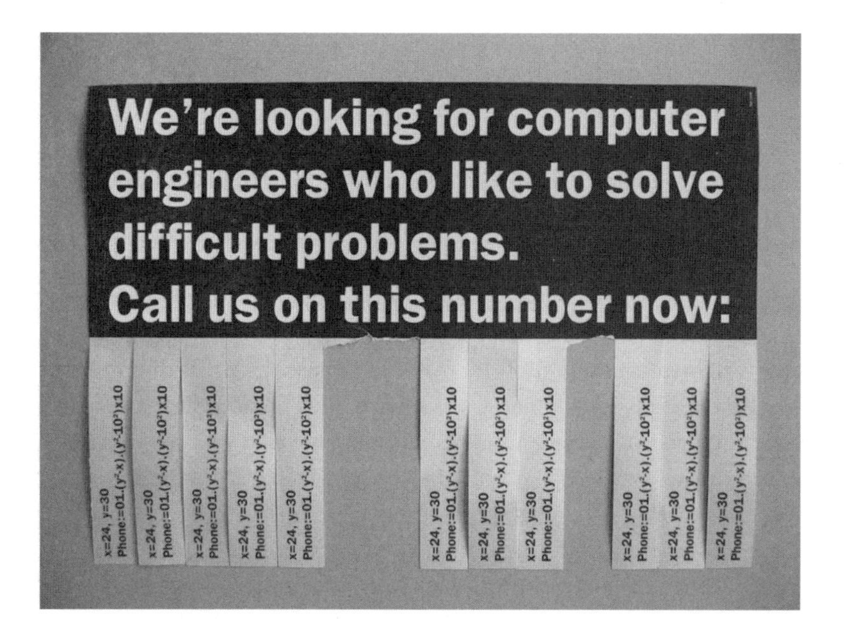

Keep your hands off the marshmallows!

Coherence is a key factor in explaining systematic above-average company performance.[2] McKinsey's genius as a brand is simply that it stuck with its promise for over seven decades. Most brands, like children and politicians – although for different reasons – find it quite hard to keep their promises. Many brands, for example, cannot resist the temptation to sacrifice consistency for short-term revenue gains (graphically illustrated by the 'marshmallow test', which we examine in the next chapter). Some introduce ill-conceived line extensions, just to create additional revenue streams. Bic – best known for its pens and stationery products – once introduced a perfume for no apparent reason, and Pepsi once launched a blue cola called Pepsi Blue that only served to weaken Pepsi as a true cola brand – since everyone expects a real cola to be brown.

Other brands find it hard to be coherent in the picture they present through their advertising. Not so long ago, for instance, we finished a three-month project with a brand-positioning concept that all key players embraced. But when we presented the first proposals based on the approved brand concept, one human resources executive caused quite a stir by saying: 'It is nice, but we are not going to do the recruitment campaign based on the brand positioning.' Fortunately, the client decided to stick to the brand concept instead of allowing immediate inconsistencies.

McKinsey has been very strong at resisting the temptations of grabbing profits that could only be gained through incoherent activities. For example, in 1969 there was a proposal to form a joint venture with another company, DLJ, with the goal of identifying and buying companies that were turnaround candidates. McKinsey would make the company profitable again and then it would be sold off. Bower was deeply opposed to the idea because he felt McKinsey would be moving away from the professional model of detached objectivity and becoming operating businessmen, entagled in the running of a business. The plan was dropped.

Later, when Enron – a big McKinsey client – collapsed into bankruptcy in December 2001, McKinsey reviewed its own work to see if there was any evidence linking the firm to the massive fraud behind Enron's business model. There was no trace of it and McKinsey was not even called as a witness in the legal case.[3] Despite Enron being one of its largest clients, McKinsey had not fallen into the trap of trying to earn more money by engaging in the kind of ambiguous activities that brought down Arthur Andersen, Enron's accountants.

To be sure, McKinsey strayed somewhat from its path during the dotcom boom when it accepted stock as payment – making it no longer independent – and served second- and third-rate clients. But these have been temporary inconsistencies, and the brand has survived, along with McKinsey's unique corporate culture.

Why the brain favours coherent brands

McKinsey's coherence goes a long way towards explaining its success as a brand, in the minds both of clients and of potential employees. Like Google, Starbucks and Apple, McKinsey invests little in advertising. Its strength stems not from adverts but from having a clear business strategy that drives everything the firm does and thus radiates out of all the points of contact the company has with the outside world. It has become part of what in Chapter 3 we called the 'brand socialisation' of senior management. Coherence in branding is about consistency in strategy and execution, above and beyond being consistent only in what you advertise.

While McKinsey is not widely known beyond the commercial world, within the higher echelons of the business community it is a household name. For example, MBA and other bright students sooner or later get in contact with the McKinsey brand and learn its value and significance. McKinsey has always attracted the best people, has been selective about the assignments it takes, delivers high-quality work and remains close to most of the world's most powerful CEOs. But how has coherence turned McKinsey into such a strong brand?

Repeat, repeat, repeat

Coherence is crucial for brands in the same way as rehearsals are critical for actors and musicians. Whether one is practising for a high-school play or for Shakespeare, repetition makes sure that everything an actor is supposed to do and say comes out in the right way at the right moment. But how does this work?

Research conducted in the 1970s by Tim Bliss and Terje Lømo shows how McKinsey's consistency as a company translates into neurological success as a brand. Bliss and Lømo knew that the brain contain billions of neurons, each connected with around 1,000–1,500 other neurons through links called 'synapses'. Through these synaptic interconnections, cells can activate each other. So, for example, the neurons representing a CEO's most relevant goal of, say, getting 'highly confidential, superbly reliable strategic advice' may activate the McKinsey brand name and those of some of its competitors.

But what Bliss and Lømo have demonstrated is that when neuron A repeatedly activates neuron B, the activation will gradually become easier and faster. Repetition makes the communication between synapses more efficient and this leads to a higher excitation of the cells involved. Coherent branding means repeating a similar message. In the case of McKinsey, this means that the goal of getting 'highly confidential, superbly reliable strategic advice' may more rapidly and forcefully activate the McKinsey brand name. So in the brain of our CEO the names of its competitors are repressed, McKinsey enters her awareness as the suitable and only option and she may immediately ask her PA to get hold of McKinsey.

Neuroscientists call this long-lasting improvement in communication between two neurons 'long-term potentiation' (LTP). When we think of the link between two neurons as a road between them, we can say that long-term potentiation means that when such a route is travelled more often, what is initially a bumpy sandy path gradually becomes an efficient motorway. We must take this quite literally, as repetition actually results in detectable, physical changes in brain structure that have been extensively studied.

Eric Kandel, who received the Nobel Prize in medicine for his research, found that repetition and LTP are the foundation of the process of memory creation. More specifically, conversion of a fleeting memory into a longer-term memory requires 'spaced' repetition of that memory. This is true for primitive life forms as well as for higher vertebrates and humans. In Kandel's words, 'Practice makes perfect – even in snails.' More recently, scientists have also found that repeated activation of one memory actually *weakens* competing memories. This facilitates the retrieval of repeated memories over memories that are not repeated, or are repeated less often, creating a winner-take-all effect.[4]

> repeated activation of one memory actually *weakens* competing memories

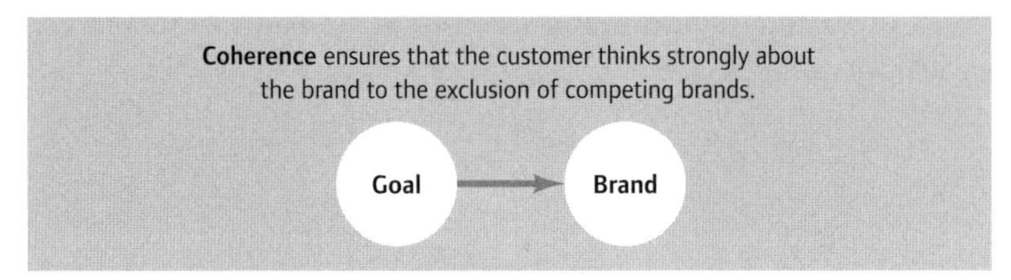

FIGURE 5.1 Law No.2: Coherence

Preventing brand memory loss

In short, because McKinsey has repeated its distinctively relevant message since the 1930s, it has strengthened its associations with the cocktail of goals and the reward centres of senior management in corporations around the globe. As a result, the McKinsey brand is much more easily and vigorously activated in their brains than the brands of McKinsey's competitors and can even repress those brands. This can of course translate into a strong market share in the high end of the consultancy market and higher client loyalty. Indeed, around 80 per cent of McKinsey's work is from returning clients. Repetition strengthens memory. And as long as this memory is distinctively relevant, the brand that has repeated its message most frequently will win the battle for choice.

For brand marketers, this is an important lesson. It provides a strong explanation of why coherence is crucial. For a brand to be top-of-mind at the moment of choice, it is necessary that it is stored in our long-term memory. This means that the brand's key promise must reach our brain repeatedly at certain intervals. If not, associations that are not reactivated will gradually grow weaker. Your customer will start to suffer from memory loss as far as your brand is concerned.

What is coherence in branding?

Marketers who are coherent in their branding approach communicate one specific promise across the two dimensions of *time* (i.e. through the years) and *space* (i.e. at all customer touch points). Figure 5.2 illustrates this. Coherent branding can be recognised when a specific brand promise (that is distinctively relevant) is repeated and fulfilled always and everywhere. It means that your branding activities are in *harmony*: your brand promise is kept and inconsistencies are banned. For coherence to work, however, your brand promise must also be *specific*. It should not be broad-ranging, but unambiguous in the mind of your customers.

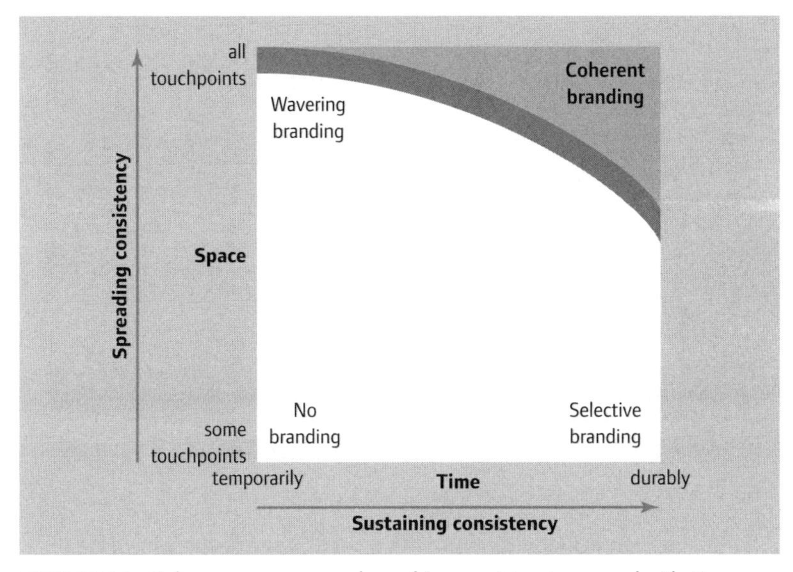

FIGURE 5.2 Coherence means a brand is consistent across both time and space

If any of these conditions are not met, your customer base is likely to suffer from brand memory loss.

Coherence as harmony

Coherent branding can be likened to harmony in music and in colour. Imagine what we would get if we were to translate each of a brand's branding activities into a different musical tone. If coherent, they would together sound like a harmonious song or symphony without false notes.

Think for example of how Coca-Cola has branded itself. Its promise has been coherent at least since it introduced the line 'Have a Coke and a smile' in the late 1970s. It turned into 'Coke is it!', 'Can't beat the feeling', 'Always Coca-Cola', and 'Taste the Coca-Cola side of life' among others. But the premise was always the same – that by drinking Coca-Cola life becomes a little more fun and rewarding.

Scene from Coca-Cola's Happiness Factory Commercial

If transposed into notes, 40 years of Coca-Cola branding might make for a musical symphony. Unfortunately, most campaigns are better not translated into music, lacking appropriate tempo, clever rhythm or the essential unbroken and flawless melodic theme.

Reiteration alone can never make your brand coherent

Yet mere message repetition is not enough. Both McKinsey and Coca-Cola have repeated a specific brand promise throughout their history and this is crucial from a neurological standpoint. Why?

Because the more specific the brand's message over time, the more likely the original 'paths' in the brain are travelled and thus strengthened when repeated.[5] Moreover, a vague claim is less likely to be relevant to customers and can never guide business decisions. So do most brands meet this criterion? Not really. Many brands are touting promises that are much too broad, especially in business-to-business branding. If we look at the well-known phrases adopted by some of the corporate banks to signify their brands, and use these as an indication of their positionings, the picture is not so satisfactory (see Table 5.1).

TABLE 5.1 Corporate banking phrases used in branding

Barclays Capital	**BNP Paribas**	**UBS**
'Earn success every day'	'The Bank for a Changing World'	'You & Us'
Credit Suisse	**Commerzbank**	**Citi**
'Thinking New Perspectives'	'Ideas Ahead'	'Citi Never Sleeps'
Deutsche Bank	**Morgan Stanley**	**HSBC**
'A Passion to Perform'	'World Wise'	'The World's Local Bank'

True, Coke's line 'Taste the Coca-Cola side of life' may not be telling in and of itself. But it is supported by 40 years of coherent advertising. Some of the corporate banking phrases shown in Table 5.1 are not just abstract in themselves. Many have not been supported by concrete deeds and cannot serve to guide strategic and operational business decisions. What is more, such phrases are not really tailored to banking but are interchangeable with the slogans used by ICT companies or accountancy firms. They lack the specificity needed to create coherence and are in danger of coming across as hot air. As such, they are not 'assets' in the volatile economy that emerged after the 2008 credit crisis and that demands a back-to-basics mentality from bankers.

Be flexible yet specific

Many non-governmental organisations (NGOs) suffer from this very same problem and the business-to-consumer sectors are not necessarily much better at creating specific claims. Of course, a brand concept must be sufficiently broad to encompass various products and services, span different regions, unite different functions and subcultures within an organisation. Yet it must not do this by sacrificing specificity. HSBC's 'The World's Local Bank' is a good contrast to being broad and meaningless. ING Wholesale Banking (ING WB) is another example from my own practice at THEY. ING WB has launched its new positioning campaign around the idea of being a no-nonsense bank. The project started at a time when the full extent of the credit crisis was becoming apparent. Together with ING WB, we created a creative concept called 'the bottom line'. We positioned ING WB as a no-nonsense bank by virtue of its focus on what matters most for its clients. Thus, ING WB is not just looking after its clients' profits and revenues. It also emphasises key issues like reducing complexity for clients. Moreover, the concept allows ING WB to talk in a more focused way about whether there is trust in the relationship – something many banks talk about. In short, the 'bottom line' concept allows ING WB to talk about the same range of topics that other banks do, but in a way that is more relevant, distinctive and coherent. The 'bottom line' is an example of a positioning that is both broad and specific. It makes a claim that can enforce consistency. In fact, people inside the bank spontaneously started to think in terms of the concept when making presentations and attending internal meetings. Additionally, it can drive an internal cultural programme to help people act in ways more in line with the 'bottom line' mentality.

Does coherence mean we should endlessly sell exactly the same products and repeat the same commercials? Of course not. That would be boring. The trick is to have variety around a theme. Think of Coca-Cola again. It has used various slogans and many different commercials and print adverts. But the basic promise has remained the same. So the *form* in which the brand is presented must vary, in design, in tone or in phrasing, while the message itself is unchanged. Thus, we can build a brand in a way that is

ING as a bottomline bank

always fresh yet coherent. To do that, we need to formulate a brand promise that is both precise and elastic.

The need to ban inconsistencies

Even regularly reaching your customer with a specific promise is not enough. You must also eliminate inconsistencies. Being inconsistent is probably worse than not communicating at all. It creates confusion at best and bewilderment at worst. It can lead to negative emotions such as aversion and dissonance[6] and your brand can be forgotten, repressed or devalued.

> you must eliminate inconsistencies

- **Forgetting your brand.** Inconsistency cancels the process by which the brain converts a transient brand memory into a permanent one. In other words, inconsistency or incoherence sets in motion a process by which customers start to forget your brand.
- **Repressing your brand.** Incoherent brands send conflicting signals to the brain that can repress the brand, bringing other more coherent brands into a more favourable position, as the brain has a tendency to create categorical and well-defined thoughts. If Coca-Cola suddenly said that its drink added sobriety to our lives instead of happiness, we would very quickly lose track of what it stood for. Incoherence can result in a cascade of what neuroscientists call 'inhibitory signals'. Coke would be repressed, allowing Pepsi and others to win the battle for choice.

Incoherence can destroy financial brand value. Smart branding means repeating a specific brand promise, delivering on it and eliminating inconsistencies.

- **Devaluing your brand**. The brain registers errors between the reward a brand promises and that which it delivers. It adjusts a brand's attractiveness downwards, when a brand delivers below what our brain expects.

Estimating the costs of inconsistency

The idea that consistency is important in branding will be verbally endorsed by most marketers. Yet in practice there is probably no branding concept that is more often ignored. Coherence is easily forgotten in the heat of the battle. Moreover, traditional arguments for coherence are weak. It is supposed to lead to increased brand awareness, greater brand recognition, trust, clarity of purpose for employees, and so on. But such arguments struggle to be heard against a quarterly sales target that underpins the performance promises the CEO has made to shareholders and analysts.

To be chosen by the brain's algorithm, the brand must repeat its promise through the years and not contradict itself. If it does, it risks losing its entire historical investment. If we look at advertising alone (which is always only a fraction of the total branding costs), Coca-Cola has made a cumulative investment of at least $20 billion in its current brand promise since the late 1970s. That is why it is so strongly ingrained in our brains and so difficult to beat. So why would its shareholders endorse a change in its brand strategy that would effectively throw this investment out of the window? Investors have every reason to object to incoherent branding, as it is against their longer-term financial interests. Incoherence is the main form of marketing short-termism. It destroys brand equity, slows a brand's sales growth, pushes its margins down and increases churn rates.

In the next chapter, we will look at a way to measure consistency, to get a better idea of when this issue arises. But to get an idea of the costs, just add up your advertising budget for the years during which you are communicating your current brand promise. That gives you an idea of what you lose when you abandon consistency.

Betting $500 million against coherence

Would you be willing to bet, say, $5 million of your budget against the law of coherence? Most marketers would say no – even though many brands are incoherent. Yet Volkswagen bet 100 times as much against the law when it introduced the Phaeton.

Superb car, wrong brand

Volkswagen's introduction of its top-end limousine, the Phaeton, was the idea of Volkswagen chairman Ferdinand Piëch, who saw the addition of a flagship model as a way of upgrading the Volkswagen brand.[7] Piëch wanted VW engineers to create a car that would surpass the prestige of market leaders Mercedes Benz and BMW. Rumour has it that Piëch gave his engineers a secret list of ten parameters the car needed to fulfil which were so ambitious that some engineers left and others thought they were impossible. One of the requirements, reportedly, was that the Phaeton should be capable of driving all day at 300 km/h (186 mph) in an exterior temperature of 50 °C (122 °F) while maintaining the interior temperature at 22 °C (71.6 °F). In addition to such extreme standards, a special glass factory (Die Glaeserne Manufaktur) with a wooden floor was built for the assembly of the Phaeton, so that clients could see how their car was built. The Phaeton had to compete head-on with other high-end flagship saloons traditionally out of Volkswagen's league, such as the Audi A8, the Jaguar XJ, the BMW 7 series, the Lexus LS460 and the Mercedes Benz S-Class.

But Volkswagen had forgotten about coherence. Not only does coherence have a strong neurological basis, it also has a strong psychological component. Psychologists have found that there is a strong tendency in every one of us to seek out stimuli that are in line with our existing beliefs and attitudes, limiting our exposure to stimuli that conflict with those beliefs and attitudes. This fact limits what marketers can and cannot do in branding. For example, if you are a Detroit carworker you are likely to read articles that praise the virtues of US-built cars and will avoid reading articles that praise foreign vehicles. Thus you can avoid uncomfortable feelings associated with contradictory information – a phenomenon known as cognitive dissonance – and experience only affirmation of your own views – cognitive consistency.[8]

Not for the people

If we were to follow the 'cognitive consistency principle', as psychologists call it, we would expect one of two things to happen to the 'People's Car' brand as a result of the Phaeton introduction. Either customers would reject the model because it contradicted the Volkswagen image of selling 'solid, precise, quality-driven, high-value vehicles'.[9] In that case, a high-end VW would seem less credible or would be seen as a slightly bigger yet much more expensive car, not a high-value one. Or people would start to see Volkswagen as a high-end brand. This, then, would have given

The Volkswagen Phaeton

Volkswagen's mid-range models a 'class for the masses' kind of appeal, upgrading the brand as a whole. The latter is, of course, what Volkswagen had hoped for.

But Phaeton sales fell short of expectations, largely because a car with list prices of €90,000–180,000 was indeed incompatible with people's existing VW brand associations. List prices in the USA were reduced by $10,000 to stimulate sales. Apparently, the mid-market 'Volks' reputation was so entrenched that the Phaeton concept was rejected as incoherent. It simply fell short of the expectations and associations people had of the top-end saloons it was competing with.

Jeremy Clarkson, presenter of the BBC television programme *Top Gear*, captured it as follows. 'The first time I clapped eyes on the new VW, it was parked outside the Burj Al Arab hotel in Dubai among a row of Rollers and S-Classes. Certainly, the Phaeton was big enough to mix it in this crowd but its styling was a little too plain, a little too dainty to cut much ice. Think of it as a stickleback in a tank of tropical fish.' And then in Clarkson's less flattering words, 'I can imagine that a few Americans are idiotic enough to part with sixty big ones for a car with a bloody great VW badge on the front, but since your chairman says the US doesn't figure, I'm afraid I'm rather lost.'[10] A big VW badge does not match with a high-end price tag. It is incoherent, because VW is associated with the Golf and the Polo models – cars for trainees instead of bosses. It was not that Clarkson was unimpressed by the car's range of excellent features. He cited superb engineering, unbelievable silence, great handling even at 320 km/h, a staggering engine, fantastic attention to detail, etc. But all that was overridden by the existing brand image, which even the engineers at Volkswagen were not able to break out of.

Not only did the Volkswagen brand limit the Phaeton, the Phaeton sub-brand also influenced the Volkswagen brand. When an incoherent message is sent out repeatedly, it can begin to alter the general brand image and become linked to the original association network. This can be for the better or for the worse. In the case of VW, its expansion into the luxury market with the Phaeton and also the Touareg sports utility vehicle caused a struggle across its model range to overcome a growing perception that its vehicles were expensive. This happened especially in the United States. So not only did the Phaeton apparently fail in its own right, it also caused trouble across the brand's entire model range. A *Financial Times* report quoted Jamie Vondruska, who runs a VW fan website, vwvortex.com, as saying: 'Phaeton and Touareg gave the impression that VW had abandoned its roots. They left VW purists scratching their heads and wondering where they were going.'[11] Trading up is more difficult than trading down. It is easier for BMW to introduce a BMW 1 entry model than it is for Volkswagen to launch a new flagship model.

The role of price and propositions

As the Phaeton story illustrates, coherence is not an option but a necessity. The psychological demand for consistency can insulate a brand against inconsistent messages for a while by blocking them out. But in the long run they will contaminate the brand image in a way that sends conflicting signals within the brain, weakening the chances of the brand being selected by the brain's algorithm.

Discounts are often incoherent

Some brands remain incoherent because they can only bring themselves to develop a short-term sales strategy. Marketers often lack the ability or willingness to look beyond immediate earnings pressures and may end up in a sales trap. Price discounting by high-quality brands is one form of incoherence. While the brain's algorithm favours coherent brands, the algorithm of many marketers seems to value short-term above long-term profits. When we are planning for the long run, we are basically textbook 'rational'. But when it comes to the possibility of getting instant reward, marketers often cannot resist the temptations of shoring up quarterly sales results by offering discounts. From the point of view of evolution, it is understandable that the goal to snatch immediate rewards has a very powerful influence on our behaviour. But it can compromise our aim of reaching the more valuable but longer-term aim of coherence. It is a conflict of goals. What was an optimal strategy for our prehistoric ancestors is a suboptimal course of action for twenty-first-century marketers living in a complex commercial society.

Economic evidence indeed shows that faith in short-term tactics – as the alternative to long-term coherence – can be misplaced. A short-term focus can destroy a brand's long-term ability to charge premium prices and thus to earn higher margins – a key component of superior returns. Price reductions (a key instrument for boosting short-term revenues) coincide with strong but short-lived uplifts in sales. This makes promotions look highly profitable, so managers push for more discounts.

The unintended consequence of regular promotions, however, is that they divert consumers' attention away from quality and customer value. Instead, they turn attention towards price. Over time, consumers become more price sensitive, and the product gradually becomes commoditised. Thus the brand becomes hollowed-out and its ability to command higher margins is undermined. The volume that customers buy at full price steadily decreases. Yet, despite the growing evidence that long-term marketing strategies – other than price promotions – yield positive long-term returns, companies continue to manage their brands with a short-term perspective.[12]

Price tactics are a common but dangerous form of inconsistency for many brands. Artificially boosting this quarter's revenues using discounting undermines a company's ability to sustain revenue in the next quarter. The sum of these short-term gains does not compensate for the long-term slide of margins that it causes. Long-term policies such as investing in advertising and product development are more effective ways of sustaining the strong returns that generate shareholder value.

Dove's coherence in propositions

Some brands understand coherence very well. Dove, Unilever's skin care brand, is an example. For decades its positioning was based on one key attribute, what it called 'a quarter moisturising cream'. And all products in its portfolio were based on this component.[13] It was the element that created coherence for the brand. When Unilever effectively upgraded the Dove positioning in 2005, it kept the quarter moisturising cream attribute but added a much more powerful idea on top of it that had a strong emotional benefit: authentic beauty.

One of the most acclaimed efforts that launched this new positioning was a 'viral' called '*Evolution*', a clip that Dove posted on YouTube in the autumn of 2006 (check it out if you have not seen it yet: search on 'Dove Evolution' at YouTube). Its purpose was to invite women to participate in one of the Real Beauty Workshops for Girls that it was organising.[14] The positioning and the viral clip flowed from a worldwide study that it sponsored in 2004 called 'The real truth about beauty'. A key finding from the study was that only 2 per cent of women around the world considered themselves beautiful. In the words of the researchers:

> Beauty is not only a word that women are very unlikely to choose to describe their looks; it is also one which many actually feel 'uncomfortable' using to describe themselves. This level of 'discomfort' illustrates the degree to which women have become distanced from today's idea of female beauty.[15]

Dove was prompted by this staggering observation to unearth the deeper insights and drivers of female behaviour regarding beauty products – Dove's business. It found that beauty had in many ways become synonymous with mere physical attractiveness – an ideal that is portrayed in mass media and ingrained in popular culture. Dove's key insight was that it is

> *this* ideal that many women measure themselves against and aspire to attain. However, because this ideal is extremely difficult to achieve, women find it difficult to think of themselves as beautiful. This can contribute to unhappiness and low self-esteem and self-worth – especially among those women (often younger) who are more likely to take their cues from popular culture.

Dove then decided to focus on the theme of authentic beauty in a way that was distinctively relevant, and stuck with it. It famously portrayed older women, unseen in traditional beauty adverts, which caused a global stir and broad approval. Not only has Dove's

global campaign emanated from this single unifying idea since 2005, it now also launches new products, such as its Pro-Age line, based on this positioning – further enhancing consistency in branding. Interestingly, the Pro-Age range of products is positioned against the traditional 'anti-ageing' creams and lotions that dominated the shelves, and so also created distinctive relevance.

'And action!'

The brain's algorithm favours brands that have been built in a coherent way, even though the brains of marketers are easily seduced by short-term gains that disrupt coherence. Let me repeat the message.

Step 1: Make your brand promise specific, yet broad

To help your brand to be chosen by the brain's algorithm, you must ensure your customer's goals and your brand are uniquely and strongly associated. You can do this through communication (advertising, PR, social learning, etc.) and through delivery – when customers actually experience that the brand satisfies their goals. The brain then assigns the brand a certain value so that it can compare the brand with others.

Vague and unclear brand promises, like the ones we saw in the corporate banking examples (Table 5.1), make it harder for the brain to assign a clear value to a brand. Such a brand cannot strongly activate the reward and motivation systems. By contrast, the more specific the brand's message over time, the more likely that the original 'paths' in the brain are strengthened when it is repeated. Coherence requires the repetition of a specific brand promise.

At the same time, however, the brand concept must be broad enough to encompass a wide variety of messages and products and address a broad cocktail of needs. The creative concept that holds it all together must be both broad and specific. It must facilitate the repetition of a specific message in a variety of ways for a variety of products and services for a variety of customer goals across a variety of customer contact points. HSBC's tagline 'The World's Local Bank' is an example of a statement that has this potential.

Step 2: Stick with the promise and keep repeating it

To establish strong associative links between your brand and your customer's cocktail of goals, you must repeatedly activate this link. That is why you must bring everything you do into line with the brand strategy. Coherence requires focus. Every customer contact point (products, website, personnel, communications, and so on.) must reiterate or prove the brand promise. Moreover the brain keeps track of the gap between the promised and the delivered reward, and can devalue incoherent brands that do not perform as expected.

Branding thus becomes more than advertising, as it should be. Some of the world's strongest brands (McKinsey, Leica and Google) have negligible advertising budgets compared with their size and value. Instead, their whole business strategy is aimed at bringing distinct customer relevance to the various segments, industries and geographical regions they operate in. And they devise business models that best capture some of the value they create for their customers so as to enjoy good profits from it.

A company like Leica has the brand in mind even when the first lines are put on the drawing board for a new product. So your business strategy and your brand strategy become inseparable. To build relevance in a coherent way, you must keep your brand in mind whenever you make decisions in product development, customer experience development, design of service concepts, pricing, training of service personnel, PR and communications. In short, you must stick to your promise and reiterate it. That is what it means to be coherent.

> your business strategy and your brand strategy must become inseparable

Step 3: Keep your eye on the ball

Inconsistencies, such as a Volkswagen with a high-end price tag, have an important effect on customers' brains. In the first place, they cancel the learning process that is maintained and accelerated by repetition of the brand promise. The brand starts to be forgotten by the subconscious choice processes in customers' brains. Its position against consistent competitors is weakened.

Secondly, inconsistencies prompt the brain to learn the new brand promise. It starts to update its conception of the brand. The brain keeps track of errors in its prediction of rewards. It remembers the gap between what it expects and what it encounters. A brand that does not deliver is less likely to be chosen in similar circumstances in the future. This can be desirable when you want to reposition the brand fundamentally. But to do this, you must be coherent in communicating and delivering the new promise. In all other cases, stay consistent.

So unless there is a compelling need to reposition, you must ruthlessly ban inconsistencies. We saw how Volkswagen caused dents in its brand by its $500 million attempt to rebuff the coherence law with the Phaeton introduction. Discounting a high-value product or service – a common form of inconsistency – can erode your ability to command a premium price. In the next chapter, we look at how the Starbucks brand took a slide through inconsistency and how it is seeking to revive it, not least by rebuilding coherence. Being inconsistent is expensive. It can hit your share price and throw out your previous investment in the brand promise up to that moment. You induce brand memory loss in the brains of your customers and prospects. In the worst cases, you generate disappointment and avoidance.

Step 4: Forget accountability

For years, improving the accountability of the marketing organisation has been a top priority of CMOs and marketing executives in developed markets. While the idea to measure efficiency and effectiveness has great merit, the emphasis on accountability can be blinding. Why? Because too often it is limited to marketing communications, which are a small part of the execution of the strategy. Coherence applies to the whole business and brand strategy. Therefore paying too much attention to accountability can distract from the need to create coherence in the entire strategy. As long as accountability does not include measuring how coherently the company's brand strategy is executed, it is of limited value. Let's not forget: branding is more than advertising.

Conclusion

Creating coherence in branding is a second major way of feeding into the brain's algorithm for making brand choices. This is the second law of branding and it states that the higher the coherence of a company's branding efforts across time and space, the higher is the chance that the brand will be chosen. Our brain favours brands that stick to one specific idea which is repeated always and in everything they do. The conversion of a fleeting memory into a permanent one requires repetition. Coherent brands fulfil this condition while incoherent brands cancel the memory-formation process, diminishing their chances of being stored, of being activated, of winning the awareness competition and hence of being chosen. In the next chapter, you will learn how to implement the law of coherence.

PRADA

Chapter 6

Aligning the business with the brand strategy

We have seen that the brain makes brand choices using a subconscious algorithm, selecting brands that have been built according to the three laws of relevance, coherence and participation. In the last chapter, we looked at the *what* and *why* of coherence. But *how* do you sustain brand coherence and how do you spread it in the organisation? What do you need to do to bring everything into line with the brand strategy? These are the questions this chapter addresses.

When the coffee goes cold

Most marketers, of course, try to be different in a relevant way. But such efforts only become what we call 'branding' if they are carried out coherently. Only then is a brand created that the brain's algorithm can select. One of the more complex brands to build coherently is that of coffee retailer Starbucks. Its story is highly instructive. Named after the first mate in *Moby Dick*, Starbucks was launched in 1971 and had become one of the world's strongest brands by the mid 1990s. In the early days it was a small store selling whole-bean coffee. The shift came in the 1980s, when CEO Howard Schultz changed its mission from selling beans to selling a coherent coffee-drinking experience.

'The story is kind of boring,' Schultz later said of the company's rapid expansion to some 15,000 coffee shops in more than 30 countries. 'We keep doing the same thing, year in and year out' – an explicit commitment to coherence. In Schultz's view, the Starbucks brand is so solid because it has been built on a distinctively relevant experience and not on advertising and promotions. 'The one thing I think is really important is the sense of community and human connection in every Starbucks store you go into.'[1] Over the period from 1992 to 2006, Starbucks outperformed the Dow Jones index by around 3,500 per cent. Then Wall Street quite suddenly went cold on its shares, partly because of the economic slowdown, but partly because of incoherence – as we shall see.

The problem of brand dilution

Schultz left his CEO position with the company in 2000, only to take back the steering wheel in January 2008 when Starbucks faced declining sales. What had happened? In a leaked memo, Schultz identified the key problem as 'the commoditization of the Starbucks experience'.[2] In his view, many decisions were made that seemed individually sound but had the cumulative effect of damaging and diluting the brand. For example, in thousands of stores Starbucks had switched to automatic espresso machines that were faster and more efficient but which eliminated the 'romance and theatre' of fresh coffee making. The new machines were also higher, blocking customers' view of the coffee being made, diminishing the feeling of personal attention paid to their drink. Moreover, the machines were operated with coffee beans that could be kept longer but spread less aroma, thus providing less coffee smell in its stores. Other issues included the design of stores, which had become more bland.

How did this happen? Perhaps Starbucks' management had overlooked the fact that the *brand* ought to have been leading in these decisions. Perhaps executives misinterpreted their own brand or failed to realise they were making incoherent decisions. Maybe they underestimated the impact of these decisions. In any case, if the Starbucks brand had been leading these choices, different trade-offs might have been made between short-term profits and long-term brand equity so that both aims could have been reached.

Marshmallows and your brand's tipping point

Creating coherence is largely a matter of branding technique. For instance, it helps if you work from a good strategic and creative brand concept and have a way to keep track of how coherent you are. If you have a portfolio of sub-brands you need tools to align them, and if you want to focus your organisation on delivering the brand promise you need a way to stage brand-led organisational change. Many of these technical elements can in fact be learned, developed or obtained from creative and strategic branding agencies.

But experience shows that there is also something much more fundamental required in order to get coherence off the ground – the ability to sustain a strategy. This may sound simple, but it isn't. There are strong opportunistic forces in most organisations. Quarterly earnings pressures, impatience, political ambition and other factors often tempt managers to act in ways that are inconsistent with the strategy. And the poise and focus that can prevent this are mostly a matter of character. In the end, creating coherence depends upon your ability to control your impulses in the service of a higher goal so that brand building can reach the tipping point after which brand strength shoots up. It is a human quality.

Take Starbucks again. Howard Schultz joined in 1982. But it took 10–20 years of diligent work to turn Starbucks into a power brand. Already personally wealthy, the fact that he has been content to pursue the same strategy for decades suggests that he has that precious ability to wait and resist distractions, rather than being driven by the need for instant rewards. It is fair to say that Schultz has made some inconsistent moves along the way, as when Starbucks launched a magazine. But he has always returned to the original strategy of creating an intimate, homely experience around coffee. Psychologists, in an experiment dubbed 'the marshmallow test' (see below), found that such self-discipline is an underlying character trait that manifests itself when we are about four years old. It is a key factor for success in life in general, and for creating coherence in particular.

The marshmallow test

A famous experiment conducted in the 1960s by Walter Mischel, a personality psychologist, identified what you need to sustain coherence.3 Mischel's study involved putting marshmallows in front of a group of four-year-olds. He told them they could have one now, but that if they could wait several minutes, they could have two marshmallows. He then observed and recorded what happened.

Marshmallows, being made of sugar, trigger our dopamine system – the circuit in the brain that predicts and registers reward. It is difficult for children to resist these forces, because the circuits for purposeful behaviour that could override the urge for instant satisfaction are not yet fully developed at the age of four. As expected, some children simply grabbed the marshmallow in front of them and ate it as soon as the researcher left. Others, however, managed to wait. How? Some covered their eyes. Others talked quietly to themselves, sang, created games with their hands and feet, and even tried to go to sleep during the waiting. These children duly received two marshmallows each.

Mischel followed the group and found, 14 years later, that the 'grabbers' generally had lower self-esteem and were viewed by others as more easily frustrated. The children who waited and thus delayed gratification were more socially competent: personally effective, self-assertive, and better able to cope with the frustrations of life. This group even scored about 210 points higher on their Scholastic Aptitude Tests.4 Moreover, these children tended to be more intelligent and more achievement-oriented.

To function effectively, we must voluntarily postpone immediate gratification and persist in goal-directed behaviour for the sake of later outcomes. The ability to delay gratification through self-discipline (as measured by the marshmallow test) turned out to be a better predictor of future success than any other measurement.

Resisting the Sirens

The insight is that in order to build a brand, you need an above-average ability to delay gratification and resist short-term impulses. It is safe to assume that many other great brand builders, like George Merck (Merck), Sam Walton (Wal-Mart) and David Packard (Hewlett-Packard) possessed this skill. But the most vivid description of it is found in Homer's *Odyssey*. In it, Odysseus sails back victorious from the Trojan War to his homeland of Ithaca. His arrogance arouses the wrath of Poseidon – god of the seas – who throws his return into disarray. Odysseus then wanders across the seas for years and at a certain moment approaches the Sirens – legendary and beautiful female creatures, who lure men with their 'mellifluous' songs. They bring certain death upon those who give in to their sweet melodies. Having been warned in advance, Odysseus orders his men to tie him to the mast of the ship and put wax in their own ears. Thus they are able to resist the temptations of the Sirens and keep their course. Odysseus is in danger of being seduced by the lure of instant gratification. But his intellect is stronger than his desires and he sticks with his longer-term purpose. In the same way, brand builders must have the self-awareness to know when to 'tie themselves to the mast', so to speak. They must know when to have the rest of their team 'put wax in their ears' so that together they continue the strategy, instead of succumbing to the temptation of inconsistent short-term returns.

Reaching the tipping point of brand power

But what is a marketer's marshmallow test? To a large degree, this is defined by the reward systems that are in place in an organisation – the performance indicators and intangible social feedback systems embedded in corporate culture. That is why I have argued in Chapter 1 in favour of including brand value in the long-term incentive plans of executives. It would make coherent decision making easier and more likely.

In the words of Erik van der Meijden, CEO of ICT company Getronics, this would encourage management teams to invest more in the brand. They might at first make some trade-offs in order to show short-term profits to shareholders, but in the longer term they would be more inclined to build brands that require lower advertising investments (like Google, Apple and Starbucks) because their promise pours out of every point of contact with customers, not just the advertising campaign)[5].

This is what happened at Starbucks. It stuck to the strategy, resisting the temptation to go astray and fall into incoherent actions. Schultz helped create a company that operated a unique and coherent system of actions and activities that were relevant for its coffee-loving clients. And when you do that, you will sooner or later reach a tipping point after which your brand strength explodes. It will perpetuate itself. Starbucks aligned a sufficient number of touch points and crossed this tipping point probably somewhere around 1995. Its brand gained momentum. From that point on, its share price rocketed. In little more than 10 years, Starbucks created a brand that was stronger than the one its competitor Maxwell House had taken more than a century to build.[6] And coherence played a major part in it – at least until Starbucks made incoherent moves that weakened its brand again (see Figure 6.1).

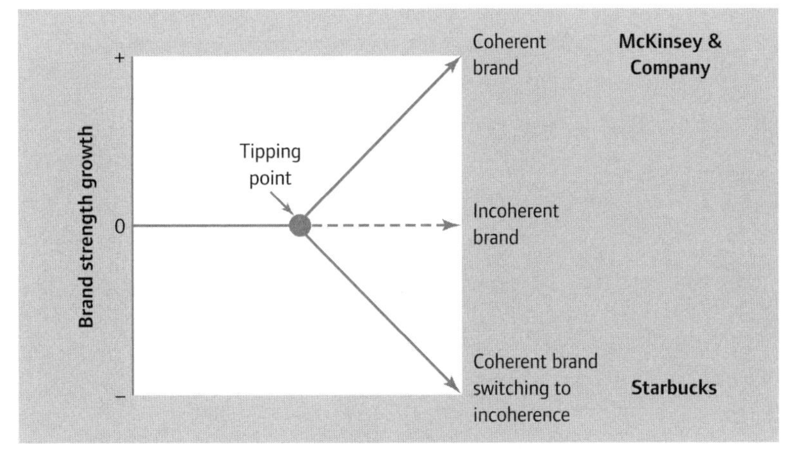

FIGURE 6.1 Reaching the branding tipping point

Defining the creative brand concept

The process of creating coherence can be made easier by defining a relevant creative brand concept. This concept must embody the brand promise and must have the potential to guide all major strategic decisions affecting the brand. For example, 'Making authentic beauty shine' could summarise Dove's brand concept and hold together everything the brand does. It provides direction for its communications, marketing and new product development.

Three types of concept

Our experience shows that there are three types of creative concept that can facilitate coherence.[7] They are not mutually exclusive.

1. Central idea

Coherence can be based on a strong, all-encompassing promise. Dove's current positioning is an example. It claims a uniquely relevant market position for the brand. Such an idea is sometimes elusively called a 'Big Idea' in marketing jargon. A good unifying idea is relevant to customers, different from the competition and offers new avenues for communication, product development and service management. Many strong product brands are based on unifying ideas, Axe ('irresistible attraction') is another example.

2. Core mentality

A second way to foster coherence is by using a mentality or ideology to align all activities. A mentality is generally more flexible than a central idea. Also, it allows a brand to shift the attention from *what* it does – which is not always unique – to *how* it does it or how it looks at the category or a certain segment of life. This can make it easier to stand out from the competition. Service brands tend to prefer mentalities above ideas as unifiers; product brands tend to use either. Examples of unifying brand mentalities include the famous 'Red' campaign for *The Economist*, 'The Coca-Cola side of life' (Coca-Cola) and 'Go jet set, go!' (Virgin Atlantic). One key difference with a mentality is that in most cases an idea emphasises what the brand offers, whereas a mentality highlights a certain approach, an attitude or a way of thinking.

3. Visual form

Visual identity is a third but weaker option to create coherence. ABN-AMRO, the Dutch bank taken over by Fortis and RBS in 2007, used this approach. It switched its brand promises at least three times in the five years preceding the merger, but maintained a strict corporate identity (brochures, websites, product packaging, front-desk uniforms, interior designs, architecture of buildings, and so on.) Thus, it unified its broad range of activities at least visually. On the downside, a visual identity offers little guidance in making strategic business decisions. Some location brands also use visual form as a way to create coherence. One of the most striking examples is French ski resort Avoriaz. Created from scratch in the 1960s, its unique architectural style creates strong visual unity, although it complements a strong central idea of being a self-contained, remote resort as the basis of its brand.

A brand concept that customers and CEOs understand

One obstacle to the creation of coherence is that management teams often do not put the brand at the heart of their decision-making processes. One thing we do in our brand consultancy practice at THEY to cope with this is to analyse which are the most important themes at our clients' board meetings. We then illustrate how executives might use the brand concept to guide decisions on these issues. As Getronics CEO Erik van der Meijden notes:

> I think many boards of directors feel that branding means advertising. That is why they delegate it to the communications department. But when the brand is translated into terms that boards are more familiar with, it can start to drive decisions on how we interact with customers, where we invest or divest, our partnerships, the innovation process, product development, our corporate culture – in short, the things that build a company.[8]

Between the end of 2006 and the end of 2008, Starbucks lost 40 per cent more in share value than the market average.[9] As previously discussed, it is reasonable to assume this was partly because of the incoherent strategic and operation decisions that weakened its brand. What could help such a company to regain its steam is first to create a clearer description of its brand. It may have to be 'downloaded' from the mind of its founder – who lives and breathes it – and be made explicit in a way that can more strongly guide decisions throughout its organisation. A brand must be explained in such a way that executives understand what the brand means for all the major decisions they face.

If you can't measure it, it does not exist

When leaders have the right traits and the right brand concept to guide coherence, it can be useful to find a way to measure coherence. It is hard to manage something that is not measured. Even informal or intuitive ways of measuring consistency are better than not measuring at all. One technique used to do that is what we call brand coherence profiling. It is a method of mapping a brand's activities on a two-dimensional coherence plane, using a simple grading scheme. The technique uses a five-point scale, shown in simplified form on the left-hand side of Figure 6.2, to assess whether an advert or a product is consistent with the brand's key promise. Companies can use it internally as an informal self-reporting measure or externally in quantitative customer research.

> it's hard to manage something that is not measured

A coherence profile allows you to trace consistency through time. Moreover, because colours can be assigned to each of the five points on the scale it is possible to present the data in a way that is simple to read, for example as a moving computer graphic. Experience shows that a simple graph like the one shown in Figure 6.2 can improve the understanding and awareness of the level of coherence built into a branding campaign. It can benefit the marketers themselves as well as their agencies.

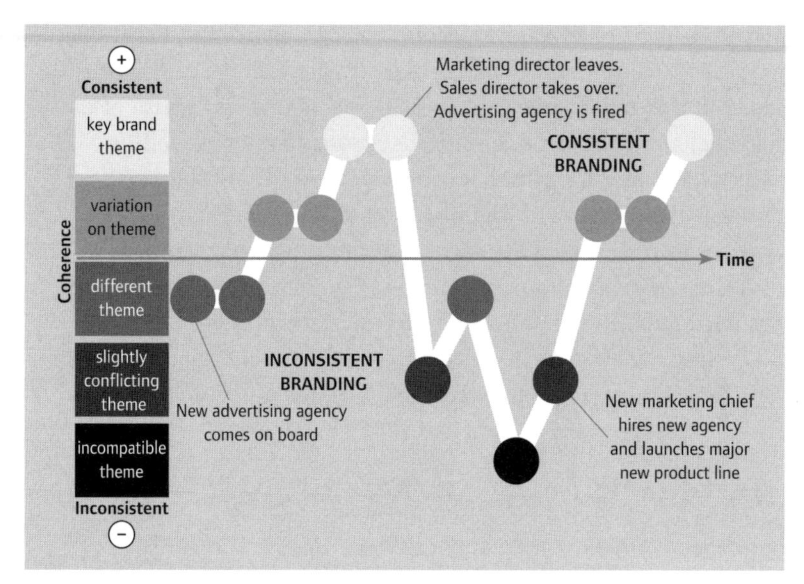

FIGURE 6.2 Example of a brand coherence profile

Aligning the brand portfolio

In many cases, companies operate a large portfolio of products and services under one brand name and this presents an enormous coherence challenge. Portfolios are often a hotchpotch of logos, unrelated products, inconsistent positionings, old or acquired labels and patchy use of the main brand in the names of the products and services. All these inconsistent products and services blur the mental representation of the main brand. Portfolios are common breeding places of inconsistency.

The need to reposition the portfolio

It is useful first to distinguish between two main brand portfolio models.[10] The first is the 'house of brands' model, in which a company operates a variety of unrelated brands that each have their own name and identity. Procter & Gamble and Unilever are main examples of companies using this approach, operating separate brands like Becel, Sun, Dove, Magnum, Axe, etc. The second model is a 'branded house', meaning that a range of products and services are marketed under one brand name. IBM,

Apple and Disney are good examples. Interestingly, this model is associated with higher financial brand value than the first model.[11] Companies using the first model have no need to create overall coherence (Unilver needs little overall coherence between Becel, Dove and Magnum, for example). Only branded house models require coherence, so Unilever would like its Becel portfolio to be coherent while IBM wants its entire portfolio to be coherent. Such portfolio projects usually start with management asking questions like the following:

- We have just acquired and merged with another company and are faced with a huge portfolio. How can we bring these products under fewer main brands?
- Our portfolio has grown organically and prolifically. How can we rationalise it?
- Are we consistent in the use of the brand name within our portfolio?
- How should we use the brand name for new products and services?
- Can we align the myriad of products and services we have, so that we create one coherent brand experience? (This question is especially asked by location brands like countries, regions, cities, theme parks, airports, world expositions.

Creating portfolio coherence means that we position the brands in it in such a way that we create *portfolio* success rather than individual successes.

Creating the naming structure

The first step we take is to set a context, by defining the range of general naming options that actually exist and that are feasible in any situation. Figure 6.3 shows the four options we have found most useful. They vary in where they place a proposition in distance away from the main brand. Although there are many differences in terms of visual identity, in practice the naming and positioning variants companies use can almost always be traced back to one of these four options.

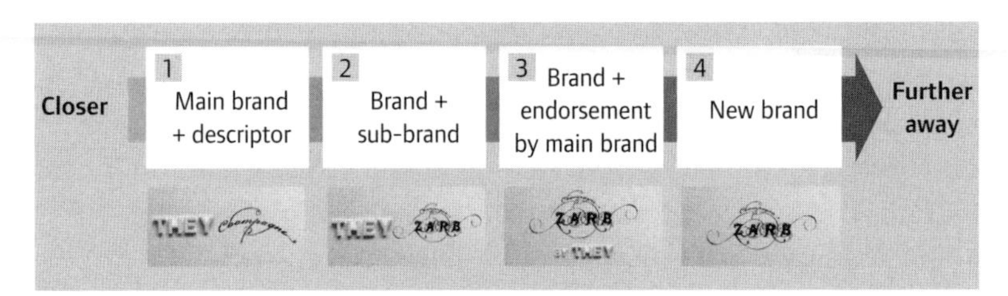

FIGURE 6.3 Four generic brand-naming options

Once the options are clear, the question becomes when to use which option. This is the pivotal issue. One way to solve it is based on the strategic role a product or service plays within the overall portfolio. We use a set of strategic portfolio roles for this purpose that are mutually exclusive and collectively exhaustive (MECE) – and which are incorporated in each of the four naming options.

One common role, for example, is that of core brands – propositions that represent and underline the most central brand associations. Marriott Hotels, the Disney Store, Johnson & Johnson Baby Shampoo are examples of core brands. In our model, core propositions are placed as close as possible to the brand name. A second role is that of silver-bullet brands. These are propositions that have an identity of their own that add new and often innovative associations to the reputation of the main brand (for example, Apple's iPhone, American Express's Blue, BMW's Z4, the *Financial Times: How to Spend It*). Silver bullets are placed slightly further away, using the brand plus sub-brand name formula.

By examining the portfolio using such strategic roles, we can create a coherent positioning and naming structure for the entire portfolio. In our experience, this generates valuable strategic discussion within executive teams. The method is simple and straightforward, but highly effective because it separates issues that are normally grouped together when naming and positioning decisions for sub-brands are made intuitively.

The portfolio alignment game

In the case of more complex portfolios it is useful to map out the brand's business on what we call a brand portfolio orchestration game board.[12] Disneyland Resort Paris serves as an example of an approach any executive team can use (see box). Based on an extensive analysis of the business, a strategic game board is created that reflects the brand's key product–market combinations. For Disneyland this could consist of at least two target groups and three product categories: location and infrastructure, hospitality and retail, attractions and shows (see Figure 6.4). Next, in concentrated interactive sessions, executives allocate all sub-brands to the cells of the game board and assign a strategic role to each sub-brand. This allows the team to analyse their entire brand portfolio, for instance identifying 'white spots' – cells that represent strategically important market areas where the company does not yet have any offerings – and priorities for business development. The result should be a coherent positioning for all sub-brands within the portfolio and a list of inconsistent sub-brands to sell or reposition. The portfolio could be further analysed in terms of innovativeness or profitability.

EXAMPLE

Steps in the portfolio orchestration game

Step 1 – Construct the game board and pawns

Based on analysis of the business and identification of the full list of sub-brands, a game set is created (board and pawns).

Step 2 – Assign all pawns to a cell on the game board

In concentrated interactive sessions and discussions between members of the executive team, all sub-brands are assigned places on the board and hence in the brand portfolio.

Step 3 – Assign strategic roles to every pawn

Each sub-brand on the board is assigned one strategic portfolio role (out of the six possible roles) by the team. This involves a high-level discussion of short- and long-term priorities and choices about the role of each sub-brand in building the overall brand and in realising the business strategy.

EXAMPLE

Step 4 – Analyse results and create implementation plan

The team then analyses the outcomes. As each strategic role is tied to one naming option (see Figure 6.3), a full naming and positioning structure results from the strategic choices made by the team. The colour coding facilitates a unique, full analysis of the balance and completeness of the entire portfolio. As a follow-up, an implementation plan is created which is then put into action by the team.

Figure 6.4 shows a small selection of Disneyland's propositions, allocated across the game board. Space Mountain might be a silver bullet for Disneyland whereas Mainstreet is a core brand. Upon analysis, Disneyland might notice that it has few propositions for business people or that it could benefit from extra silver bullets in its infrastructure. In our experience, the brand portfolio orchestration game is extremely effective in helping executives create coherence in complex portfolios. It facilitates high-level discussions and decision making by bringing objectivity to the process, and creates a clear action list. Once implemented, the result is a clear and coherent brand portfolio with well-positioned sub-brands that strengthen, not distort, the main brand.

Staging brand-led organisational change

Every point of contact with the organisation can reinforce or contradict the existing brand associations in customers' brains. For example, when a receptionist picks up the telephone and talks using slang, this can undermine the upmarket image of a private bank. In its most advanced form, therefore, sustaining coherence means aligning the entire organisation so that everyone thinks and behaves in a way that supports the brand.

sustaining coherence means aligning the entire organisation

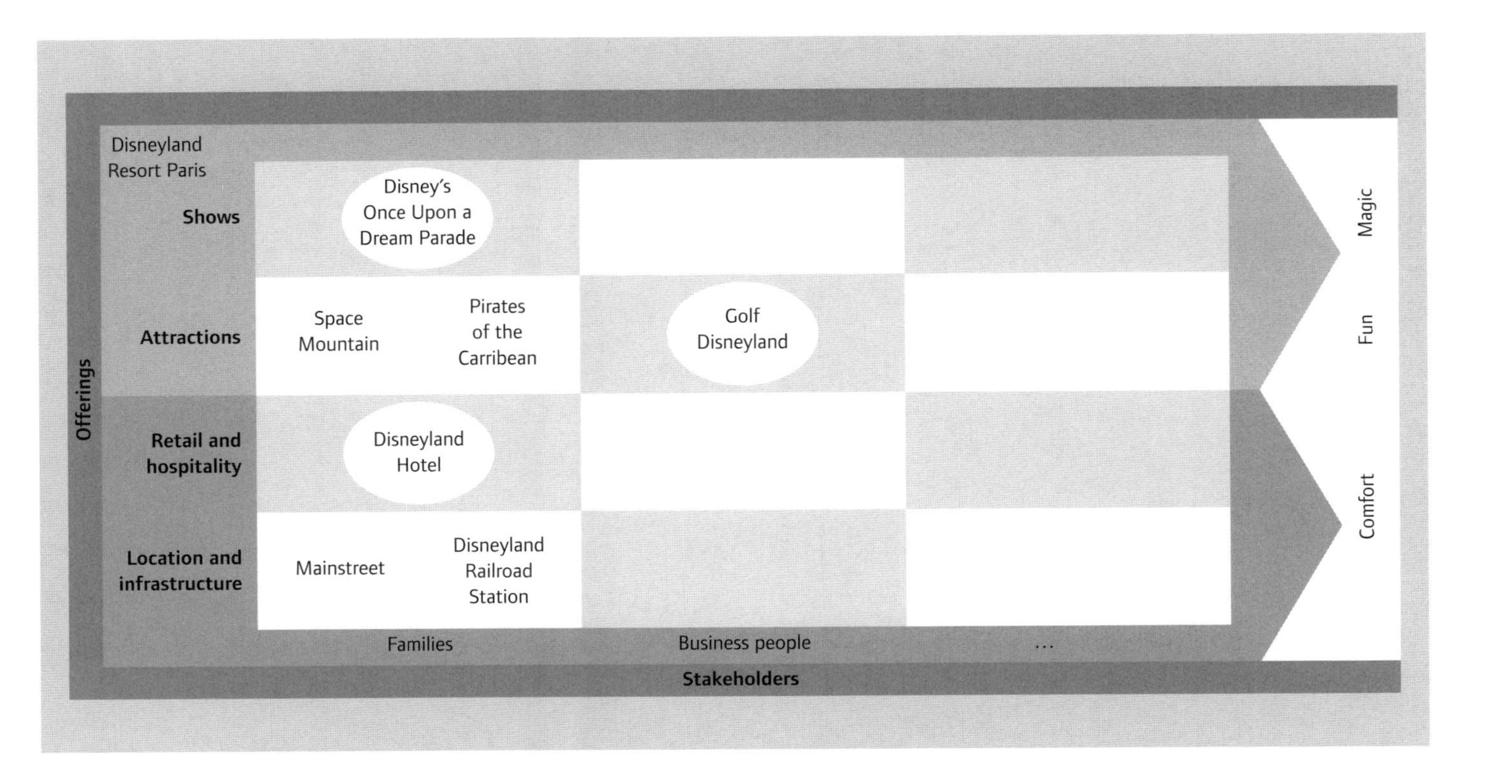

FIGURE 6.4 Creating balance and synergy, using the brand portfolio orchestration game

In many cases, this requires carrying out brand-led organisational change. All too often, a new positioning only results in a new advertising campaign. Especially in the case of service companies, such an approach can wreak havoc. When a brand relies on employees' behaviour to validate the new promise, an internal change programme is vital to the brand's success. This requires a lot more than what is commonly done under the flag of 'internal branding'. Organisational change has received little attention in the field of branding, perhaps because change is an especially complicated process. A 2006 *McKinsey Quarterly* global survey showed that only 38 per cent of executives thought their company's most recent transformation had at least a 'mostly' positive impact on performance.[13]

Despite these difficulties, the rewards are there. A study by Booz Allen Hamilton, for example, found that companies that placed the brand at the centre of their strategic decision-making and operational processes enjoyed profit margins nearly twice their industry average (see Figure 6.5).[14] These brand-focused companies really 'sweat the details', gearing the entire organisation towards fulfilling the brand promise.

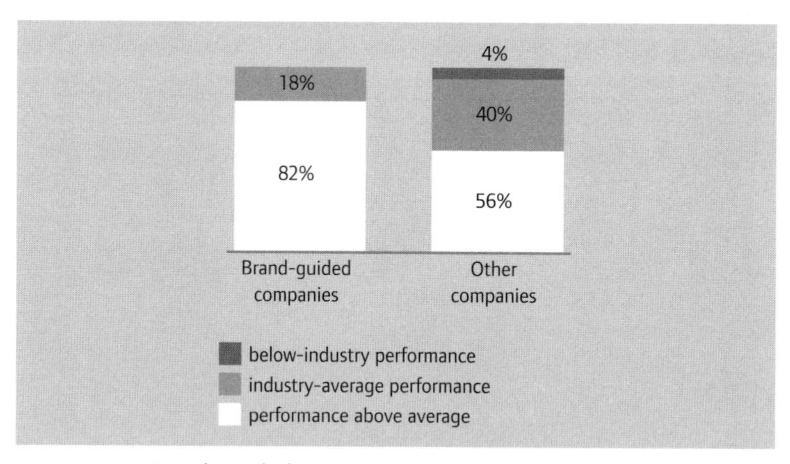

FIGURE 6.5 Brand-guided companies are more profitable

Source: Booz-Allen Hamilton

One model we have found helpful in understanding how to foster coherence through brand-led change is shown in Figure 6.6.[15] Its premise is that people often resist the change process more than the change itself. The left-hand side of the chart, therefore, summarises the ingredients of a more people-friendly process.

The right-hand side of Figure 6.6 shows the stages people move through. The creative brand concept serves as the basis of a meaningful corporate story that details why change is necessary and what a better future would look like.[16] A broad range of media (including corporate films, launch events, workshops, work-group sessions and advertising campaigns) can be used to move the organisation through the five stages shown on the right-hand side of Figure 6.6 over a period of months or even years. Of course, to foster coherence, as many employees as possible should internalise the brand concept as fully as possible. Ideally, people develop a sense of pride about what the company does and commit themselves to its purpose. It helps when the ideas behind the brand and the change process are genuine. Some of the ideas about participation, presented in Chapters 7 and 8, can also be useful.

Telecom provider Orange, for example, organised awareness and identification workshops with employees when it launched its new positioning under the banner of 'The future's bright, the future's Orange'. This helped everyone at the company to become aware of the brand's promise and become energised by the perspective it offered. Moreover, people were presented with opportunities to become comfortable with the new brand concept and to define their own specific role within it.

In another example, Philips – one of the world's largest electronics companies – understands very well that its claim of 'Sense and simplicity' requires it to live and breathe the implications of this positioning. Consequently, it has linked the bonuses of its top marketers to their ability to embody 'simplicity' in their own personal conduct in the eyes of their subordinates. The idea is to create real commitment to the brand from its top people. Examples such as these show the wide-ranging efforts needed to create coherence in branding, which stretch beyond the creative skills of the marketer or the advertising agency.

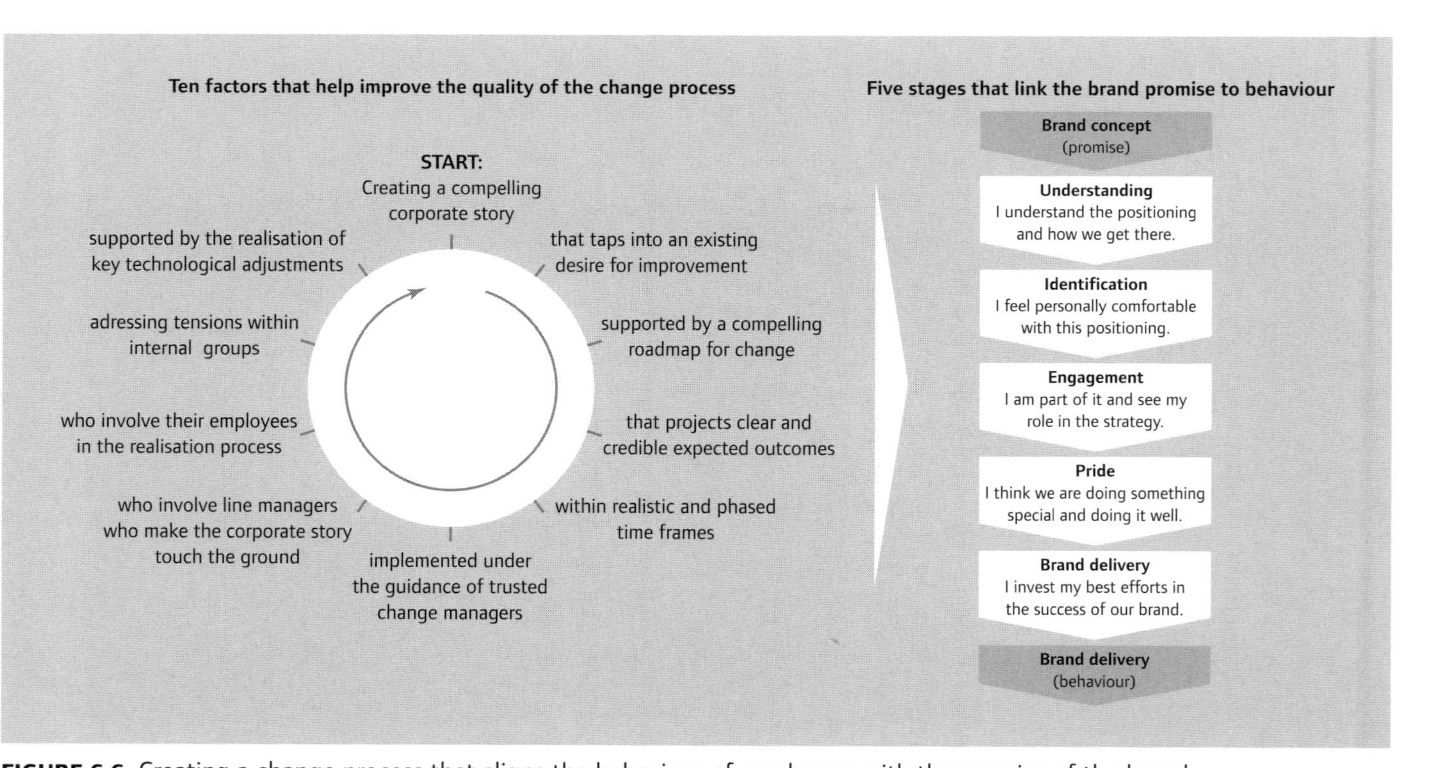

FIGURE 6.6 Creating a change process that aligns the behaviour of employees with the promise of the brand

Talking the walk

To create coherence, advertising should be one of the outcomes of the process, not the starting point. Ideally, it should be used to communicate the brand strategy. Coherence means you should not walk the talk but talk the walk. That is: first you show, then you tell. The following steps can help you achieve this.

Step 1: Do the marshmallow test

In order to create coherence, you need people who have the personality and the stamina to sustain the brand strategy – provided it is a good strategy, of course. You need people who can pass the marshmallow test. The first thing to do is to get such people in the right seats. Without strategic self-discipline, branding is virtually impossible. So train yourself to note when you are drifting off strategy, and return. Of course, you must challenge the strategy. Sometimes you must change it. In that case, be consistent in the new strategy. When you stick to the course, your investments become compounded; at some stage you will reach the tipping point and the strength of your brand will take off. Be prepared, however, to put in years of consistent effort before that happens.

Step 2: Make the concept meaningful to customers and executives

Create a brand concept that contains a relevant promise for customers – they must understand and recognise it. But in order for it to drive the organisation, executives must understand its implications for the decisions they make, and every other decision maker must understand its consequences for their day-to-day work. This is essential for fostering coherence.

Interestingly, a good creative brand concept provides meaning and perspective – also for board members. Take the example of HSBC. Speeches and meetings become much more compelling when talk about innovation, market share, growth potential, geographical reach, profitability and strategic acquisitions is placed in the context of being 'The World's Local Bank'. It can motivate people at all levels of the organisation. It adds meaning and significance to their working lives. It adds human sense to otherwise sterile concepts. It also provides management with a soapbox, an opportunity for showing leadership. If you need more convincing, think of Barack Obama and his concept of hope and change.

In the light of this, the moment when a founder hands over to a successor is a crucial moment for the brand. Usually the brand is in his or her head. For others, however, it is much more difficult to understand the brand's implications for the strategic and operational business decisions they face daily. The brand must, therefore, be explained so that everyone can understand it. This is not only difficult; it is also too often overlooked.

Step 3: Apply the tools

Finally, you must track coherence, align the portfolio and bring the behaviour of the organisation into line with the strategy. We have reviewed tools that can enable you to do this. Staging brand-led change is the most complicated one. Changing an organisation is difficult. What makes it even more challenging is that in the case of branding, the change process must be guided by the brand concept. Yet brand specialists are often not skilled at leading real change programmes, while change consultants generally lack the requisite creative and strategic branding skills. Getting them to work together is the only option.

Conclusion

The conversion of a fleeting memory into a permanent one requires repetition. Coherent brands meet this requirement while incoherent brands cancel the memory-formation process. Creating coherence requires stamina and integrity. Like Odysseus, marketers must be able to resist the temptation of quick but irregular wins which involve deviation from the strategy. At the same time they must read the signs of change and create variation and renewal based on the original brand promise. Creating coherence, then, is always a compelling personal endeavour. In the next two chapters, you will learn how to use the third component of the branding-with-brains framework: the law of participation.

Chapter 7

LAW No.3: Participation

We have seen that the brain uses a subconscious algorithm for choosing between brands stored in our long-term memory. This algorithm favours brands built according to the three laws of relevance, coherence and participation. This chapter presents the third law of branding. It states that marketers must enable customers to interact with the brand, so that they can help to define the way in which the brand fulfils its promise. Participation may revolutionize the branding industry in the coming years, moving from push to pull branding based on customer involvement. So how does this law work and what does it mean for your brand strategy?

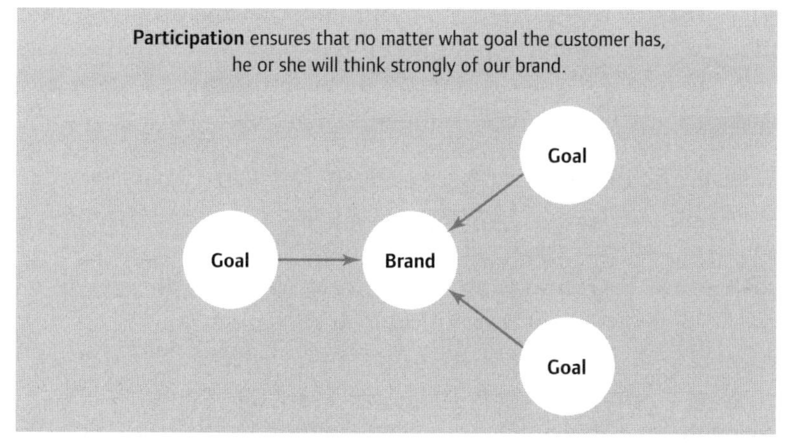

FIGURE 7.1 Law No.3: Participation

Running to a new rhythm

A good way to understand participation is to look at a product called *Nike+iPod* that Mark Parker and Steve Jobs, CEOs of Nike and Apple respectively, launched together in May 2006 in New York.

Nike Plus, as it was later called, is a technology that allows your running shoes to communicate with your iPod. It consists of a small sensor under the liner of the shoe that measures footfalls and sends this data in real time to the iPod. The iPod then calculates your speed, distance and calories burned. From the iTunes store, you can download to your iPod special training sessions made by world-class coaches that you can play while running. A voice-over guides your run. Apple has filed a patent to capitalise on a technique to change the music tempo based on the pace of your running.[1] Imagine Robbie Williams singing faster or slower to match your running pace. During your run, your data (distance, time, speed, calories burned) is shown on the iPod screen and provided by the voice-over. This makes your workout more effective and, above all, more fun – as millions of runners have discovered.

Then when you return home and, still sweating, sync your iPod with iTunes, the data of your run is uploaded to the nikeplus.com site. There are several online applications to use with your exercise data. For instance, you can directly see the result of your run – in neat graphs – and compare your performance with previous runs.

You can also choose to measure yourself against the results of others around the world on the 'leader board'. You can track all your runs, set new goals, get training programmes or enter challenges with runners around the world. You can plot your runs on Google Maps if you want or find new runs plotted by others in your area. Moreover, it provides a platform for virtual racing, progress tracking, motivational goal setting, forums and global community comparison tools (over 100 million miles have been run collectively). All this happens within a branded context, taking the proposition beyond just a shoe, a sensor, a receiver and an iPod.[2] Essentially, the lonely activity of jogging is turned into an entertaining community event. Nike and Apple do not organise this community; they facilitate it within a branded environment. Thus,

Nike Plus engages customers in an experience that customers partly create themselves.

Why the brain favours participatory brands

The neuroscientific underpinnings for the advantages of participatory brands like Nike Plus are relatively new. It had long been thought that the adult brain does not generate new cells and cannot change or repair itself – obliging us to live with the brain cells given to us at birth. But recent research has refuted this idea.[3] Thousands of new cells are born every day in a process called 'neurogenesis', especially in areas related to learning and memory (for example, the hippocampus). The adult brain is a much more dynamic organ than scientists originally imagined, creating new hopes for the treatment of brain damage, for instance. Interestingly, participatory branding facilitates the process by which new brain cells are created and retained, and improves the chances of a brand being remembered when it matters most.

Creating deep impressions

Participation is good for brains in the same way as playing outdoors is beneficial for most children (compared with passively watching several hours of television a day).[4] Through play, children optimise the development of their brain. Research has shown that, in general, exposure to participatory, enriched environments (such as the outdoors) doubles the growth of new brain cells and connections and strongly improves memory performance. It also improves learning of cognitive, emotional, social and motor skills. At the other extreme, intense exposure to impoverished information – such as being in constant readiness to react instantly to messages like emails, SMS, voicemail, etc. – can knock up to 10 points off your IQ.[5] As a result, some scientists like Princeton's Elizabeth Gould now think that the structure of our brain is strongly influenced by our surroundings (danger, continued stress, poverty, monotony, information bombardment, etc.).[6] The process by which new brain cells are created and integrated in brain functioning takes little more than a month. But after this period, the effect of participatory environments on the brain can become so strong that it not only delays memory loss when we grow older, it can even repair memory failure after the damage of brain cells due to injuries or diseases like Alzheimer's.[7]

participation is good for brains

Why? One key reason is that the brain creates twice as many new brain cells and connections when interacting with enriched environments as it does when interacting with impoverished surroundings. In a laboratory, the simplest example is a mouse living in surroundings with mates, treadmills, sticks, compartments and seesaws, compared with a mouse living in an environment without any such facilities.[8] For children, the outdoors provides such an enriched environment. In the same way, participatory branding experiences provide enriched environments for customers. An 'enriched' environment offers multiple opportunities for meaningful, customer-driven interaction – Nike Plus is an example. But how does participation's effect on the brain work?

We have seen that the brain contains billions of neurons, each of which is connected with around 1,000 to 1,500 other neurons through links called 'synapses'. The brain contains roughly as many of these connections as there are stars in the known universe. Through these synaptic interconnections, cells can activate each other. So, for example, the neurons representing a jogger's goal of using a protective and smart tracksuit may activate the neurons representing the Nike brand name. We have seen that repeated activation strengthens such connections, so that a coherently built brand is activated more quickly and more forcefully by a customer's cocktail of goals. Participation, on the other hand, can do two things:

- **Multiply existing connections.** First, participation can strengthen the brand's existing links with customer goals through the formation of additional brain cells and synaptic connections. The extra interconnections in such a rich network allow a cascade of further cross-activation.[9] This is important, as the intensity with which a brand is activated is roughly equivalent to the sum of the signals coming in through the synapses. More connections mean more signals, which means a stronger activation, which means a higher chance of being remembered. So Nike Plus effectively multiplies the neural connections the brand has with the customer goal of 'improving running performance'. This means that the Nike brand will be activated more forcefully by this goal than competing brands.

- **Link the brand to additional, individual customer goals.** Secondly, what may be even more interesting is that, through participation, the brand can become linked to other important customer goals. In other words, the cocktail of goals to which the brand is connected is both extended and personalised. For example, the Nike Plus voice-over can help you – if you select a training programme – to manage your tempo and the number of calories you burn. You can use Nike Plus for setting and attaining calorie-burning objectives so that your brain may thus begin to associate Nike with the goal of weight loss, which can be strongly linked to your self-image. The brain may start to see Nike as a way to manage and improve your health, stamina, energy level and sense of physical self-worth. Because you influence the process, you may come to link the Nike brand to more of your personal goals. And each of these associations can activate the brand. As a result, you may think of Nike more frequently because it becomes linked to a wider variety of relevant goals than it ever was as a mere maker of sportswear.

In short, participation helps a brand to be activated more forcefully and more frequently. Brands that can enrich the interaction with their customers are thus more likely to be selected by the brain's brand-choice algorithm.

Factors of enrichment

Enriched environments share a number of characteristics that promote neurogenesis in a way that benefits a brand (see Table 7.1). The Nike Plus experience embodies a number of them. First, Nike Plus allows freedom of movement. Because control of the entire interaction process rests largely with the user, they will employ Nike Plus in the way that is most relevant to them individually. Participation leads them to associate the Nike brand with their personal goals.

TABLE 7.1 Factors that make up an enriched environment

Make participation rewarding
The interactive brand environment must be meaningful and rewarding for customers. There must be something of value to be gained from participating.
Provide opportunities for learning
The growth of new connections is especially strong when interaction facilitates learning (e.g. information, knowledge, skills, etc.).
Give the customer control
Connection growth is stronger when the learner is in control of the process and experiences room for voluntary action and freedom of movement. Think of Apple stores where visitors can freely wander around and test products.
Make it socially stimulating
Interesting interaction with other people lowers stress and adds positively to the development of new brain cells and interconnections.
Minimise stress and pain
Stress impairs memory formation and retrieval.

Source: Adapted from: Dr Joan Tierney (2006), 'Enriched Environment: Putting Guidance into Practice – Why Bother?' Presentations from Traumatic Brain Injury Functional Rehabilitation Conference, New Zealand.

Secondly, the Nike Plus website has been designed to be meaningful and rewarding to runners. Clever feedback mechanisms play a crucial role in this. You return home feeling satisfied with yourself. You link some of these rewarding feelings to the brand. Then you upload your data and watch a chart of your run. A meaningful and rewarding activity, performed within the context of the Nike and Apple brands, ends but your brain will store it as something to repeat in the future.

Thirdly, the whole experience is coherent. It provides no inconsistent signals that cancel the learning process. The associations thus learned can be reactivated regularly to become stronger. Finally, Nike Plus allows forms of social interaction, which further enhance the building of new connections in the brain.[10]

LEGO's experience store also makes clever use of the third law. The shop's designers have created play spaces in the middle of the store with dozens of cylinders containing the LEGO bricks within children's reach, thus encouraging a direct experience of its products. The store, designed by Fitch, breaks with the tradition of placing closed boxes of LEGO bricks on long shelves. It also breaks with the old rule that you are not allowed to play with the toys in the toyshop, which most kids were inclined to ignore anyway.

Instead, it stimulates people to interact with the brand. Children can talk their parents into playing with the bricks in the store. For parents, this can evoke strong memories of their own childhood when they played happily with LEGO themselves. As a result, fresh associations are created and old ones are reactivated, giving LEGO an advantage over competing brands that do not allow participation. Brands that tempt their customers to try, play, practise, learn, exercise, adapt, interact or socialise with them are more likely to win the battle for awareness and be chosen.[11] Neuroscience indicates something that few marketers realise: participation is a superior branding approach.

Count me in

Participation is not simply letting customers tinker with your brand. It means giving them control within certain limits. As we shall see, the potential to give them such control varies from industry to industry, although the reasons why customers want to participate seem to be relatively common across categories.

> participation means giving customers control within certain limits

What you get and how you get it

Participation has two dimensions: process flexibility and outcome control.[12] Figure 7.2 explains how these dimensions apply to branding. Take Disneyland, for example. When you visit it, the end result (experiencing Disney magic) is explicitly defined by Disney throughout every detail of the park. But the process by which it is experienced is left up to you. You can decide which rides to visit, what shows to watch and where to eat.

> participation has two dimensions: process flexibility and outcome control

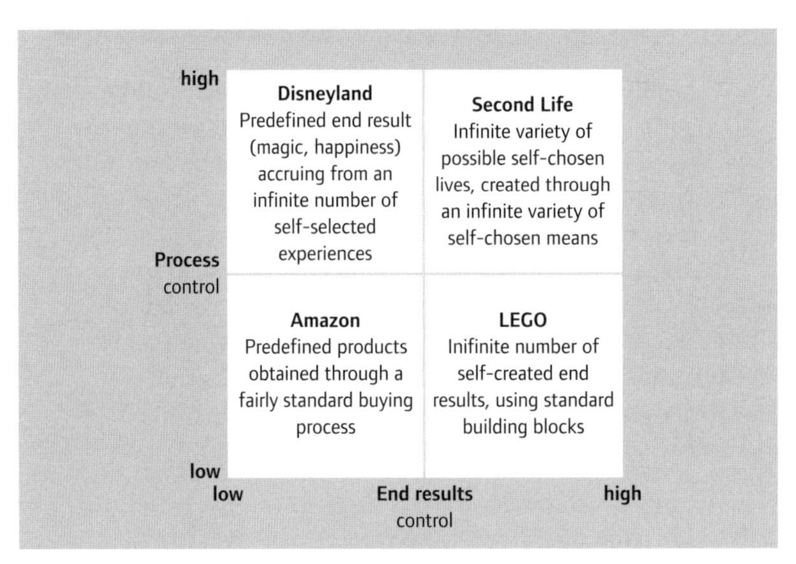

FIGURE 7.2 Examples of relinquishing the control of process and end results to customers

With LEGO it is the exact opposite. The process is fixed (fitting prefabricated bricks) but the end result is open. You decide what you create out of the bricks – a garage, a car, a doll, a house. At Amazon the situation is different again. Both the end product and the purchasing process are rather fixed. You get a book, a DVD or other item from the Amazon stock delivered to your door and your influence is limited to the choice of the item, the payment option and delivery method. The purchase process is also relatively fixed: you click the buttons at the Amazon website. Second Life is at the other end of the spectrum. The end result is open: you define your own life and what its purpose is. Little is fixed. The process is open as well. You decide how your life is lived, with what identity and looks.

Changing the rules of the game

Traditionally, when an advertiser like Unilever or Renault sent out a brand message to customers through the mass media, the message was rather passively absorbed (provided it reached the customer). Brand associations were formed as a result of absorbing the message. Let, assume that, in the traditional model, 70 per cent of the effect was attributable to the message, and 30 per cent was generated by the recipient (by paying active attention or by consciously evaluating the message).

Companies like Heineken, Procter & Gamble, FedEx – in fact *all* major brands – have carried out their advertising in this way for many decades. In the case of brand participation, however, the branding effect is less attributable to the brand owner and more to the recipient, who accounts for – say – 70 per cent of the brand memory-formation process. The brand owner plays a smaller role in the branding process than was previously the case. Participation means customers build the brand.

If you add all that up, participation may look disheartening at first, especially if you are Unilever or P&G and your global advertising spend is upwards of €3 billion a year. It means, after all, a radically different allocation of funds – away from sender-controlled channels and towards customer-influenced forms of interaction where the marketer deliberately cedes control. It means that the effectiveness of, say, 70 per cent of your €3 billion marketing investment would depend on your customers, if you were to invest it completely in a participation strategy. However, precisely because customers participate, the net branding effect is stronger.

Gauging your industry's participation potential

The key to participatory branding, therefore, is to *organise self-organisation*: to initiate the conditions within which customers can create their own benefits and do the branding themselves. The starting point for doing this, however, is not the same in every industry. Some product categories allow interaction more naturally than others.

Figure 7.3 shows that different sectors have different levels of participation capacity. For example, medical clinics (bottom left) have less room to give customers control than has the hotel business.

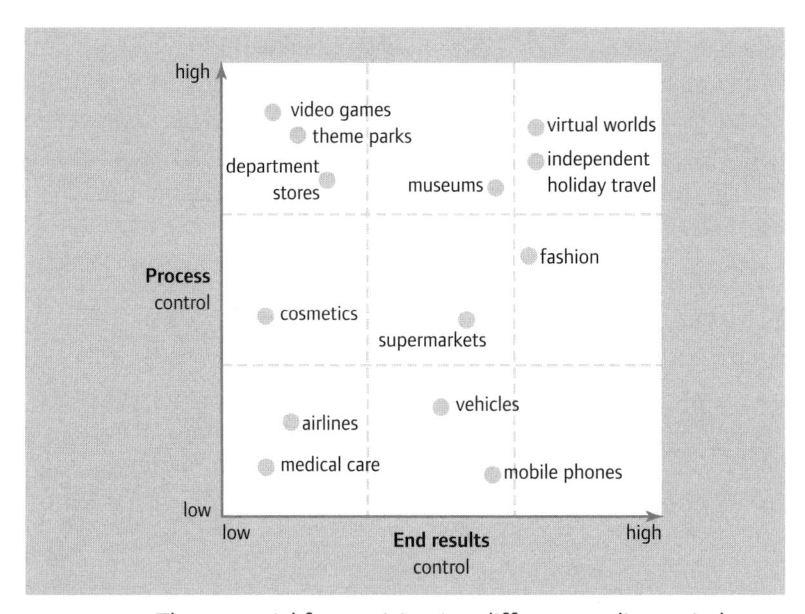

FIGURE 7.3 The potential for participation differs according to industry

Video games (top left) are a different case altogether. Take *Grand Theft Auto*, for instance. Sales of the fourth release in the first seven days were worth $500 million, more than double the box-office results of the best-selling film of all time. The different possible end results of the game are limited: you win; or you lose, in which case you die. The rules of the game are fixed, as is the way the game is controlled. But apart from that, the choices you can make when hunted by the police, for instance, are multiple. All decisions are up to you and there are many options. Every time you play the game it is slightly different, giving gamers a great sense of freedom.

From oldies like *Donkey Kong* up to today's best sellers, games are strongly participatory brands, which surely explains part of their huge success. What is more, the key to games such as *Call of Duty* is not just manipulating the joystick but also deciphering the rules, which is mentally challenging. Popular entertainment culture is getting more intellectually demanding by the year and may be sharpening – rather than 'infantilising' – our brains, as Steven Johnson noted in his book *Everything Bad Is Good For You.*[13]

Some brands increase their participatory power by entering new industries. Designer Giorgio Armani comes, of course, from the fashion industry (mid-right in Figure 7.3) and is now entering the hotel business, where there is similar room for participation. Armani is opening a luxury hotel in Dubai in 2009 at Burj Dubai, the world's tallest tower. A second Armani hotel is planned for Milan, followed by Marrakesh and New York. The Armani Hotel Dubai includes restaurants, 160 guest rooms and suites, and a spa covering more than 40,000 square metres.[14] The Armani hotels are all marked by Giorgio Armani's design aesthetics, allowing participation within a branded context. By entering the hotel industry, Armani expands its options for creating brand participation among a well-defined segment of customers.

Nintendo, the game-system maker, has stretched its participatory power by broadening the application of its Wii console in a way that is drawing in new users. The Wii made its mark as a gaming system that got people off the couch, to play games like tennis and golf with motion-sensing controllers. In 2007, it introduced a virtual personal fitness trainer in Japan, Wii Fit + Wii Balance Board, complete with exercises, progress monitoring, goal-setting functions and so on.[15] These accessories target a mainstream audience and are especially popular among women. Your body mass index is the key factor for tracking your progress in a phenomenon called 'exercise gaming'. There is nothing to stop Nintendo from building a community over the internet, with tools similar to those pioneered by Nike Plus, where people can do their morning exercises together while in their own homes, discussing tips or exchanging exercises. Similarly, Nokia extended its reach by creating the Nokia Sports tracker. This is a GPS-based activity tracker that works on smartphones and measures information such as running speed, distance and time, but also stores maps of your runs.

Some brands are better at inducing participation than others within the same industry. For instance, with its innovative interface the iPhone shifts the level of process control upwards for mobile phone users. This will result in a stronger branding effect than competing handset brands will be able to offer, giving Apple an edge in creating a strong brand position within the global handset market.

Why people participate

But why would people make the effort to participate? Surely they can also consume more passively? Yes, but as Figure 7.4 shows, there are several reasons why people want to engage.

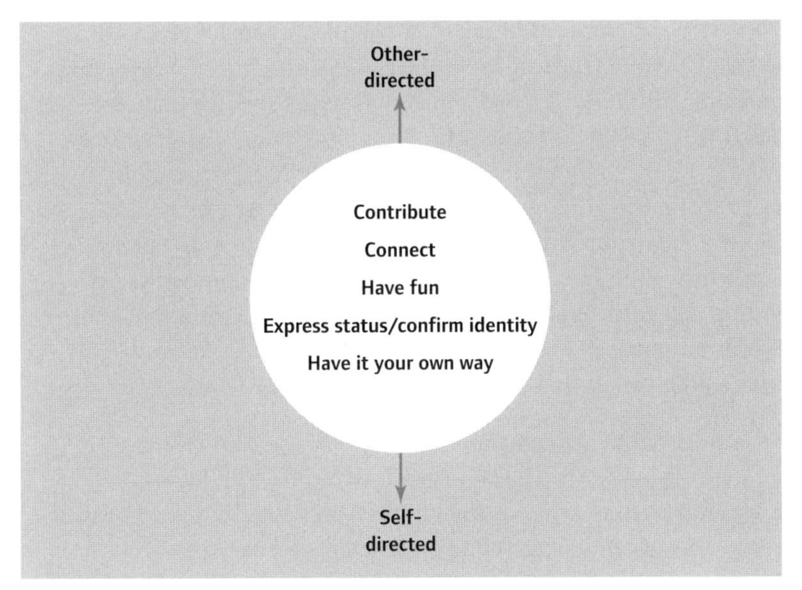

FIGURE 7.4 The five most common drivers of participation

The desire to have it our way We have learned that we can be very demanding. We can increasingly get what we want, in the way we want it, when we want it, armed as we are with readily available information sources, comparison sites, personal shoppers, and so on. By participating, we take our faith in our own hands and define, co-create and co-produce the products, services and experiences we buy – from sport shoes to cars, from hotel stays to financial services. Puma's Mongolian Shoe BBQ is a good example, where customers can assemble and completely customise their own shoes online and then have them delivered to their home address. Another example is when the CD-ROM drive of your PC is broken and you go to the manufacturer's forum to find repair tips from other users of the brand instead of calling in someone to repair it.

To express status and confirm identity Sometimes people participate to gain recognition. This can take many forms: for example, being an expert, being creative, being cool, being accepted, etc. Mexx, for example, organised a competition where a girl and her best friend could upload their best dual photo to the site, to become the next 'XX Girls'. The winners would win a professional photo shoot and go on to be part of Mexx's XX perfume campaign.

As girls were encouraged to ask their friends to vote for them, Mexx enabled girls to generate buzz for themselves and for the brand. It is increasingly difficult for us as consumers to distinguish ourselves through what we buy. Mass-market brands are accessible to almost anyone in our affluent society. Consequently, customers can no longer rely on the product or service to provide them with instant recognition and admiration from their peers. It is thus up to us to tell the story. Brands that can provide us with the ingredients for this story can gain an edge. Participation by telling stories helps us to achieve a status or identity dividend from our product and service purchases in this new context.[16]

Have fun Participation can simply be enjoyable and entertaining. Games are a good example and so are 'flash mobs' – sudden, short and concerted group acts in a public place. In one example, described in *Harper's Magazine*, Macy's rug department was the site of a flash mob when, all at once, 200 people wandered over to the carpet in the back left corner and, as instructed, informed sales staff that they all lived together in a Long Island commune and were looking for a 'love rug'. Just as suddenly, everyone disappeared again.[17]

The desire to connect Community websites like Facebook are about connecting with other people, keeping up with their whereabouts and informing them of yours. Equally, being part of Nike Plus can mean you are a member of a global running community that creates a sense of mutual understanding and belonging. People participate to connect with like-minded people (especially by means of blogs, forums and communities) and share experiences with others. Such media offer a sense of community. Hence their name, 'social media'. In some cases, people are there because of pressure from their peers who want to connect with them, or because they hope to make new friends themsleves through such communities.[18]

The desire to contribute Adding something to a product, service or community can be motivated by either reciprocity or efficacy. For instance, you can put in information on a forum hosted by Leica, on the premise that you will receive useful assistance or input in return when you are in need. Alternatively, you could contribute because you like the idea that others can benefit from your input.

In some cases, the value of participation depends on the number of other people participating. Social networking is hard if you are the only one. The number of other people participating can also be a signal that participation is interesting, thus stimulating others to engage.

> participation presupposes that the brand is relevant to customers

It is a mistake to think that people will participate in just any platform. It is not enough simply to put a site online with the brand's television commercials and some downloadable content. Participation presupposes that the brand or product is *relevant* to customers. Customers do not participate just for participation's sake. The interaction itself must be rewarding but the brand has to have value to them as well. In other words, for participation to work the brand must implement the law of relevance. The law of coherence must also be applied to ensure that participation does not mean the brand getting torn apart by customers doing their own thing with it. The third law is consequently the most challenging one because it requires us to implement both the first and the second laws.

A different kind of marketing

The third law of branding points us in the direction of a specific use of media and branding platforms, aimed at inducing participation. This has several consequences for the marketing function. Participatory branding represents a different approach to branding, one that contravenes many of the old rules that marketers have come to rely on.

Make your brand strategy open-ended

While many participatory platforms use the internet, it is a mistake to think that participation is just a virtual phenomenon that uses social media. The physical world offers many examples (as we will also see in the next chapter). The New York Prada store designed by Koolhaas, which opened in 2001, is an example.

It is a store whose meaning extends beyond its walls because of its ability to transform itself from a fashion shop into a gallery, a seminar room, or an exhibition space. The store was designed so that its function could easily be changed. By staging forward-looking community events that allow participation and interaction, the Prada brand stretches its meaning. It becomes richer and less confined, without losing its allure and relevance as a barometer of contemporariness. This is the essence of the third law of branding. It is about giving customers autonomy in defining the brand. It is about organising self-organisation by customers, both online and offline.

At the world exposition in Hanover, I was commissioned by the Dutch government to study the nationally branded pavilions – absorbing, participatory environments – for their effects on national reputations. On average, I found, 2.7 million people focused themselves for about 20 minutes each in the branding campaign of a given nation. Imagine having the full attention of your target audience for a third of an hour. It is a marketer's dream. For the immensely successful Dutch pavilion, a six-storey brand experience designed by MVRDV (see facing page), we calculated the value of the pavilion's image effects at around €350 million – more than ten times the initial investment.[19] This is quite an astonishing figure of a degree that we will not find for non-participatory campaigns.

The French ski resort of Avoriaz, which we discussed briefly in Chapter 6, is another interesting case. It is a village with a characteristic design language reflected in each and every building – from the apartments to the church, from the 'bus' stops for horse sleighs to the baker's shop. Moreover, the functional and visual design of the resort itself intensifies the experience of its harsh physical surroundings. Avoriaz is also completely environmentally friendly, closed to cars, largely self-supporting, aesthetically blending in with its natural background. It is coherent in every way. As in every village, it allows visitors almost complete freedom over how they spend their time. But almost everything you do is within a uniquely relevant and coherent branded experience that allows strong process control in producing an intense and pleasurable winter holiday.

There are no traditional media

Unfortunately, participation is still being pioneered only by a small group of marketers. The strategies that many brands are currently formulating are often mere box-ticking approaches. All too often, we see little more than a television commercial launched online. A MySpace page is opened and the obligatory viral (often the television commercial itself) is put on YouTube in the hope that people will start forwarding it so that word-of-mouth will do the rest. Obviously, the results are often lacklustre. Others put all their faith in the deployment of so-called 'non-traditional' media. This approach can be effective. To be sure, traditional mass media like television and radio have become less suitable to targeting specific audiences (although interactive television may change this). Audiences are generally fragmenting. For instance, in 1960 the average US household had access to 5.7 television channels. Today, the same home has more than 100.[20] But simply substituting traditional media (television, radio, print) with non-traditional media (such as viral films, in-game advertising, interactive banners) does not do the trick. Why not? Essentially because traditional media do not exist. There is only traditional media *usage*. Traditional media can be made participatory, and conversely, non-traditional media can be used in a boring, non-interactive way.

Traditional media become less effective. But what to think then of the very effective campaigns in traditional media, such as the Sony Bravia (bouncing balls), the Adidas 'Impossible is Nothing' (featuring Muhammad Ali) and the Coca-Cola Side of Life (Happiness Factory) campaigns? Moreover, there are many campaigns that are less successful, despite their heavy use of so-called non-traditional media. These include advertisements in Second Life, interactive banners in MySpace, virals and in-game campaigns. Despite television being traditional, Unilever is stepping up its investment in interactive television adverts – a potentially more participatory variant of a traditional medium. It launched its first one for Axe in 2005. Interactive adverts allow participation in ways that will grow ever more sophisticated in the coming years.[21] Whether an interactive advert will work depends on the degree to which its content induces participation.

The point is this: from a branding perspective, the idea that non-traditional media are inherently more effective than traditional ones is dangerously misleading. Media do not hold the key, and the distinction between traditional and non-traditional media is futile. Creativity is what counts. There are many examples of traditional media being used creatively and successfully to stimulate participation. Figure 7.5 provides some examples. It is better to distinguish between participatory and non-participatory media usage rather than between traditional and non-traditional media.

Certainly, some media enable more participation than others. Marshall McLuhan distinguishes between hot (low in participation) and cool (high in participation) media.[22] The internet allows a great deal of interaction, while radio offers little. But almost all media – even ones less suited for interaction – can be used to create participation. The reality show *Big Brother* (see Figure 7.5) is an example of a traditional medium, television, turned into a participation platform, for instance by inviting viewers to select the person who has to leave the house, and adding a website where viewers can choose their own camera angle. The programme is a hit in 70 countries, thanks largely to its participatory format.

Co-creation and a more open strategy

In strategy terms, participation implies that a business may shift from a transaction base (selling a product or service) to an ongoing relationship with customers (continuous interaction and adjustment of the product or value-creation process). Prahalad and Krishnan describe the business implications of this profound shift towards 'co-created value' in their book *The New Age of Innovation*. They see this participatory business model as the exact opposite of the Model T Ford, a standardised product of which Henry Ford famously said: 'You can have any colour as long as it's black.' In the view of Prahalad and Krishnan, the future growth of today's companies rests on their ability to access a global network of resources provided by others to co-create unique experiences for customers one at a time.[23]

Participatory

Big Brother
Big Brother follows a group of strangers living together in a house fitted out with dozens of cameras and microphones recording their every move 24 hours a day. One by one, the houseguests will vote each other out of the house. At the end of three months, the last remaining houseguest will receive the grand prize. Viewers can vote for who they wish to see evicted and can choose camera angles on the show's website (realitytv.about.com)

Batman
The Dark Knight is an alternative reality game created by Warner Brothers and 42 Entertainment to promote *The Dark Knight* Batman film. The game includes a storyline in which the players are characters: citizens of the fictional Gotham City. The game requires searching for clues to continue the story on the internet, on the phone, and at real-life events (batman.wikibruce.com)

Traditional ← → Non-traditional

Adidas – Impossible Is Nothing
The *Impossible Is Nothing* campaign encourages everyone to take their first step in reaching their impossible goal. Through stories of real people attempting and achieving what once seemed like impossible goals, Adidas hopes to inspire people to think about their own obstacles and how to overcome them. More than 30 international sports stars and lesser-known athletes tell their 'impossible' stories using their own hand-drawn illustrations and paintings (press.adidas.com)

BMW Films – *The Hire* series
BMW's groundbreaking *The Hire* film series ignored conventions and created the phenomenon known as online films. The web has never been the same since. These eight short films by critically acclaimed Hollywood directors effectively revolutionised the world of interactive entertainment, while showcasing BMW's unique high-performance vehicles (bmwusa.com)

Non-participatory

FIGURE 7.5 Traditional media can be participatory

As this inevitably means customers influencing the meaning of our brand, branding itself becomes more open-ended. This could contradict the law of coherence. Each customer might create a different brand meaning, at odds with the meaning intended by the brand owner. But this is not necessarily the case when you set the boundaries within which participation takes place.

The trend towards a more participatory type of branding fits into a much broader development that writer and semiotician Umberto Eco has described in *The Open Work*.[24] In it, he signals a tendency in modern art (music, painting, poetry, literature, etc.) to create works that are 'open' or 'unfinished'. They leave room for the performer or audience to interpret them – unlike, for instance, the representational paintings of Titian or Canaletto. Similarly, in classical branding, marketers broadcast a finished, closed brand via the mass media to a mass audience. The type of branding advocated in this chapter breaks with this classic paradigm. Marketers in the new approach present a more open and unfinished brand and solicit participation from customers, who can interpret or adapt the brand to their own needs and preferences. Thus, they create their own variation on the brand's key theme. Eco first signalled this trend in the 1960s in the arts. Around forty years later, the marketing field has begun integrating this avant-garde artistic invention into its commercial strategies.

How to get in

Integrating participation in your brand strategy can make a huge difference to the effectiveness of your branding activities. However, it requires a number of changes in thinking to implement it. The following steps are designed to help.

Step 1: Understand the importance of participation

Brands that are able to induce participation can facilitate a learning process during which new brain cells and connections are created. Participatory brands are better remembered at the moment of choice and are more likely to be chosen. To that end brands must enrich the interactions customers have with them, offering meaningful opportunities to try, play, practise, learn, exercise, adapt, interact or socialise with them.

Step 2: Open up

Participation requires you to let go of the traditional centralised branding philosophy. It means allowing customers to control what they get and how they get it. We have seen that different industries have different capacities for participation. But we must let go of the old idea that a marketer dictates the meaning of the brand. This sounds simple, but it is difficult to do. The prize for those who can wisely relinquish control is a brand that is favoured in the brains of its customers.

Step 3: Think virtual and physical

Forget the distinctions of 'traditional' and 'non-traditional' media. Opening up your brand is done not only by using the internet (e.g. Nike Plus), but also through more traditional media and branded physical places (e.g. branded stores, world exhibitions, resorts, etc.). An often overlooked possibility for participation is the product experience. Brands like Leica and Apple pay great attention to the packaging of their products. Unwrapping your newly bought camera or laptop becomes a more intense, more rewarding interaction with the brand that helps to build its position in the brain.

Conclusion

The law of participation states that we must give customers the opportunity to influence the results the brand provides, the process by which those results are created, or both. Participation stimulates the creation of new brain cells and connections between the brand and the customer's cocktail of goals. Participation extends and personalises the cocktail of goals to which the brand is connected and multiplies the number of connections. As a result, participatory brands are activated more forcefully and more frequently and are thus more likely to be chosen. Customers appear to have at least five participation drivers: a desire to have it our way, a desire for fun, a desire for identity, expression and status, a desire to connect and a desire to contribute. To benefit, however, marketers must open up their brand to customer influence and stop talking about traditional versus non-traditional media. Instead, they must promote self-organisation by customers and distinguish between participatory and non-participatory media usage.

So how can you develop the concept of participation for your own brand? This is the topic of the next chapter.

Getting your audience to enter the game

In the previous chapter, we saw that our brains favoured participatory brands over non-participatory competitors. We also saw, however, that it was not enough simply to offer the possibility of interaction. Participation must be rewarding in its own right, while reinforcing the distinctive relevance (Law No.1) of the brand. It must be staged in a way that is consistent with the brand's identity (Law No.2). And finally, customers must feel the benefit of engaging.

The idea that participation in itself must be rewarding for participants has not yet caught everyone's attention. Brands open pointless MySpace pages, put me-too content on YouTube or ask people to send in user-generated content to win the obligatory trip to New York. All this is done for no better reason than that 'this is what customers want nowadays' or because everyone else is doing it. A recruitment advertising agency once told our mutual client: 'You know, it is amazing how many people are on those social communities nowadays.' The account manager then said: 'We must be present there also, but in such a way that we can control what is being said. We advise you to open a blog for potential recruits at your corporate website.' The client nodded pensively. But why would potential recruits want to spend their free time at the edited weblog of a corporate website? It underlines a painful point: very little thought is put into creating something really engaging for the target audience.

We the people

The success of Barack Obama's 'Change' campaign to become the Democratic nominee and later President of the United States in

2008 is a strong example of eliciting participation. Whether or not you agree with his policies, it is fair to say that Obama touched many hearts and minds in the United States and abroad. He pitched his brand of change with a glow and eloquence that are seldom seen and that many have compared to those of Martin Luther King and John F. Kennedy. The campaign – and possibly Obama's way of marketing his policies – can be analysed in terms of our three laws.

- Obama's message of change and hope was made distinctive from the message of rivals and relevant to a sufficient numbers of voters and officials to give him momentum. It tapped brilliantly into the American Dream and America's cultural and political history, instantly positioning Obama as a new-generation statesman.
- The coherence with which he spread his message made it sink in and lent him the credibility he sought. His non-partisan style of politics emphasised his statesmanship. And his main message neutralised his partisan opponents.
- His ability to encourage a legion of volunteers and donors to participate in his campaign enabled him to clinch the nomination and lead his party.

Consider this last point more carefully. He was the first politician in history to use the full range of modern social media and networking tools to mobilise supporters. He employed a grass-roots operation that brought record numbers of new, young voters to the polls. It motivated an unprecedented number of internet donors to send money, creating the best-funded campaign in American history. He ran an organisation of enthusiastic volunteers who spread his message from door to door and rallied voters behind him. In short, Obama marketed his participatory brand in a way that many commercial brands could learn from.

The key to his success was that the Obama brand made it individually rewarding to participate. He often emphasised that he was there through and for the people. He thus enabled Americans to play a part in bringing historic change to their country. The message of hope – a key facet of the Obama brand – reinforced this, as hope can be defined as a realistic anticipation of reward.[1] By

contributing, the people of America increased the chances that their reward – changing the political status quo in America – would materialise. In bringing this about, Obama created a self-fulfilling prophecy: his ability to mobilise people at the grass roots provided proof of his electability, which attracted yet more people, augmenting the snowball effect. Very soon, people were joining an apparently winning team that would bring long-sought change to their country.

Mobilising your customers

Like many participation campaigns, Obama's was subject to the 'network effect' – the phenomenon that the value of something depends on the number of people already doing it or using it. People were wary at first of joining an outside contender. But when early supporters joined, many others dared to jump on the bandwagon. Social media such as MySpace work in much the same way, depending upon others to use them too. However, it is not always necessary to create a network effect to elicit participation. In other cases, such as Nike Plus, the example we looked at in the last chapter, participating is beneficial for a sole individual. You can track progress in your speed or endurance entirely on your own. With or without the network effect, participation is a superior yet still underused way of building brands. To use it we must learn to mobilise minds and develop relationships in a way that is different from conventional marketing tactics.[2]

So what is the key? How can you tempt an audience to do something? How can you get them to engage in your brand? The answer is: by setting before them a sufficiently tempting opportunity to co-define what they get from your brand and how they get it. That is easily said, of course. But how do you create a sufficiently tempting opportunity to participate? To address this question we must first understand how the brain weighs costs and benefits, as this puts us in a better position to evaluate participation platforms. Secondly, we need tools for crafting more tempting engagement strategies that offset the costs of participation with satisfying rewards for target groups. Finally, we must challenge the assumptions behind our conventional approach to communication planning, as they are biased against participatory branding.

we must understand how the brain weighs costs and benefits

Convincing the brain to participate

The marketing environment today is littered with uninspired participation platforms that fail to convince customers that the benefits are worth the effort.

Neuroscientific research shows that choice processes happen mostly subconsciously but can often be viewed as cost–benefit assessments.[3] It turns out that in many decisions, including the decision to participate, the brain integrates a range of signals into an evaluation. To do this, it has to consider many elements. Suppose, for example, that you walk into a Starbucks during an afternoon break. Deciding whether you want a Frappuccino or an apple juice – a simple choice – requires considering a whole range of factors, not just taste. Your brain might consider their relative price, your energy level, the time of day, the weather, and so on.

An area of the brain called the prefrontal cortex is responsible for making these evaluations. It can do this even when it has no direct experience to go on. In this case, it draws indirectly on our previous evaluations and their effects, the goals we have pursued, our perceptions of the emotional and behavioural reactions of others, and other factors. Our brains can compare apples with oranges and guide us through an unknown city or the first month in a new foreign job.[4] What is more, they work for us largely subconsciously, rapidly and relatively effortlessly. But how do we get this brain area to advise our clients to participate in our branding platform?

Anticipating rewards

The strongest force to engage us is the anticipation of reward, the expectation of personally relevant benefits from participating. So what exactly is a reward? Our brain considers as a reward everything that contributes to our chances of survival. When a potential reward comes within our reach, specialised brain circuits (the dopamine system) start to influence our choices and behaviours.

In the beginning, rewards were very basic things. Food, sex, shelter and the like elicited strong reward signals – and still do. But we have seen in Chapter 3 that more abstract phenomena – ideas, self-image, social expectations – can acquire similar reward value. As soon as we can gain such rewards from participating in something, our brains may – subconsciously – steer our decisions and actions towards participating.

The marshmallow test cited in Chapter 6 shows that it requires effort to postpone such gratification. In other words, the more instantly a reward can be gained, the more likely people are to engage. From this, we can draw two important conclusions.

- First, we must design participation platforms to provide at least some instant gratification and immediate reward, even though the main benefit may take a while to obtain.
- Secondly, engaging large groups of customers for longer periods of time works best when we provide intermediate rewards.

So in developing brand participation strategies, the key is to make participation itself rewarding. Around 2.5 million people participate in Nike Plus not only because of the Nike brand. Hundreds of Batman fans played *The Dark Knight* alternative reality game not just because of their love for the Batman brand that staged it (see below). Hundreds of *Lost* fans participated in the Darhma Initiative as volunteers to save the world not just because of the *Lost* television series itself. All these people got involved because they saw participation itself as rewarding.

A cornerstone of designing participation strategies, therefore, is to map out relevant reward opportunities along the participation journey and to create the prospect of new rewards from further engagement.

If you do not think your strategy through, and just ask people to upload their own videos to your participation site, for example, you risk getting so little response that you end up paying, say, €15,000 per film.[5] Nevertheless, many marketers seem to neglect this rather basic principle and fail to offer meaningful benefits. Why? Perhaps it's because the enormous branding power of participation is not yet common knowledge. Or perhaps it's because people still don't think hard enough about what they need to offer in order to persuade customers to take part.

Mapping participation value

One way to assess the likely success of a participation strategy is to draw a participation value map such as the one shown in Figure 8.1. This value map models the cost–benefit assessment our brain makes. It can be used in quantitative research. On the horizontal axis are the potential rewards of participation that we discussed in Chapter 7. Not all of these rewards need to be obtainable in any situation; they merely represent the most common ones that occur individually or in combinations.

On the vertical axis we find the costs of participation to the customer. These include the necessary financial outlay, the amount of time, attention and energy demanded, and the degree of previous disappointment (which provides an obstacle to engagement). This last point is particularly important. Our brain has been shown to keep track of our past actions. It stores experiences (subconsciously) that influence our future decisions and, among other considerations, seeks to avoid regret.[6]

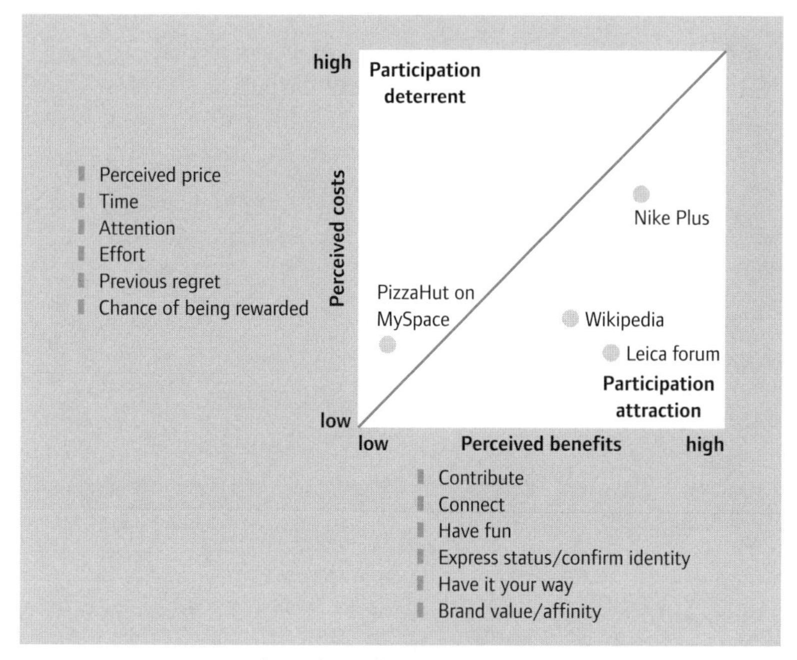

FIGURE 8.1 Mapping the value of participation

These factors allow us to evaluate our platform and help to map it on the cost–benefit plane. Platforms above the diagonal line shown in Figure 8.1 are unsuccessful in eliciting participation. To measure yourself, it can be helpful to include several platforms that do well and do badly on the factors indicated, so as to create reference points. But to map it, we must first design it.

Creating a participation strategy

To make a meaningful attempt at engaging your target group, you need to create a blueprint for a participation strategy.

To design a participation strategy in detail, we must draw the participation journey and the rewards customers can reap along it. This can take the form of a phased storyline with participation rewards marking the stages. Think of it as planting a trail of Easter eggs that your customers can uncover. In creating it, we must start with the contents instead of the media – those come later.

Figure 8.2 shows the seven basic building blocks of a good participation strategy. We will review each of these items below.

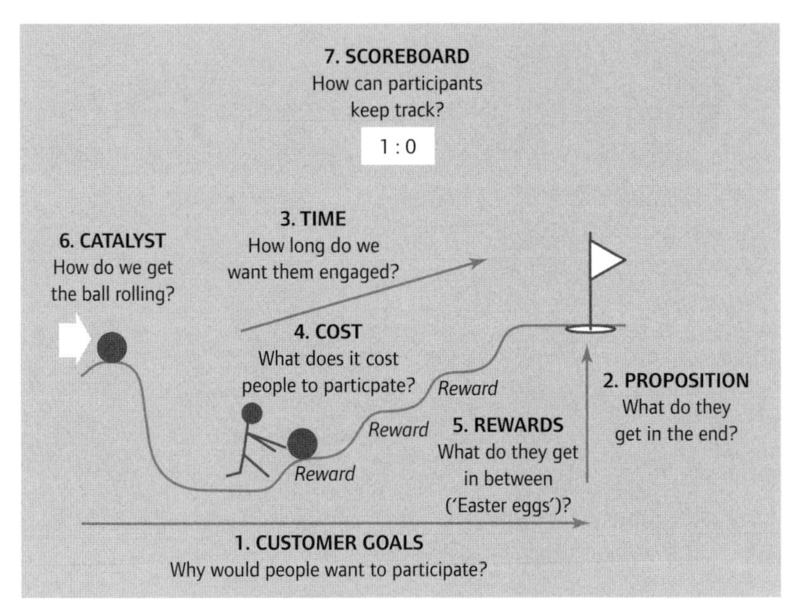

FIGURE 8.2 Blueprint for a participation strategy

1. Customer goals These are the basic needs in our customers that we are addressing in order to engage them. Nike Plus, for example, targets the insight that running builds health in your body but brings loneliness to your mind. In the case of Obama, the insight was the desire among citizens to establish a more unified political approach to solving America's most pressing problems. A strong insight is needed to motivate people. Platforms that lack it will not be very successful.

2. Proposition The proposition is a statement of the overall advantage that people gain from participating with the brand. The proposition can be either an end benefit or an influence on the process by which the brand delivers it. In the case of the Obama campaign, the proposition was securing the presidential nomination to bring about change. With Nike Plus, the proposition is that you have much more fun running; running becomes more social and more interesting (by having instant performance feedback).

3. Time This refers to the period during which we want to engage people. In the case of the Obama campaign, the primary period was clearly marked to run from January 2008 until August 2008 when the nominee was chosen. With Nike Plus, the period is variable: in most cases it is decided by the runner. Specifying the time frame is crucial in order to provide enough reasons for people to *remain* engaged.

4. Costs Participation always requires an investment from the participant in terms of time, effort or money. Obama's supporters, for example, were asked to donate small amounts of money (e.g. $25), or to put in time to persuade other people to vote for him, or to put in effort to distribute promotional materials. With Nike Plus, costs include buying the shoe sensor and the iPod receiver, the effort of downloading training programmes, sweating and doing the actual running. It is wise to specify the costs, to see if the participation rewards you aim to offer will compensate for them.

5. Rewards Participation must be rewarding. If you want to engage people for more than a few seconds, you need to provide intermediate rewards – or at the very least promise them. These rewards – and this is crucial – must be related to the brand in order to strengthen it. Figure 7.4 shows common participation drivers. A brand can select the ones most suited to its brand identity and translate them into meaningful participation rewards.

> rewards must be related to the brand

In the Obama campaign, people could contribute to his underdog campaign, for example by convincing people to go to the ballot box and vote for *him*. There were 52 intermediate state elections held to win 'delegates'. These delegates eventually decided who would be the nominee. The intermediate 'rewards', in other words, were the number of state delegates that were won during each stage. Participants would know they had contributed towards Obama winning them. In the case of Nike Plus, the intermediate rewards are provided by the music you listen to as you run, the training programmes that tell you your progress, the personalised charts of the results from your run.

When rewards do not reinforce the brand identity – as with many sweepstakes and contests – then participation does little to build the brand.

6. Catalyst To get the participation process rolling, you need to arouse a customer's curiosity, either by posing a question, creating a disturbance, withholding something from people or offering them something they can help to define.[7] Nike Plus was launched by an announcement that the CEOs of the partner companies were holding a joint press conference. People were not told what would be presented: something was withheld from them and this caught the media's attention.

In the case of Obama, he made his announcement to run for president by presenting himself as a disruptive force. He underlined the audacity of his intentions to the media who were following the much more experienced and well-known candidates he was facing.[8]

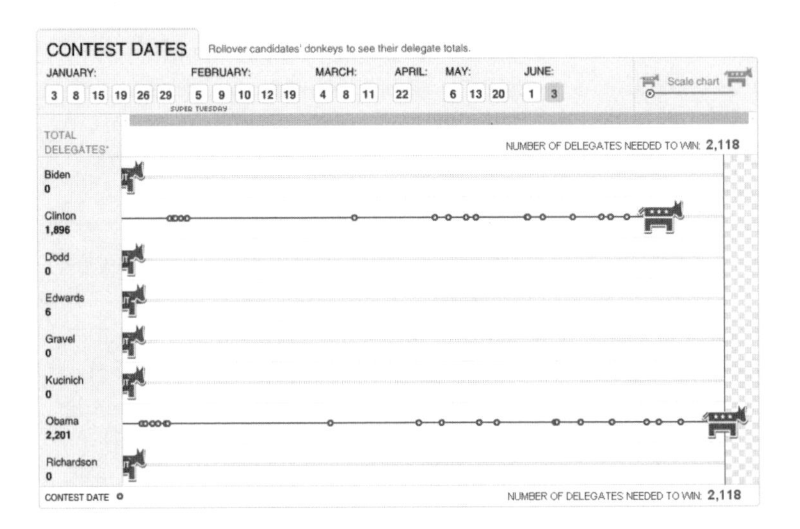

7. Scoreboard This is how you measure progress in the participation process. In the Obama presidential campaign these were the opinion-poll results and the total number of delegates won, as the screenshot above shows. In Nike Plus there are several scoreboards. The iPod display, for instance, provides details about time, distance and calories burned. Then there are the personalised charts comparing your last run with previous runs. There is also the worldwide ranking of people's running times over the same distance (e.g. 5 km) called the 'leader board'. All these elements encourage the runner. Scoreboards allow participants to keep track of the rewards collected so far.

Why so serious?

The promotion for the Batman film *The Dark Knight* is another good example of a successful participation strategy. It combined many of the elements of our blueprint. The film opened on 17 July 2008 in Australia, but its promotional campaign started 18 months before the premiere. The campaign centred on a game that was entirely consistent with the Batman brand concept and the premise of the film. In the game, participants follow clues given to them by, among others, the Joker – the villain in the Batman series. We can illustrate the blueprint by looking at this in more detail.

There were several customer insights behind the Batman game. One of these was that true Batfans would be dying to know more about the new film before its release. The game's proposition was that participants could uncover and experience the plot line of events in Gotham City – the fictional city where the Batman series takes place – in the period between the end of the last film (*Batman Begins*) and the opening of the new one (*The Dark Knight*). It covered the 'inter-film' period. No one other than the game's participants could learn about these developments. This of course made participation unique and irresistible for fans.

The catalyst for the game was buzz and gossip. A number of events were created. The film's official website went live. Election posters for Gotham's district attorney Harvey Dent appeared around Los Angeles. The film website then redirected participants to a similar campaign poster at **ibelieveinharveydent@warnerbros.com**. Next, the owner of a comic-book shop in Los Angeles reported that Joker cards saying 'I believe in Harvey Dent too!' had been left all over his store. A few weeks later, dollar bills with Joker faces were found at the San Diego Comic-Con convention. The bills led to **whysoserious.com**, a webpage that recruited people for jobs as Joker henchmen. The page contained coordinates to a place near the convention centre. It also featured a countdown clock that went off the next morning at 10 o'clock. At that time and in that place, a phone number was written in the sky to mark the game's official launch. After participants solving all the clues, wearing Joker masks and collaborating with friends online, one fan was 'abducted' and 'killed' in place of the Joker. The participants in San Diego received clown masks as a reward, while online players were rewarded with the first teaser trailer for *The Dark Knight.*[9]

The participation period was a lengthy 18 months. Yet there was no permanent engagement possible, as episodes of the game were delivered in unexpected chunks. During all that time, the game was essentially free. Participation costs were generally just time and energy. But to participants, it was rewarding at every stage. Each episode revealed more 'inside' stories from Gotham City and provided tangible rewards like Joker masks, film previews, film tickets, etc. All rewards were coherent with the story. Participants understood that the whole game was a build-up to the official release date of the film in July 2008. This worked as a kind of scoreboard to keep track of where they were in the game.

Thus, *The Dark Knight* game pulled people in. It made them do things. It made participants experience the Joker's sardonic ways and twisted thinking. Interestingly, by building the promotional campaign around the antagonist (the evil Joker), the game's creators boosted the demand for the protagonist (Batman) to enter the scene. Batman himself played no serious role in the game, and this only enhanced anticipation of the film that would finally unleash the battle between good and evil on screen.

The smart and creative storytelling techniques used in this campaign are only beginning to be applied to branding in general. The intricacy of *The Dark Knight* game, developed by 42

Entertainment, is so far unique in the world of marketing. But given its success, we will surely see more campaigns like this in the near future. They will make people aware of the power of participatory branding. This kind of 'transmedia storytelling' – in which various media are used to open up the brand's world – will increase the demand for screenwriters and playwrights capable of creating this kind of drama and intrigue. In due course, they may become part of creative teams.

The end of conventional communication planning

We have seen that Nike Plus, *The Dark Knight* and the Obama campaign are prominent examples of participatory campaigns. They are a logical next step in an evolution from campaigns that grab attention to campaigns that elicit engagement. Figure 8.3 illustrates this transition.

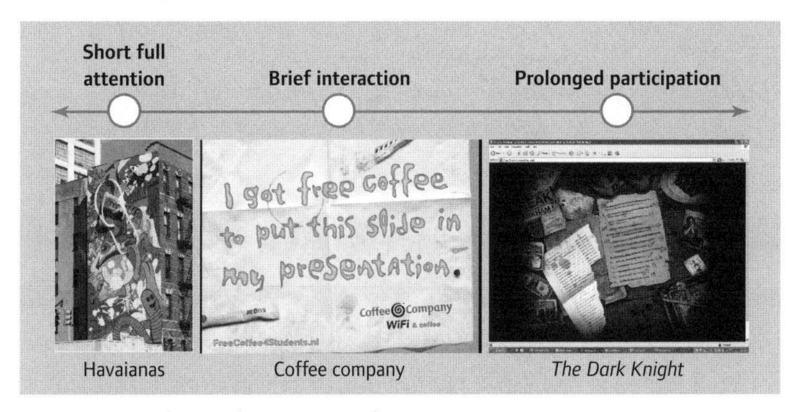

FIGURE 8.3 The evolution towards participation

A recent Havaianas campaign, for example, reflects the first step. It used brightly coloured decorations on the sides of gloomy buildings in New York to grab attention. The campaign turned heads by cheering up the streets, transforming apartment blocks into communication media. A campaign we did for coffee company included rewarding students with free coffee if they put a prepared slide in their presentation and uploaded a photo of it – 'Participatory slidevertising'. Warner Brothers made the leap to full-fledged participation with *The Dark Knight* campaign. It brought a cartoon to real-life gaming, engaging Batfans over a longer period of time – a state-of-the-art example of participatory branding.

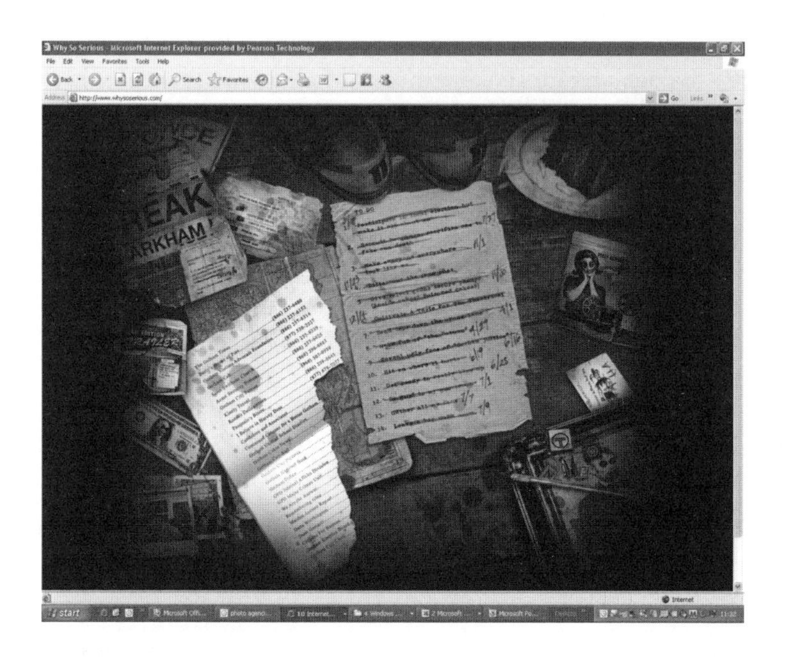

> participatory branding is different from traditional brand communication

But most marketers find it hard to create participation campaigns. Some do not realise that participatory branding is different from traditional brand communication. The problem is not that it requires some kind of exotic new skill to do it well. It simply means using branding creativity in new ways. But today's communication and media-planning approaches are strongly biased against participation.

Table 8.1 summarises the four most significant biases against participation and the following steps consider how they can be overcome.

TABLE 8.1 Eliminating the biases against participatory branding

Bias	Typical remark	Necessary action
1 The 'I love talking' trap Marketers are habitually focused on sending their message, instead of on interaction.	**We must tell customers what we want them to know** 'If we don't tell customers what they must know about our product, they will not buy it.'	**Open a dialogue** Earmark a percentage of your budget specifically for participatory programmes, measure your success and improve on it.
2 Target group myopia Participation is aimed at the classic communication target group.	**Our customers are different** 'Our target group is not interested in participation.'	**Define a participation target group** This group is comprised of people most receptive to engagement.
3 Media reach doctrine Participation platforms are judged on their ability to reach all members of the target group.	**The platform is too niche** 'We don't reach enough people through a participation platform.	**Create indirect reach** Define a 'trickle-down' approach that benefits from PR and word-of-mouth to spread the message.
4 The sweepstake fallacy The participation platform offers rewards that are unattractive and unrelated to the brand's identity.	**Offering a decoy is not enough** 'The easiest way to engage people is to allow them to win a nice prize.'	**Create relevant and coherent rewards** The benefits you create for participants must be worth the effort for the people you seek and be in line with the brand promise.

Step 1: Open a dialogue

The first bias against participation is that most brand managers are habitually focused on talking and not on listening. Marketers and many advertising agencies have no inclination to embark on a dialogue with customers. Often, there is a fear that participation may distort the brand's message. Communication managers find it reassuring to run an advertising campaign. It provides a sense of grip on the relationship with customers. You do something. You tell customers what you want them to know. By contrast, if you were to raise the issue of participatory branding with the typical marketer, the response might be: 'But if I don't tell customers about our product, how do I make them buy it?'

Participation requires that we give up some of this control. It leaves open the way in which the customer interprets our message. You have to understand that participation may not always be directed at immediate sales. But in the longer term, it offers much greater rewards, as customers personally identify with your brand and end up doing some of the work for you, boosting sales down the line.

The remedy To counter this first bias, you need to allocate a significant percentage of your budget for participatory media usage. This means branding initiatives in which customers do something or tell you something back. State this percentage explicitly in the communication plan. And define indicators to gauge the level of participation that you have elicited.

Step 2: Redefine your target group

The second bias against participation is that target groups are usually not defined based upon their propensity to engage. Traditionally, marketers divide their targets into two groups:

- the marketing target group – the broad class of people to whom they aim to sell their product or service, and
- the communication target group – a subset of the marketing target group towards whom they focus their advertising efforts.

The problem is that the prime targets for your advertising (your communication target) are not necessarily the people most inclined to participate in your branding platform. As a result, many marketers make remarks like: 'Our core target group is not interested in participation.'

But this can be a dangerous illusion flowing from an ingrained segmentation model. The solution is to change the way you define audiences. Simply turn the issue around and identify a participation target group that is willing to engage. The trick is to aim for the people who are already enthusiastic about your brand and make them even more so, turning them into ambassadors.

The remedy We need, therefore, to create a new target group. The participation target group can de defined as the people within the marketing target group who are most likely to participate in a branding platform. Generally, only the most dedicated brand users participate. Do not expect to get a representative sample of your client base to engage.

Forrester Research has created a continuum of social media users, ranging from fully active 'creators' to sidelined 'inactives'.[10] The use of social media is not the same as the inclination to use Nike Plus, play the Batman game or enter into any other kind of branded interaction. Yet the logic behind this model – that people differ in their propensity for engagement – is crucial to developing participation strategies. For example, it is vital to develop different modes of participation based on the different degrees of participation readiness of your audience.

Figure 8.4 shows a generic classification of levels of engagement. Different offerings must be created to suit each level. Moreover, it must be possible and easy for users to move up to a higher level of participation. The Nike Plus website, for example, offers different features for different users. Heavy users can use the blogs, use the worldwide rankings and create collective goals with other users. Medium users can use the personal running graphs, and light users can simply download some running music or a training programme and leave it at that.

Step 3: Look for indirect reach

The third bias against participation is that marketers often view participation platforms in terms of the classic criterion of 'reach' – the percentage of people within the communication target group contacted by a given medium. An oft-heard dismissal of participation proposals is: 'We don't reach a sufficient number of people through a participation platform.' We call this the reach doctrine and it blocks innovation in your marketing.

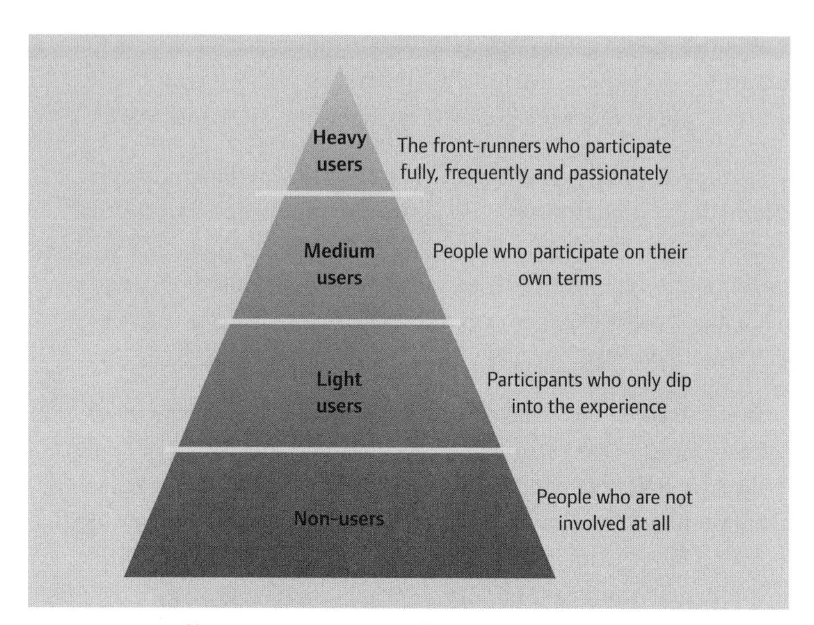

FIGURE 8.4 Different groups have different levels of participation

The reach doctrine implies that to be effective you need to send out your message to your whole target group. (It is thus related to our first bias.) It is based on the assumption, prevalent in the 1950s, that people do what you tell them to do in your advertising. So, if you do not reach everyone, you supposedly miss crucial sales opportunities. Today's marketing environment, in which people are increasingly media-savvy, adept at blocking messages and more focused on peer reviews, makes the reach doctrine outdated.

What is needed for successful participation can be a smarter 'trickle-down' effect – a scheme defining how recognition of the platform can be extended from dedicated users to the whole marketing target group (see Figure 8.5).

Most people who come across a participatory platform hear about it from friends or colleagues. It is satisfied participants who draw others into the platform. They get talking outside the brand and build upon the story themselves (as with the Pokémon game, for instance). Strong platforms, like Nike Plus and *The Dark Knight*, thus enjoy a member-gets-member effect, because it is 'cool' and worth referring to others. Often the platform itself is advertised in

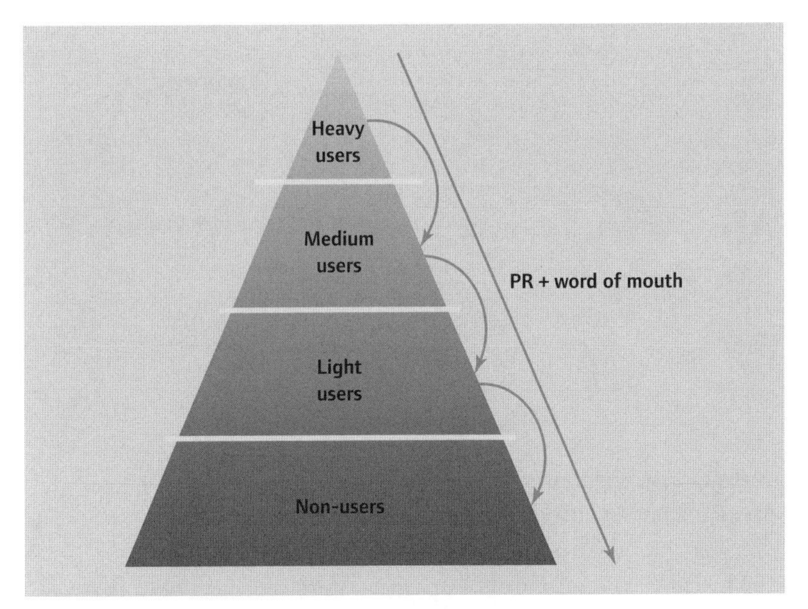

FIGURE 8.5 Strong platforms generate PR and word-of-mouth to build reach

some form. For Nike Plus, for example, a television commercial was developed. *The Dark Knight* relied on gossip. A successful participation platform is so appealing that it attracts media coverage and peer-to-peer conversation simultaneously, with the one feeding off the other, rapidly generating PR and word-of-mouth. In this way, Nike and Warner Brothers eventually achieved a reach far beyond their expectations. Thus, reach is not the primary product but the spin-off of an interesting participation platform. The lesson is that whereas a hoarding can raise awareness, a strong participation platform can generate a phenomenon.[11]

The remedy Eliminating the reach doctrine may require a clearer view of the costs of contact of a participatory branding platform. Figure 8.6 outlines how this reasoning may go. The figure shows that costs per person reached may be greater for highly participatory platforms (the curved line) than for non-participatory platforms like traditional advertising campaigns (the straight line). In the long run, however, participation is a more effective means of branding because it increases the likelihood that your brand will be selected by the brain's brand-choice algorithm, and that revenue

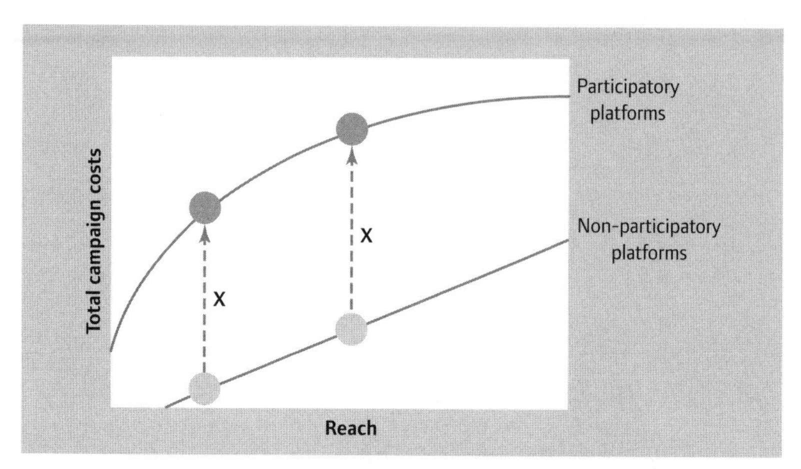

FIGURE 8.6 Platforms with greater participation and higher revenue will also have higher costs per contact

earned by the brand will grow. A participatory platform may also cost more per person reached (indicated by the factor 'X' on the figure). But because revenues will also be higher in the longer term, the level of profit or return on investment will not be eroded.

Step 4: Provide rewards that fit your brand

The fourth bias against participation is that rewards are often irrelevant and out of step with the central brand message. Often, little effort – to the point of contempt towards the customer – is put into defining valuable engagement rewards. A typical remark might be: 'People are always willing to engage if they can win a nice prize.' In other words, marketers are essentially trying to trick people into engagement by giving away an iPod or a trip or a car. We could call this the sweepstake fallacy.

All this achieves is to draw people to a prize frenzy. You are certainly not engaging them in your brand. The brain is prone to remember how it gained rewards. But if the rewards you offer are unrelated to your brand, people do not remember your brand. Obama allowed participants a role in changing their nation. Nike Plus offers participants a more interesting way to become better and fitter runners. *The Dark Knight* allowed participants to enter the world of Batman and experience in advance the new film. In each of these cases, the rewards are expressions of the brand staging the experience.

The idea is not to engage people in winning prizes. The aim is to make them participate in your brand. If not, your campaign is close to worthless from a branding perspective. Moreover, it is questionable if a prize attracts the people you want to attract. It is certain that they will not generate the type of buzz around your brand that you seek.

The remedy Any rewards should be closely linked to the brand. In many cases, the pleasure of participation is its own reward. You must think strategically and creatively to come up with satisfactory intermediate rewards that are in line with the identity of the brand.

The exit of traditional media planning

Media play an important role in building brands. The main part of communication budgets is generally consumed by buying media space. But the law of participation has the potential to disrupt the media-planning landscape in the coming years. Increasing fragmentation of media will mean that the return on investment of traditional media usage will plummet further. Other ways must be found, and are being found, to create sufficient indirect reach – for example, by stimulating worth-of-mouth.

Media planning as a separate function will therefore undergo considerable change. It will probably be absorbed into a discipline that answers the key strategic issue of participation: how do we reach the maximum number of people with a more participatory form of media usage? Such a discipline will depend on a further integration of the separate functions that, today, we call creation, account planning and media planning. Marketers and agencies that are able to blend these disciplines into a seamless function will be winning. Needless to say, the internet will command an ever more pivotal role in this.

One of the most interesting consequences of the rise of participation is that the boundary between your communication and your offerings will blur. Nike Plus is a service, but at the same time it is a branding platform. The same goes for *The Dark Knight* campaign: it is both an advertising campaign and a product that people consume. This may prove to be a shift that will change the face of the marketing industry.

Conclusion

Participatory branding is an underused way of building stronger brands. The first reason for this is that many marketers have never realised that participation can be such a powerful creator of brand associations. Secondly, those who have tried have run into resistance from the conventional communication-planning process – which is predisposed against participation campaigns.

Still, neuroscience indicates that richer, more interactive environments enhance the memory-formation process. This means that participatory branding helps build stronger brands more quickly. But how do you engage people?

We saw that the brain's decision to participate could be understood as a cost–benefit assessment. So it is useful to draw a participation value map (see Figure 8.1) to assess your engagement strategy. This tool makes it easier to balance the advantages and disadvantages of participating from the viewpoint of the participant.

The strongest force to engage us is the anticipation of reward: the expectation of personally relevant benefits from participating. This means we must map the participation journey through time and the rewards customers can reap along the way. This is needed to *keep* people engaged. To develop a strong participation strategy, we need:

1. *A strong participation plan.* The plan must cover the seven building blocks discussed in this chapter:
   - Clear customer insight
   - Strong proposition
   - Assessment of the engagement period
   - Understanding of the costs to participants
   - Definition of rewards that offset those costs
   - Catalyst
   - Creation of a scoreboard to measure progress.

2 *Elimination of planning biases.* The standard communication planning process is overly conservative. It works against the development of successful participation strategies. The target group is often wrongly defined, the concept is unfairly judged on direct reach, and the rewards are badly conceived. To change this, four remedies must be adopted:

- Allocate a meaningful percentage of the communication budget specifically for participatory branding.
- Define a participation target group.
- Think of reach as a crucial spin-off, not as a given characteristic of a participation platform.
- Take your audience seriously by putting effort into providing relevant and coherent participation rewards.

Now that we have covered the three laws in depth, the final topic we will look at is ethics. The application of neuroscientific techniques to marketing has raised moral issues. Is it justifiable to apply medical techniques – designed to cure people – to sell them products and services? In an increasingly socially conscious society, this is a question many companies and organisations must address. It is the topic of the next chapter.

Chapter 9

Is this book morally wrong?

The three branding laws we have discussed flow from neuroscientific research. Some of this research has been awarded the Nobel Prize in medicine. But may we use knowledge intended to improve people's health in order to sell them more branded products and services?

In a globalising world where the good citizenship of companies is increasingly scrutinised, it is worthwhile to consider this issue. Just ask Nike, or Nestlé, or a handful of other global brands whose reputations have been put at risk by the discovery of questionable practices at some point in their supply chain. There would of course be little point in this book if it were proposing an approach that was effective but immoral. That is certainly not the case. But there are those who might question our moral standards. So what are the arguments to support our case?

The limits of neuromarketing

Naomi Klein's book *No Logo* has become a symbol of criticism against the practice of branding.[1] Broadly speaking, it suggests that brands have become omnipresent commercial manipulators. A recent article in the *Guardian* about neuromarketing added fuel to this argument:

> If businesses can know more about what and how we think than we do ourselves, they'll also gain the power to control our perceptions and even our behaviour in ways we won't be able to detect. If it achieves even part of its potential, neuromarketing promises to tip the balance of power in the marketplace from the buyer to the seller.[2]

I am deeply sceptical about whether neuromarketing can really do this. Our brains cannot be micro-managed by marketers, only influenced. Moreover, knowledge about how our brains work can help us be on our guard against certain marketing techniques. For example, when we notice that our brain seems to have settled on buying something we can ask ourselves: 'How important is it that I buy this product?' This requires a high degree of self-awareness, of course. So there is a case to make for the protection of those who naturally lack this ability, such as children.[3] This is especially so because, as we have seen, branding influences our subconscious attitudes and decision processes. At the same time, knowledge of how our brains work can increase our self-understanding and hence our proficiency in self-management – starting from early adulthood.

our brains cannot be micro-managed by marketers, only influenced

But the theme is a familiar one. As early as 1928, Sigmund Freud's American nephew and PR mastermind Edward Bernays considered manipulation of the masses – which he called the 'engineering of consent' – a perfectly legitimate thing:

> The conscious and intelligent manipulation of the organized habits and opinions of the masses is an important element in democratic society. Those who manipulate this unseen mechanism of society constitute an invisible government, which is the true ruling power of our country. We are governed, our minds are molded, our tastes formed, our ideas suggested, largely by men we have never heard of. This is a logical result of the way in which our democratic society is organized.[4]

Objections to such ideas are at least as old. They are raised regularly against neuromarketing, for example by consumer organisations like Commercial Alert in the United States. To highlight the possible moral objections that some might have against this book, therefore, let's call upon a hypothetical consumer activist who can state such views more succinctly.[5] Her opinion about this book might be as follows:

> Marketing is the means of separating people as quickly as possible from as much money as possible. *Branding With Brains* strongly increases marketers' effectiveness in selling products and services customers do not really need. The book does this by stipulating three laws aimed at manipulating the subconscious brain. Thus, marketers can now reach their commercial aims without people's consent and without customers knowing it.

The key question is: when does influence become manipulation?[6] If you are a marketer using this book, you may have to answer this question at some point. To help you, we will consider three ethical frameworks that have gained widespread acceptance in Western thinking. They are the moral theories of Immanuel Kant, Aristotle and John Stuart Mill (see Figure 9.1). They will provide you with well-grounded perspectives and arguments so that you can form your own judgement in your own situation.

		Ethical aim	
		just individuals	just society
Ethical starting point	moral principles	**ARISTOTLE** (virtue ethics)	
	moral rules	**KANT** (deontological ethics)	**MILL** (Utilitarianism)

FIGURE 9.1 Three ethical perspectives

Immanuel Kant and Branding With Brains

Immanuel Kant was one of the most influential Western philosophers and the founder of an important ethical theory. Born in 1724, he was one of the great proponents of the Enlightment, for which he formulated 'Dare to know' as the motto (*Sapere aude!*). Kant urged man to free himself of dogma and superstition, and to rely instead on his mental capabilities.

According to Kant, the whole purpose of philosophy is aimed at answering three questions: What can I know? What may I hope for? What ought I to do? The third question defines the essence of the field of ethics. Kant developed a new theory that to this day represents one of the main ethical perspectives.

Ethics are all about intentions

The core idea of Kant's moral theory is that man in general is a rational and self-conscious being. Man is therefore never bound to act on circumstance, instinct or emotion alone. In Kant's view, man has the capacity to choose based on free will. Whether there really is such a thing as free will (neuroscientific research has raised doubts about this) is not really relevant to Kant. Sufficient is the fact that we appear to ourselves to be free. Hence, we find ourselves confronted with moral questions that we must solve.

Acting morally based on free will means, according to Kant, that we act based upon principles that as a matter of duty we impose upon ourselves. For Kant, morality is not a matter of effects or end results but of intentions. So if a marketer truly aims to be fair but his act turns out to be unfair for a particular customer, the marketer may have made a mistake but has not acted in a morally unjustifiable way. Thus, Kant searches for the rule or principle that a free, rational and morally just person would out of duty impose on his or her intentions. He then introduces his cardinal rule called the 'Categorical Imperative': 'I should always act in such a way that I could want my behaviour to become a universal law.' The adoption of this rule, then, is his universal measure of ethical behaviour. Let's see what Kant's imperative means in practice.

> according to Kant, morality is a matter of intentions

An ethical test

Take the following real case to get a feel for Kant's ethical theory. During the credit crisis of 2008, the BBC World Service interviewed a couple in California whose interest payments on their mortgage had risen while the value of their house had dropped by about 40 per cent. Fortunately, their income was sufficient to pay the interest – unlike that of thousands of others in the United States at that time.

This Californian couple did not face any urgent problem. Nevertheless, they decided to stop paying the interest on their mortgage. 'You see,' the woman said, 'it no longer made financial sense for us to do so.' What was going on?

The house, the reporter found out, was now worth less than the mortgage. The couple had borrowed $500,000 to buy the house, but it was now worth around $300,000. They faced a loss of $200,000 *if* they had sold the house at that point. To avoid this loss, they stopped paying interest. The consequences of stopping their interest payments were clear to the couple. They knew, of course, that the bank would take the house, evict them and then sell the house to recoup the loan. But then came the twist. 'The bank cannot come after us for the remainder. We will have to rent for five years but then we will buy a new house and start all over again.' The couple thus cut their potential loss. They deliberately left the bank with the loss, because they felt it was in their self-interest.

'But you did sign the contract to borrow the money. And you did promise to pay it back. And you could afford it,' the reporter pointed out. 'Yes,' the woman said, 'but you have to take care of yourself. No one will do it for us.'

Applying Kant's moral formula

We do not need an eighteenth-century German philosopher in order to form an opinion about mortgage payment. But for a more objective discussion about the ethical aspect of this case, it is useful to use Kant's framework. How would he view this story? There are four steps in Kant's formula we can take to judge this.

- *Step 1: Formulate the rule you propose to follow.* We might say that the rule our couple is following is: 'I intend to break my promise for personal benefit.'
- *Step 2: Formulate it as a law that anyone in these circumstances must follow.* When we translate this into a universal law we get: 'Anyone must break his promise when he can gain from it.'

- *Step 3: Consider whether your rule would lead to contradictions or irrationalities.* Now when we look at what this means, we see that this moral law would create a world in which no meaningful agreements could be made. It eliminates trust. It would make it impossible to do trade or even run an economy. In this world, nobody would have trusted our couple enough to have given them the loan to buy their house in the first place. Or the bank would have withdrawn it at any moment it thought it could make a better investment anywhere else.
- *Step 4: If there are no contradictions or irrationalities, the action is morally permissible.* In the final step, we must thus conclude that the rule creates severe contradictions. It is irrational to want the world that is its consequence. Therefore, according to Kant's categorical imperative, acting the way the California house owners did is not morally permissible.

The morality of this book depends on your intentions

So, according to Kant's formula, are you acting against accepted moral standards if you apply the principles of this book? According to Kant, this does not depend on what is in the book, but the intentions with which you use it.

Suppose your intention were – as our consumer activist suspects – to manipulate people's subconscious minds and sell them products and services against their consent. Applying the four steps of Kant's formula, you would clearly be in the wrong. You would create the moral law that everyone who wants to sell something must try to influence everyone else in an insidious way to buy against their will. Ultimately, this view of the world would have everyone seeing everyone else as an object solely for their own use. It would be self-defeating and therefore immoral. In Kant's view, we should never treat people solely as a means to an end; we should also consider them as ends in themselves. Even if manipulating people's subconscious minds by using the ideas in this book is impossible (which I think it is), that does not matter. In Kant's view, it is all about your intentions.

Yet if you are using this book to create stronger brands that are more relevant or meaningful for clients, that is an entirely different matter. You are not viewing customers merely instrumentally, as wallets with legs that you must empty as quickly as possible. You also respect them as autonomous human beings.

Aristotle and Branding With Brains

Aristotle (384–322 BC) is another towering figure of Western thinking. He was a student of Plato and the tutor of Alexander the Great, and considered to be the founder of modern science. Probably few people have influenced Western thinking more than Aristotle.

Much of his writing has not survived, but his ethical theory has. It has had great influence on Western moral philosophy throughout the centuries. And it is still interesting and influential. Many modern self-help books on personality and character-building are – sometimes implicitly – based on Aristotle's work. His book *Nicomachean Ethics*[7] describes a second influential ethical perspective.

Ethics are about character

To Aristotle, the goal of ethics is the essentially practical one of helping us to achieve happiness in life. Contrary to Kant, Aristotle believed ethics could not consist of general rules. Every situation and person are too different. Acting ethically requires that we possess the right 'disposition' so that we act justly in any situation. To acquire it, we must first understand what our function, our goal, as a human being is.

> we must possess the right disposition to act justly in any situation

Our highest goal in life, according to Aristotle, is to thrive and be happy. We all want to do well in life. And according to Aristotle this is an inborn tendency. The result is that *everything* we do is ultimately aimed at making us flourish.

Yet living well is something we have to learn. It is not a feeling or a state of mind, as these are only temporary things. Instead, living well is a permanent way of *acting* that is based on *virtues* like courage, compassion, cleverness, wisdom, and so on. How does lifelong virtuous action enable us to flourish? The reason is *not* just because society rewards virtue. In Aristotle's view, living virtuously leads to well-being primarily because it means acting in the way a human being is designed to function. To be virtuous is to be an excellent example of what it is to be human. It conforms to our highest nature; it actualises our potential. Acting according to our nature makes us happy and successful. True virtuous action, therefore, is always inwardly driven.

However, we are not born with the skills and the disposition needed to act virtuously. We must acquire them through example, practice and experience. This process starts in early childhood. In fact, for Aristotle, an upbringing in good habits is necessary in order to benefit from the study of ethics. When we grow older we start acting for ourselves instead of by imitation. From then on, we must steer ourselves towards practising virtue all our life. 'Anything we have to learn to do,' said Aristotle, 'we learn by the actual doing of it.' Only by repeatedly acting virtuously can we learn to do so quite naturally in every situation. By practising virtue, we can make it part of our character. Happiness and success then become a habit.

Aristotle's ethics, therefore, are akin to a skill that must become ingrained in our personality. His goal is not to devise a formula that helps determine what to do in a certain situation, like Kant did centuries later. His theory is aimed at understanding what it is to act virtuously, so that we can improve the education of our children and consciously guide the development of our own character throughout life.

Aristotle's moral checklist

So are you acting unethically if you apply the principles of this book? According to Aristotle, an act is virtuous only if it meets five conditions. Let's review those first:

1. Is the act good or just? Our deed is only virtuous when it is an example of behaviours that are considered good, right or just in the society in which we live. For example, in one of the opening sequences of the Disney version of *Aladdin*, the main character gives away his only piece of bread to two poor children who are in even greater need of food than he is himself. This is a generous act and, in our society, generosity is considered something good.

2. Is the act performed deliberately? We must deliberately choose what we do in order for our act to be virtuous. For Aristotle, it is not enough just slavishly or absentmindedly to do the right thing. We must do it deliberately for it to be a virtuous act. Aladdin, to continue our previous example, is fully aware of what he is doing and of the fact that to give his bread away is a good thing to do.

3. Is the act chosen for its own sake? Our highest goal in life is to do well, to flourish. There is nothing more relevant and nothing we rate higher than that. Therefore, it is not a means to an end. As virtuous acts make us feel happy and do well, they are desired for their own sake. In 2006, FC Barcelona – the Spanish soccer club – chose UNICEF as its main shirt sponsor. Instead of asking for money, the club is donating to UNICEF nearly €2 million per year to use its logo on the club's shirts. Is this a virtuous deed? If Barcelona did this to help the world's poorest children and as a result the club's sense of well-being improved, it could be considered virtuous. If it did it only in order to look good or to prevent its other commercial sponsors from being overshadowed by its main shirt sponsor, it is not virtuous. Aladdin gave his bread to street children who gave nothing tangible in return, and Aladdin does not meet them again. He chose to be generous for the sake of being generous and thus passed the third test.

4. Does the act performed flow from our character? An act is only virtuous if it is in accordance with our fixed qualities and traits. It must flow from our permanent disposition. An isolated act of bravery from a coward who subsequently reverts to type is not therefore a virtuous act. A brand launching a campaign or a new product that is not consistent with its brand personality is not acting virtuously. Aladdin, in Disney's classic production, turns out to be generous of heart. Time and again he shows himself to be a virtuous person. He strays now and then but feels bad about it and then returns to being virtuous again.

5. Does the act hold the mean between extremes? Aristotle says that a key characteristic of acting virtuously is keeping the mean between extremes. Not too much, not too little. The mean, however, is not absolute but relative to ourselves. Aladdin, in the scene mentioned above, has just obtained a loaf of bread with relative ease. He gives it away to someone in much greater need, who does not possess the skill or the talent to obtain food. Giving it away thus effectively holds the mean between extravagance and selfishness for Aladdin.

According to Aristotle, we act virtuously and will flourish when we do something good and do it deliberately, for its own sake, in line with our character and in a balanced way. Aladdin's act meets all of Aristotle's criteria for virtuous behaviour. How does this book meet those criteria?

The morality of this book depends on your disposition

Suppose you use this book's ideas to manipulate people's subconscious minds and sell them products and services against their consent. It is clear that this is not a virtuous deed according to Aristotle. Manipulation is considered a vice. You would fail the first test straightaway.

But suppose you are Leica. In the words of Andreas Kaufmann, its owner and CEO, Leica's aim is to provide photography enthusiasts with cameras and lenses that allow them 'to create works of art'. Leica helps people to carve out a frame of time and hence a memory. By embodying all its knowledge and expertise in its cameras and lenses, Leica gives its clients a top-quality tool with which to document life.

Leica could use the laws of relevance, coherence and participation to build a brand that better helps its clients achieve this. Would that be a virtuous act? Leica really serves its clients. It seeks to help people conserve memories in the most effective way possible. Leica considers it a virtue and pursues it deliberately and for its own sake. It believes in the rightness of this pursuit. Of course it also wants to make money. But if that was its primary aim, it might reduce its quality and sell an average product to a mass market. But it has never lowered its quality. Throughout its 75-year existence, it has always sought to improve quality. It is therefore not a temporary aim but one that flows from its character as an organisation. Moreover, in striving for perfection it has always held the mean between boastfulness on the one hand and understatement on the other. In short, when Leica uses the three laws of branding to improve on the aim it has pursued throughout its history, it is acting from a fixed and virtuous disposition. From the Aristotelian perspective, then, it is possible to use this book in a way that is ethically acceptable.

John Stuart Mill and Branding With Brains

The final ethical perspective considered here is Utilitarianism, expounded by Jeremy Bentham (1748–1832). Its main proponent was John Stuart Mill. Mill was an influential nineteenth-century

British economist and parliamentarian and arguably the greatest philosopher of his time. Henry Sidgwick, a contemporary of Mill, claimed, 'I should say that from about 1860–65 or thereabouts he ruled England in the region of thought as very few men ever did: I do not expect to see anything like it again.'[8] Although the roots of Utilitarianism go back to the ancient Greeks, especially Epicurus, it is a view that is quite modern, as we shall see.

Ethics are all about consequences

The aim of Utilitarianism has been summarised as 'providing the greatest happiness for the greatest number of people'. It states that the moral value of actions, by people, by institutions or by brands depends on how well those actions promote human happiness. In Mill's words:

> The 'greatest happiness principle' holds that actions are right in proportion as they tend to promote happiness; wrong as they tend to produce the reverse of happiness. By happiness is intended pleasure and the absence of pain; by unhappiness, pain and the privation of pleasure.[9]

To Mill, happiness is what we all desire, and what we value not as a means to something else but as an end in itself.

A basic premise of Mill's Utilitarianism is that we all partially depend on others for our happiness and are always happier when others treat us with consideration. To maximise individual happiness, therefore, we must all take the happiness of others into account in everything we do. It is our moral duty to try to bring about the greatest happiness for the greatest number of people because it is what we ourselves would value. Mill, then, is not an advocate of egoistic hedonism – blindly chasing our own individual pleasures. In his view, humans have a strong desire to be in harmony with their fellow humans, making it realistic to take the happiness of others into account in our actions.

To Mill, not all pleasures are created equally. 'It is better to be a human dissatisfied,' Mill famously said, 'than a pig satisfied.'[10] Humans need to be happy more than pigs do. From this, Mill concludes that there are higher and lower pleasures. Music and art, for example, require education to be experienced as pleasurable and hence they are more refined. They are higher pleasures, and the ability to enjoy them requires practice.

> according to Mill, we must consider the consequences of our actions

When faced with a choice, we must consider the consequences of our possible actions. We must then choose the option we believe generates the most happiness, not just for ourselves, but for everyone.

The morality of this book depends on the consequences of your actions

So what happens when we apply Mill's theory to this book? Is it ethical to apply it? Under Utilitarianism, this all depends on the consequences of your actions. Suppose that you were to use this book to manipulate people's subconscious minds in a way that would make them buy more products or services without their consciously willing it. What would be the consequences of your action and would that action lead to the greatest aggregated happiness?

The question, therefore, is whether people buying a certain product are happier when they have bought it with conscious deliberation, or without it. Research discussed in Chapter 2 shows that in the case of more complex products and services, people are happier with their decisions when they have made a choice for a product without deliberation.[11] We could say that if their subconscious is manipulated, they do not notice it and experience no negative feelings. In that case, manipulation of the subconscious could actually lead to more happiness. If we reason in this way, manipulating the subconscious in the case of complex choices (such as a mortgage or a car) would actually be an ethical thing to do according to Utilitarianism, because it would promote overall happiness. We seem to be assuming in this case that we are more satisfied with complicated brand choices we make intuitively rather than deliberately. Contrary to Kant and Aristotle, Utilitarianism finds no fault in this kind of manipulation because we reckon that on balance it generates more human happiness.

TABLE 9.1 A summary of the three ethical perspectives

	Kant	**Aristotle**	**Mill**
Designation	Deontological ethics	Virtue ethics	Utilitarianism
Basis	Intentions	Character	Consequences
Why act ethically?	It is our duty	It leads us to success and happiness in life	We have a natural desire to be in unity with our fellow creatures
Decision process	▪ 1: Formulate the rule you propose to follow ▪ 2: Formulate it as a law that anyone in those circumstances must follow ▪ 3: Consider whether your rule would lead to contradictions or irrationalities ▪ 4: If there are no contradictions or irrationalities, the action is morally permissible.	▪ 1: Is the act 'good'? ▪ 2: Is it performed deliberately? ▪ 3: Is it chosen for its own sake? ▪ 4: Is it in line with the character of the person or brand? ▪ 5: Does it keep the mean between extremes?	▪ 1: What are the possible actions in this situation? ▪ 2: What are the consequences of each action? ▪ 3: What is the overall happiness flowing from each option?
Ethical value of this book	▪ Depends on your intentions	▪ Depends on your disposition	▪ Depends on whether it promotes overall happiness
Accusation by the hypothetical consumer activist: 'Applying this book is unethical because it allows marketers to manipulate people's subconscious brain, selling to them without their awareness or consent.'	You are acting unethically only if your *intention* is to deliberately *trick* customers into buying your brand against their own desire. If this is not your intention, the accusation is false and, following Kant's theory, it is entirely ethical to apply this book.	Manipulation is a vice. So if exerting unfair control is what you do, it is immoral. But if you are using the three laws to advance virtuous acts by your brand, this is morally permissible and the accusation is false.	If you can demonstrate that total happiness increases due to your influence, the accusation is false.

Conclusions

Whether or not it is ethical to apply the principles in this book depends primarily on the perspective we take and on the person and situation in which we apply the three laws. The principles themselves are value-free. It is the intention, the disposition or the consequences that can make their application moral or immoral. We have reviewed three perspectives that can help us analyse this more carefully in a particular situation. Table 9.1 summarises the main differences between them. It also summarises the main arguments against the claims of our hypothetical consumer activist.

This book itself is ethical. But the application of its principles is not unequivocally morally justifiable. That all depends on the user according to the three ethical perspectives reviewed. Whether our hypothetical consumer activist is right or wrong in her moral assertions, therefore, depends on your use of this book. Manipulation is wrong in many cases, but applying this book with goodwill, integrity and proper aims is ethically acceptable. But it is like using dynamite. To destroy lives with dynamite is wrong, except perhaps in the pursuit of a just war. But using dynamite to build a tunnel that will connect an otherwise cut-off community is a morally acceptable use of explosives.

Please Recycle

Chapter 10

Come again?

Brands can have extraordinary value and meaning for customers and hence for the companies that build them. Why? Because strong brands influence the choices of the brains they are stored in, in a way that generates more stable cash flows, higher margins and bigger market shares for the organisations that build them. Brands, then, play an important role in matching supply and demand in our globalising economy – even in times of economic depression and crisis. But how can you build a brand that can influence customers' subconscious choices in your favour?

This question can be answered more fully when combining what we know about branding with insights gained from the 'hard' neurosciences. To that end, I have rendered findings from fundamental brain research into clear prescriptions for strategy in this book. I have stated that our brains make brand choices in much the same way as Google selects websites: it follows something we can call a stable but subconscious algorithm. This highly smart algorithm is designed to select the brand that seems best and most dependably to fit our purpose in that particular situation, in a process that proceeds quickly, effortlessly and almost entirely subconsciously. Hence, I have stated that all customers – and we ourselves – can be seen as subconsciously rational.

Naturally, strong brands – those that have highest value for companies – are the ones that precisely comply with the selection rules built into their customers' brains. So which brands does the brain favour? This book states that the brain's subconscious algorithm selects brands that have been built according to the three laws of relevance, coherence and participation that constitute what I call the branding triangle. The branding triangle is the foundation of all effective branding. A good deal of this book is therefore devoted to explaining these laws and how you can implement them.

For a company, this book links the macro level of a company's financial success to the micro level of the subconscious customer brain (see Figure 10.1). These laws apply equally to consumer brands as to business-to-business and commercial brands, as well as to public brands and NGOs. A key to success for all these organisations lies in knowing how to persuade the subconscious minds of stakeholders. So how do you do that? We will finish by looking once more at some of the main ideas we have discussed in this book.

FIGURE 10.1 Linking micro to macro

Make branding more effective

This book argues that there is too big a gap between the economic value of brands and the strength of the discipline that builds them. This is especially apparent at the boardroom level. Branding is often overlooked in the daily routines and strategic thinking of executives because it is seen either as a vague discipline or as a merely operational activity. I have argued, however, that building stronger brands more quickly, cheaply and reliably is impossible without active involvement from the CEO and that given the huge financial value of brands this involvement is justified. A first step to ensure this is to link executive remuneration to branding success (to include the appreciation of the financial value of the brand in the long-term incentive plan). Several strong-brand companies have already taken such measures. This stimulates executives to consider branding more closely and to find ways to integrate the brand more effectively into their strategic and operational decisions.

A second step is to understand that branding is not just advertising. From the brain's point of view, everything a company or organisation does sends a potential reward signal about the brand. Brands become strong, therefore, by integrating everything they do, so that they speak with one voice to the conscious and subconscious minds of customers. The coherence that flows from this allows some of the world's strongest brands to invest relatively little in advertising. The brand promise and delivery are enforced at every touch point, not just the advertising, lowering advertising costs while boosting branding effectiveness.

A third step is to learn how to judge creativity more objectively. The brains of customers are persuaded by brands that have been built according to the branding triangle. Thus, all customer-facing initiatives must be judged on their relevance, coherence and participatory nature. These are three branding review criteria that everyone can learn to use and that facilitate a more objective discussion at all organisational levels.

Subconscious rationality

The brain's algorithm is designed to select from memory the brand that seems best and most dependably to fit our purpose. This means marketers may have to update their understanding of how customers choose. For instance, the widely used AIDA model (see Chapter 2) is based on asking customers for conscious answers about processes they do not have the slightest conscious clue about – which makes the insights thus gleaned less than dependable.

> marketers must update their understanding of how customers choose

Similarly, it is unwise to think that customers habitually act irrationally, even though that may sometimes seem to be the case. It is better to assume that you probably do not fully understand which subconscious goals drive them. It is true that we sometimes use means (for example, smoking) to reach a certain goal (relaxation) that harms the attainment of other goals (being healthy). Our goals can be in conflict. But brand choices are always purposeful, aimed at satisfying subconscious goals. So the fact that everything we do is rooted in the subconscious does not at all mean that we are irrational. The two are not the same. Evolutionary forces have made humans and many animals goal-optimising in the way that neuroeconomics predicts on the basis of mathematical models. Of these species man is the only truly consciousness kind. Therefore, we have concluded that consciousness is not necessary for making rational decisions. It fundamentally changes the way that marketers, who try to understand customer behaviour, should look at their clients and prospects. It also changes our view of ourselves as customers making buying decisions.

be prepared for sceptical reactions when using these insights

You should be prepared for sceptical or hostile reactions when you start using the insights presented in this book. The field we have covered is a controversial one. The idea that branding is primarily aimed at influencing the subconscious choice processes of customers may be even more so. People are understandably afraid of the idea that marketers are interfering with the thought processes they themselves are unaware of. But not every claim made by neuromarketing proponents is true. Chapter 2 has therefore separated the genuine possibilities of neuromarketing from some of the neuro-nonsense. It makes sense to familiarise yourself with these ideas but also to understand the ethical aspects of neuromarketing, discussed in Chapter 9.

A law for strategists: relevance

The brain is hard-wired to seek reward, including also from brands. Being uniquely relevant, therefore, is almost all that matters. The law of relevance applies to all brands. This includes price fighters – which may be surprising to some people. Low cost can be highly relevant to certain customers. But if you strive to be a cost leader (like Aldi and easyJet), you should still work on your relevant differentiation if you want to be favoured by the brain's algorithm.

Brands are relevant to the degree that they trigger biological or cultural reward signals in our brains. This means you must educate your customers' brains on the rewarding features of your brand, by associating it with existing needs and then gradually replacing these with more abstract needs and distinctive rewards. You must, therefore, always start at the bottom, with instrumental associations, before you can gradually add more aspirational ones. As the brain learns continuously, broad shifts within society as a whole will change the needs cocktails that customers use to activate brands from memory. You must think constantly about what the changes in the world could mean for the goals and preferences of your customers, and hence the likelihood of your brand being skipped or chosen by the brain's subconscious algorithm.

This brings us to a crucial point: make sure you understand the subconscious cocktail of goals or needs that drives your customers. These cocktails consist of goals from several general categories. Customers use these to activate brands from their memory. Therefore, you must associate your brand with them. To know these goals or needs for your specific category, you must shift towards using appropriate qualitative research techniques (relying on indirect probing and observation). Also, you should adapt your quantitative research methods, using accessibility as a key measure (the ease or swiftness with which a brand comes to mind in response to the activation of a goal). Moreover, as customers select brands based on goal cocktails, brand, positioning concepts must be based on cocktails of goals instead of individual insights – as is now often the case.

Building distinctively relevant brands, therefore, requires a better use of your empathic and analytical skills when you listen to your customers. The personality traits and skills required to implement this law fall in the domain of emotional intelligence – the concept popularised by Daniel Goleman.[1]

A law for leaders: coherence

The second law we discussed was that of coherence. Contrary to what many people think, strong brands often invest relatively little in advertising. IKEA, Google and Starbucks are some examples.

The trick of strong brands is that they have a good business strategy, which they execute consistently. When you are coherent, your brand promise and your delivery upon it come pouring out of every touch point you have with customers. This creates an orchestrated repetition of your promise, which is what the brain needs to memorise your brand. Coherence is the surest way of building a strong brand while reducing advertising spend. But you do need a creative, strategic brand concept that can drive your whole business – one based on a strong core idea or a distinct mentality. The concept must be specific as opposed to vague, and flexible instead of limiting. It must be uniquely relevant for customers but also meaningful for the CEO, because he or she must start making all crucial business decisions with the brand as a touchstone. Only then will you be able to bring everything you do under one banner without being broad to the point of hollowness. And only then will you be able to stick with your focus for years – which the brain's brand-choice algorithm favours.

Interestingly, when you are coherent, you can start forgetting about accountability – which in practice is usually focused on advertising effectiveness. After all, coherence means that everything you do in the service of attaining your business strategy is aligned, so accountability boils down to measuring return on investment of the brand or company as a whole. What is more, communications as a separate and almost autonomous function that owns and builds the brand should disappear. In a world of information abundance, word-of-mouth communication and rapid dissemination of news, the monopoly of advertising on influencing brand perception has long evaporated. When brands suffer, it is not usually from a mere perception problem that a campaign can rectify. They suffer from problems in their business strategy or the way the brand actually delivers on its promise. Everything a brand does communicates. What the communication department can do, however, is tell people inside and outside the company what the brand stands for. Thus, it can play a crucial role in getting the wheels of the brand turning.

Don't get me wrong. I am not advocating the holding of a brand 'inquisition' in every company. Habitual inconsistency is the big problem, not occasional mistakes or well-prepared repositionings.

What I am advocating is that top management takes full responsibility for branding. Not everyone has the character traits needed to build a coherent brand. Whereas the first law requires empathy, the second one demands the ability to delay gratification. Coherence requires forgoing short-term profits that conflict with the brand strategy (such as excessive discounts by high-end brands). The ability, metaphorically, to tie yourself to the mast in the face of temptation is an essential one in reaping the fruits of coherence. But it takes motivation and effort to pass the marshmallow test.

> top management must take full responsibility for branding

A law for creatives: participation

The final law is that of participation. The degree to which you are able to open up your brand and allow people to do things with it improves the chances that they will choose it in the future. Participation does not favour control freaks who guard their brands with armies of lawyers. Participation means relinquishing some of the control over a brand's definition to your customers. You allow them to customise what the brand means to them. While the internet provides marketers with a large box of tools and opportunities for fostering engagement, location brands are a physical domain that offers powerful possibilities that are at least as interesting to explore. In the end, however, the key is to rethink all media so as to employ them in more participatory ways.

The prerequisite for participation is not just that the brand behind it is relevant but that engagement is rewarding in itself. You must provide customers with feedback that allows them to enjoy the fruits or the results of participation. One potential problem in getting it off the ground is that the traditional communication planning process is biased against participation. First, you must make dialogue a true priority, instead of assuming that the brand is the sender and the customer the receiver. Second, you must change your target group definition as your communications audience is not necessarily the group most inclined to engage. Third, you must do away with the classic media indicator of 'reach', as participation often generates spin-offs that fall outside the scope that is measured by the reach criterion. Finally, the rewards you create for participants must be coherent with your brand promise.

The most important character trait to use to engage customers, however, is the ability to give them an action perspective, the ability to do things within the bigger scheme of the brand. You must define ways for people to join in and benefit from that. In the end, this is a highly creative exercise. Barack Obama's presidential bid is a great example of a campaign that offered multiple opportunities for people to contribute to a bigger brand story.

Final words

The brain chooses brands in much the same way as Google selects websites: according to a stable but subconscious algorithm. Brands built according to the three laws of relevance, coherence and participation are more likely to be chosen than brands that have neglected these principles. These simple findings, which constitute the core idea of this book, have enormous consequences for anyone seeking to build a brand or aiming to mobilise minds for a longer-term cause.

My aim has been to build a stronger foundation for the allegedly 'soft' discipline of branding, not by making it more quantitative, but by making it more focused and objective. I believe these principles can help companies as well as governments and NGOs to be more productive in realising their strategic priorities.

It is perfectly reasonable to suggest that neuroscientific knowledge should not be used indiscriminately for selling people more goods. However, I have demonstrated that the moral responsibility for this lies with the user and is not inherent in the subject matter itself. I hope I have covered some new ground in this book and made a contribution to my field that others can find of interest. Whatever the final judgement, I am certain that a better understanding of the brain can help marketers become more successful, now and in the future.

However, I am also convinced that our brains are flexible enough to elude the final control of commercial or political practices. Understanding the brain may help in reaching a certain practical purpose. But it can also result in a better appreciation of how mind-bogglingly complex the brain actually is. It inspires awe. The brain must be one of the most beautiful things man has ever investigated. Strangely enough, of course, we are studying ourselves in it, because we are our brains. But can we corner the brain through the knowledge we gain about it and thus control it against our own will? I think not. For in our healthy brains we always appear – at least to ourselves – completely free.

Notes

Introduction

[1] It is the strap line of Bartle Bogle Hegarty.

[2] For the best overview to date, see: **Glimcher, Paul W., Colin F. Camerer, Ernst Fehr** and **Russell A. Poldrack** (eds) (2008), *Neuroeconomics: Decision Making and the Brain*, London: Academic Press.

[3] Quoted in Episode 1 of *The Century of the Self*, a four-part BBC documentary, 2002, by the filmmaker Adam Curtis. At the time of writing it could be found at **http://video.google.com/**.

[4] **Glimcher, Paul W.**, and **Aldo Rustichini** (2004), 'Neuroeconomics: The Consilience of Brain and Decision', *Science*, 306, 5695, 447–452.

Chapter One

[1] **Madden, Thomas J., Frandk Fehle** and **Susan M. Fournier** (2006), 'Brands Matter: An Empirical Demonstration of the Creation of Shareholder Value Through Branding', *Journal of the Academy of Marketing Science*, 34, 2, 224–235.

[2] See **Steel, Jon** (1998), *Truth, Lies and Advertising: The Art of Account Planning*, London: John Wiley & Sons.

[3] **Schultz E., Don** (2006), 'Trash Trove: Where Is the Real Brand Knowledge?', *Marketing Management*, 15, 5, 10–11.

[4] **Court, David C. Thomas D. French** and **Trond Riiber Knudsen** (2006), 'The Proliferation Challenge', *Profiting From Proliferation*, New York: McKinsey & Company.

[5] American Association of National Advertisers (ANA) member surveys (2006) and (2007); CMO Council, (2007), *Marketing Outlook* 2007.

[6] **Spencer Stuart,** 'Chief Marketing Officer Tenure Improves According to Annual Spencer Stuart Study', Press Release, Friday 1 June 2007; Karlsson, Per-Ola, Gary L. Neilson and Juan Carlos Webster, (2008), CEO Succession 2007: *The Performance Paradox*, Special Report, Booz & Co.

[7] This book distinguishes between memory-based choice (internally prompted) and stimulus-based choice (externally prompted). Most choices are at least in part memory based and this book is focused on formulating strategies to make your brand win in memory-based choice situations.

[8] **Franzen, Giep** and **Marike van deu Berg** (2001), *Strategisch Managment van Merken*, Amsterdan: Kluwer.

[9] Calculated as advertising expenditures as a percentage of net sales, based on Apple's 2008 SEC 10-K filing, Google's 2007 SEC 10-K filing and Procter & Gamble's 2008 SEC 10-K filing.

[10] Personal interview by the author, 11 February 2009.

[11] Personal interview by the author with Peter Verhoeff of Mercer, 3 October 2008.

[12] See **Harter Gregor, Alex Koster, Dr Michael Peterson** and **Michael Stomberg** (2005), 'Managing Brands for Value Creation', New York: Booz Allen Hamilton and Wolff Olins; Gromark, Johan, Thomas Bo Astvik and Frans Melin (2005), *Brand Orientation Index*, Götenborg: Label AG.

Chapter Two

[1] See **Willmott, Michael** and **William Nelson** (2003), *Complicated Lives: The Malaise of Modernity*, London: John Wiley & Sons; Schwartz, Tony (2007), 'Manage Your Energy, Not Your Time', *Harvard Business Review*, 85, 10, 63–73.

[2] **Strong, E.K. Jr.** (1925), 'Theories of Selling', *Journal of Applied Psychology*, 9, 1, 75–86.

[3] For a detailed historical overview, see **Barry, Thomas E.** (1987), 'The Development of the Hierarchy of Effects: An Historical Perspective,' *Current Issues and Research in Advertising*, 10, 251–295; the figure is adapted from the following book that provides a superb treatment of marketing funnel analysis: Riesenbeck, Hajo and Jesko Perry (2007), Power Brands: *Measuring, Making, Managing Brand Success*, Weinheim: Wiley-VCH.

[4] **Brian Haven's** blog at **http://thoughts.birdahonk.com/2007/08/rethinking-the-marketing-funne.html**, accessed 5 October, 2008; Haven, Brian (2007), '*Marketing's New Key Metric: Engagement*', Cambridge, MA: Forrester Research.

[5] **Libet, Benjamin** (1985), 'Subconscious Cerebral Initiative and the role of Conscious Will in Voluntary Action', *Behavioural and Brain Sciences*, 8, 4, 529–539; Libet, Benjamin (2003), 'Can Conscious Brain Experience Affect Brain Activity?', *Journal of Consciousness Studies*, 10, 12, 24–28.

[6] See: **Soon Chun Siong, Marcel Brass, Hans-Jochen Heinze** and **John-Dylan Haynes** (2008), 'Subconscious Determinants of Free Decisions in the Human Brain', *Nature Neuroscience*, 11, 5, 543–545.

[7] **Bargh, John A.** and **Tanya L. Chartrand** (1999), 'The Unbearable Automaticity of Being,' American Psychologist, 54, 7, 462–479.

[8] **Bargh, John A.** and **Tanya L. Chartrand** (1999), 'The Unbearable Automaticity of Being,' American Psychologist, 54, 7, 462–479.

[9] See **Dijksterhuis, Ap, Henk Aarts** and **Pamela K. Smith** (2006), 'The Power of the Subliminal: On Subliminal Persuasion and Other Potential Applications', in *The New Unconscious*, ed. Ran Hassin, James Uleman and John Bargh, New York: Oxford University Press; Pinker Steven (1997), *How the Mind Works*, London: Penguin.

[10] **Lutz, Antoine, Heleen A. Slagter, John D. Dunne** and **Richard J. Davidson** (2008), 'Attention Regulation and Monitoring in Meditation', *Trends in Cognitive Sciences*, 12, 4, 163–169.

[11] **Dijksterhuis, Ap, Maarten W. Bos, Loran F. Nordgren** and **Rick B. van Baaren** (2006), 'On Making the Right Choice: The Deliberation-Without-Attention Effect', *Science*, 311, 1005–1007.

[12] See also **Chartrand Tanya L. Joel Huber, Baba Shiv,** and **Robin J. Tanner** (2008), 'Nonconscious Goals and Consumer Choice', *Journal of Consumer Research*, 35, 2, 189–201; Montague, Read (2006), *Why Choose This Book? How We Make Decisions*, New York: Dutton, Chapter 2.

[13] See **Frijda, Nico H.** (1986), *The Emotions: Studies in Emotion and Social Interaction*, Cambridge: Cambridge University Press.

[14] See: **Nedungadi, Prakash** (1990), 'Recall and Consumer Consideration Sets: Influencing Choice Without Altering Brand Associations', *Journal of Consumer Research*, 17, 263–276; Yantis, Steven (2005), 'How Visual Salience Wins the Battle for Awareness', *Nature Neuroscience*, 8, 8, 975–977; Miyashita, Yasushi (2004),

'Cognitive Memory: Cellular and Network Machineries and Their Top-Down Control', *Science*, 306, 435, 435–440; Dehaene, Stanislas, Jean-Pierre Changeux, Lionel Naccach, Jérôme Sackur and Claire Sergent (2006), 'Conscious, Preconscious, and Subliminal Processing: A Testable Taxonomy', *Trends in Cognitive Sciences*, 10, 5, 204–211.

[15] **Yantis, Steven** (2005), 'How Visual Salience Wins the Battle for Awareness', *Nature Neuroscience*, 8, 8, 975–977; Duncan, John (2006), 'Brain Mechanisms of Attention', EPS Mid-Career Award 2004, *The Quarterly Journal of Experimental Psychology*, 59, 1, 2–27; Kuhl, Brice A., Nicole M. Dudukovic, Itamar Kahn and Anthony D. Wagner (2007), 'Decreased Demands On Cognitive Control Reveal the Neural Processing Benefits of Forgetting', *Nature Neuroscience*, 10, 7, 908–914; Miller, Earl K. and Jonathan D. Cohen (2001), 'An Integrative Theory of Prefrontal Cortex Function', *Annual Review of Neuroscience*, 24, 1, 167–202.

16 **Kahneman, D., I. Ritov** and **D. Schkade** (1999), 'Economic Preferences or Attitude Expressions? An Analysis of Dollar Responses to Public Issues', *Journal of Risk and Uncertainty*, 19, 220–242; Kahneman, D. and I. Ritov (1994), 'Determinants of Stated Willingness to Pay for Public Goods: A Study in the Headline Method', *Journal of Risk and Uncertainty*, 9, 5–38.

[17] **Walvis, Tjaco H.** (2003), 'Avoiding Advert Research Disaster: Advertising and the Uncertainty Principle', *Journal of Brand Management*, 10, 6, 403–409.

[18] **Dehaene, Stanislas, Jean-Pierre Changeux, Lionel Naccach, Jérôme Sackur** and **Claire Sergent** (2006), 'Conscious, Preconscious, and Subliminal Processing: A Testable Taxonomy', *Trends in Cognitive Sciences*, 10, 5, 204–211; Yantis, Steven (2005), 'How Visual Salience Wins the Battle for Awareness', *Nature Neuroscience*, 8, 8, 975–977.

[19] **Nairn, Agnes** and **Cordelia Fine** (2008), 'Who's Messing with My Mind? The Implications of Dual-Process Models for the Ethics of Advertising to Children', *International Journal of Advertising*, 27, 3, 447–470.

[20] **Laurent, Gilles** and **Jean-Noël Kapferer** (1985), 'Measuring Consumer Involvement Profiles', *Journal of Marketing Research*, 22, 1, 41–53.

[21] **Lapersonne, Eric, Gilles Laurent** and **Jean-Jacques Le Goff** (1995), 'Consideration Sets of Size One: An Empirical Investigation of Automobile Purchases', *International Journal of Research in Marketing*, 12, 55–66.

[22] For studies on consideration set size, see for example **LeBlanc, Ronald P.** and **Neil C. Herndon Jr.** (2001), 'Cross-Cultural Consumer Decisions: Consideration Sets – A Marketing Universal?', *Marketing Intelligence and Planning*, 19, 7, 500–506; Roberts, John (1989),'A Grounded Model of Consideration Set Size and Composition', *Advances in Consumer Research*, 16, 749–757.

[23] See: **Nairn, Agnes** and **Cordelia Fine** (2008), 'Who's Messing with My Mind? The Implications of Dual-Process Models for the Ethics of Advertising to Children', *International Journal of Advertising*, 27, 3, 447–470.

[24] See for example **Lovallo Dan P.** and **Olivier Sibony** (2006), 'Distortions and deceptions in strategic decisions', *McKinsey Quarterly*, February; Ariely, Dan (2008), *Predictably Irrational: The Hidden Forces that Shape our Decisions*', New York: HarperCollins.

[25] **Glimcher Paul W.** (2003), '*Decisions, Uncertainty, and the Brain: The Science of Neuroeconomics,* Cambridge MA: MIT Press/Bradford Press.

[26] **Packard, Vance** (1957), *The Hidden Persuaders*, New York: David McKay Co.

[27] See for example 'The Science of Shopping', **http://www.cbc.ca/consumers/market/files/money/science_shopping/**

[28] For example, see Read Montague's views in **Rowan, David,** 'Neuromarketing: The Search For The Brains "Buy" Button', *The Times Magazine*, 5 February, 2004.

[29] **Wallis, Jonathan D.** (2006), 'Evaluating Apples and Oranges', *Nature Neuroscience*, 9, 5, 596–598.

[30] *The Economist*, 'Do Economists Need Brains?', 24 July 2008.

[31] **McClure, Samuel M., Jian Li, Damon Tomlin, Kim S. Cypert, Latané M. Montague** and **P. Read Montague** (2004), 'Neural Correlates of Behavioural Preference for Culturally Familiar Drinks', *Neuron*, 44, 2, 379–387.

[32] Figure is based on eight hours of advertising-free sleep per day. For a good overview of estimates, see the blog The Elusive Advertising Clutter **http://www.hhcc.com/?p=468**, accessed 26 October 2008.

[33] For evidence of subconscious processing of information that affects behaviour see, for example: **Klucharev, Vasily, Ale Smidts** and **Guillén Fernández** (2008), 'Brain Mechanisms of Persuasion: How 'Expert Power' Modulates Memory and Attitudes', *Social Cognitive and*

Affective Neuroscience, 3, 4, 353–66; Persaud, Navindra, Peter McLeod and Alan Cowey (2007), 'Post-Decision Wagering Objectively Measures Awareness', *Nature Neuroscience*, 10, 2, 257–261; Pessiglione, Mathias, Liane Schmidt, Bogdan Draganski, Raffael Kalisch, Hakwan Lau, Ray J. Dolan and Chris D. Frith (2007), 'How the Brain Translates Money into Force: A Neuroimaging Study of Subliminal Motivation', *Science*, 316, 904, 904–906; Karremans, Johan C., Wolfgang Stroebe and Jasper Claus (2006), 'Beyond Vicary's Fantasies: The Impact of Subliminal Priming and Brand Choice', *Journal of Experimental Social Psychology*, 42, 792–798; Berridge, Kent C. and Piotr Winkielman (2003), 'What Is an Unconscious Emotion? The Case for Subconscious "Liking"', *Cognition and Emotion*, 17, 2, 181–211.

[34] **Johnson, Samuel,** 'The Art of Advertising Exemplified', *The Idler*, 40, Saturday, 20 January, 1759.

[35] **Nairn, Agnes** and **Cordelia Fine** (2008), 'Who's Messing with My Mind? The Implications of Dual-Process Models for the Ethics of Advertising to Children', *International Journal of Advertising*, 27, 3, 447–470.

[36] **Packard, Vance** (1957), *The Hidden Persuaders*, New York: David McKay Co. For James Vicary's hoax see Boese, Alex (2002), *The Museum of Hoaxes: A History of Outrageous Pranks and Deceptions*, New York: Plume.

[37] **Karremans, Johan C., Wolfgang Stroebe** and **Jasper Claus** (2006), 'Beyond Vicary's Fantasies: The Impact of Subliminal Priming and Brand Choice', *Journal of Experimental Social Psychology*, 42, 792–798.

[38] *The Century of the Self* is a four-part BBC documentary, released in 2002, by film maker Adam Curtis. At the time of writing, it could be found at **http://video.google.com/**. Episode I looks at the role of Edward Bernays.

[39] **Reus, Sjoerd Sarah van der Land** and **Marjolein Moorman** (2008), *Onbewust Beïnvloed: Hoe Reclame Werkt Zonder Dat Je Het Weet Én Hoe Je Het Meet*, Amsterdam: SWOCC.

[40] Addiction has been described as a form of 'mutiny' in the midbrain, or more specifically as chronic disruption of the balance between the midbrain dopamine system and the prefrontal and frontal serotonergic system. See Ross, Don Carla Sharp, Rudy E. Vuchinich and David Spurrett (2008), *Midbrain Mutiny: The Picoeconomics and Neuroeconomics of Disordered Gambling – Economic Theory and Cognitive Science*, Cambridge MA: MIT Press.

[41] **Riesenbeck, Hajo** and **Perry Jesko** (2007), *Power Brands: Measuring, Making, Managing Brand Success*, Weinheim: Wiley-VCH.

[42] **Nedungadi, Prakash** (1990), 'Recall and Consumer Consideration Sets: Influencing Choice Without Altering Brand Associations', *Journal of Consumer Research*, 17, 263–276; Nedungadi, Prakash and J. Wesley Hutchinson (1985), 'The Prototypicality of Brands: Relationships with Brand Awareness, Preference and Usage', in *Advances in Consumer Research*, 12, eds Elizabeth C. Hirschman and Morris B. Holbrook, Provo, UT: Association for Consumer Research, pp. 498–503; Holden, Stephen J.S. and Richard J. Lutz (1992), 'Ask Not What the Brand Can Evoke: Ask What Can Evoke the Brand', *Advances in Consumer Research*, 19, 101–107.

Chapter Three

[1] **Kahneman, Daniel** (2003), 'A Perspective on Judgement and Choice: Mapping Bounded Rationality', *American Psychologist*, 58, 9, 697–720.

[2] **Kuhl, Brice A., Nicole M. Dudukovic, Itamar Kahn** and **Anthony D. Wagner** (2007), 'Decreased Demands on Cognitive Control Reveal the Neural Processing Benefits of Forgetting', *Nature Neuroscience*, 10, 7, 908–914; Wells, D.G. and J.R. Fallon (2000), 'Dendritic mRNA Translation: Deciphering the Uncoded', *Nature Neuroscience*, 3, 11, 1062–1064; Holden, S.J.S. and R.J. Lutz (1992), 'Ask Not What the Brand Can Evoke: Ask What Can Evoke the Brand', *Advances in Consumer Research*, 19, 1, 101–107; Nedungadi, Prakash (1990), 'Recall and Consumer Consideration Sets: Influencing Choice Without Altering Brand Associations', *Journal of Consumer Research*, 17, 263–276.

[3] **Camerer Colin, George Loewenstein** and **Drazen Prelec**, 'Neuroeconomics: How Neuroscience Can Inform Economics', *Journal of Economic Literature*, 43, 1, 9–64.

[4] **Bourdieu, Pierre** (1987), *Distinction: A Social Critique of the Judgement of Taste, Cambridge* MA: Harvard University Press p.2 (emphasis added).

[5] **Montague, Read** (2006), *Why Choose This Book? How We Make Decisions*, New York: Dutton.

[6] **Frijda, Nico H.** (1986), *The Emotions: Studies in Emotion and Social Interaction*, Cambridge: Cambridge University Press.

[7] For example, see **Rushworth, Matthew F.S.** and **Timothy E.J. Behrens** (2008), 'Choice, Uncertainty and Value in Prefrontal and Cingulate Cortex, *Nature Neuroscience*, 11, 4, 389–397; Doya, Kenji (2008), 'Modulators of Decision Making', *Nature Neuroscience*, 11, 4, 410–416.

[8] **Yantis, Steven** (2005), 'How Visual Salience Wins the Battle for Awareness', *Nature Neuroscience*, 8, 8, 975–977; Duncan, John (2006), 'Brain Mechanisms of Attention', EPS Mid-Career Award 2004, *The Quarterly Journal of Experimental Psychology*, 59, 1, 2–27; Miller, Earl K. and Jonathan D. Cohen (2001), 'An Integrative Theory of Prefrontal Cortex Function', *Annual Review of Neuroscience*, 24, 1, 167–202.

[9] **Kahneman, D., I. Ritov,** and **D. Schkade** (1999), 'Economic Preferences or Attitude Expressions? An Analysis of Dollar Responses to Public Issues', *Journal of Risk and Uncertainty*, 19, 220–242; Kahneman, D. and I. Ritov (1994), 'Determinants of Stated Willingness to Pay for Public Goods: A Study in the Headline Method', *Journal of Risk and Uncertainty*, 9, 5–38.

[10] **Sontag, Susan** (1977), *On Photography*, London: Penguin Books.

[11] **Lane, Anthony** (2007), 'A Critic at Large – Candid Camera: The Cult Of Leica', *The New Yorker*, 24 September .

[12] **Lane, Anthony** (2007), 'A Critic at Large – Candid Camera: The Cult Of Leica', *The New Yorker*, 24 September.

[13] Personal interview by the author, 13 August 2008.

[14] **Bedbury, Scott** and **Stephen Fenichell** (2002), *A New Brand World: Eight Principles for Achieving Brand Leadership in the 21st Century*, New York: Viking Penguin.

[15] **Bonini Sheila, Lenny Mendonca** and **Michelle Rosenthal** (2008), 'From risk to opportunity – How global executives view sociopolitical issues: McKinsey Global Survey Results', *McKinsey Quarterly*, www.mckinseyquarterly.com.

[16] **Sachs, Jeffrey D.** (2008), *Common Wealth: Economics For A Crowded Planet*, New York: Allen Lane.

Chapter Four

[1] **Walvis, Tjaco H.** (2003), 'Avoiding Advert Research Disaster: Advertising and the Uncertainty Principle', *Journal of Brand Management*, 10, 6, 403–409.

[2] For more about ZMET, see for example: Zaltman, Gerald and Lindsay Zaltman (2008), *Marketing Metaphoria: What Deep Metaphors Reveal About The Minds of Consumers*, Boston, MA: Harvard Business School Press; and Zaltman, Gerald (2003), *How Customers Think: Essential Insights Into the Mind of the Market*, Boston, MA: Harvard Business School Press.

[3] See: **Stienstra, Jochum** and **Wim van der Noort** (2008), 'Loser, Hero Or Human Being: Are You Ready For Emergent Truth?', Best Methodological Paper ESOMAR Congress 2008; Snowden, Dave and Jochum Stienstra (2007), 'Stop Asking Questions: Understanding How Consumers Make Sense Of It All', Research Paper, ESOMAR Congress 2007.

[4] **Dichter, Ernest** (1964), *Handbook of Consumer Motivations: The Psychology of the World of Objects*, New York: McGraw-Hill.

[5] **Franzen, G.** and **M. Bouwman** (2001), '*The Mental World of Brands: Mind, Memory and Brand Success*' Henley-on-Thames: World Advertising Research Centre; Holden, S. J. S. and Lutz, R. J. (1992), 'Ask Not What The Brand Can Evoke: Ask What Can Evoke The Brand', *Advances in Consumer Research*, 19, 1, 101–107

[6] In the case of cars, for example, people will not evoke a general concept of safety but safety in the context of cars, which would be slightly different from safety in the case of insurance, air carriers or medical treatment, for example. Otherwise, the brain could end up selecting a reliable insurance brand when we actually want a reliable car.

[7] **Riesenbeck, Hajo** and **Perry Jesko** (2007), *Power Brands: Measuring, Making, Managing Brand Success*, Weinheim: Wiley-VCH.

Chapter Five

[1] **Edersheum, Elizabeth Haas** (2004), *McKinsey's Marvin Bower: Vision, Leadership and the Creation of Management Consulting*, Hoboken NJ: John Wiley & Sons; McKinsey & Company, (1999), *McKinsey & Company Inside and Out: An Introduction to the Firm*, New York: McKinsey & Company.

[2] **Collins, James C.** and **Jerry I. Porras** (1994), *Built To Last: Successful Habits of Visionary Companies*, New York: HarperCollins.

[3] **Byrne, John A** (2002) 'Inside McKinsey', Business Week, 8 July.

[4] **Bliss, T.V.P.** and **T. Lømo** (1973) 'Long Lasting Potentiation of Synaptic Transmission in the Dentate Area of the Anaesthetized Rabbit Following Stimulation of the Perforant Path', *Journal of Physiology*,

232, 2, 331–356; Kandel, Eric R. (2001), 'The Molecular Biology of Memory Storage: A Dialogue Between Genes and Synapses', *Science*, 294, 5544, 1030–1038; Kuhl, Brice A., Nicole M. Dudukovic, Itamar Kahn and Anthony D. Wagner (2007), 'Decreased Demands on Cognitive Control Reveal the Neural Processing Benefits of Forgetting', *Nature Neuroscience*, 10, 7, 908–914.

[5] According to the 'encoding specificity principle', the target item (e.g. brand attributes) must be encoded in relation to the cue for the cue to be effective (Tulving and Thomson 1973, see below). The brand's message, therefore, must emulate the cues stakeholders choose to evoke brands. See for example: Vaidya, C.J., M. Zhao, J.E. Desmond, and J.D. Gabrieli (2002), 'Evidence for Cortical Encoding Specificity in Episodic Memory: Memory-Induced Re-Activation of Picture Processing Areas', *Neuropsychologia*, 40, 12, 2136–2143; Tulving, E. and D.M. Thomson (1973), 'Encoding Specificity and Retrieval Processes in Episodic Memory', *Psychological Review*, 80, 5, 352–373.

[6] See **Festinger, L.** (1957), *A Theory of Cognitive Dissonance*, Stanford, CA: Stanford University Press.

[7] See Wikipedia, Volkswagen Phaeton, **http://en.wikipedia.org/wiki/Volkswagen_Phaeton** (accessed January 2008).

[8] Cognitive consistency (n.d.), *Dictionary of Marketing Terms*, **http://www.answers.com/topic/cognitive-consistency** (accessed January 2008).

[9] *Financial Times*, 12 March, 2007, Companies International, 'VW Chief Sets Sights On Volume Growth', **www.ft.com**.

[10] **Jeremy Clarkson,** Car Reviews, 'Volkswagen – Phaeton', 1 May, 2002, **http://www.topgear.com**.

[11] *Financial Times*, 13 February, 2007, 'VW Seeks to Tempt Back US Buyers', **www.ft.com**.

[12] **Lodish, Leonard M.** and **Carl Fl. Mela** (2007), 'If Brands Are Built over Years, Why Are They Managed over Quarters?', *Harvard Business Review*, 85, 7–8, 104–112.

[13] See also: **David A. Aaker** (2004), *Brand Portfolio Strategy: Creating Relevance, Differentiation, Energy, Leverage, and Clarity*, New York: Simon & Schuster.

[14] **www.youtube.com**, type: Dove Evolution.

[15] **Etcoff, Nancy, Susie Orbach, Jennifer Scott** and **Heidi D'Agostino** (2004), *The Real Truth About Beauty: A Global Report – Findings of the Global Study on Women, Beauty and Well Being*, Commissioned by Dove, a Unilever Beauty Brand.

Chapter Six

[1] Section title and quote are taken from: **Wiggins, Jenny,** 'When The Coffee Goes Cold', *Financial Times*, 12–13 December 2008; *The Economist*, 'Perky People', 28 May, 1998.

[2] **Schultz, Howard** (2007), 'The Commoditisation of the Starbucks Experience', 14 February, http://www.starbucksgossip.com/, accessed 19 December 2008.

[3] See **Mischel, Walter, Yuichi Shoda** and **Monica I. Rodriguez** (1989), 'Delay of Gratification in Children', *Science*, 244, 4907, 933–938; the experiment was later also described by others, including Daniel Goleman in his book *Emotional Intelligence* (see next note).

[4] **Goleman, Daniel** (1995), *Emotional Intelligence: Why It Can Matter More Than IQ*, New York: Bantam Books.

[5] Personal interview with Erik van der Meijden,19 December, 2008,

[6] **Court, David C., John E. Forsyth, Greg C. Kelly** and **Mark A. Loch** (1999) 'The New Rules of Branding: Building Strong Brands Faster', McKinsey & Company: McKinsey White Paper.

[7] These three types of coherence are based on a model created by my colleague Roland van der Vorst at THEY.

[8] Personal interview with Erik van der Meijden, 19 December 2008.

[9] *The Wall Street Journal* website, Starbucks Stock Chart, accessed 20 December 2008 (www.wsj.com.)

[10] See for example: **Aaker, David A.** (2004), *Brand Portfolio Strategy: Creating Relevance, Differentiation, Energy, Leverage, and Clarity*, New York: Simon & Schuster.

[11] **Rao, Vithala R., Manoj K. Agarwal** and **Denise Dalhoff** (2004), 'How Is Manifest Branding Strategy Related to the Intangible Value of a Corporation?', *Journal of Marketing*, 68, 4, 126–141.

[12] This approach as described here is currently in the process of being patented.

[13] 'Organizing for Successful Change Management: A McKinsey Global Survey' (2006), www.mckinseyquarterly.com.

[14] See for example: **Harter, Gregor, Alex Koster, Dr Michael Peterson** and **Michael Stomberg** (2005), 'Managing Brands for Value Creation', New York: Booz Allen Hamilton and Wolff Olins; and Gromark, Johan, Thomas Bo, Astvik and Frans Melin (2005), *Brand Orientation Index*, Götenborg: Label AG.

[15] The 10 levers for change are based upon research by **Bennebroek Gravenhorst, Kilian M., Renate A. Werkman** and **Jaap J. Boonstra** (2007), 'The Change Capacity Of Organisations: General Assessment and Five Configurations', *Applied Psychology: An International Review*, 52, 1, 83–105. The five phases of adoption stem from a 2008 THEY white paper on internal branding, by Boris Nihom.

[16] See for instance: **Isern, Josep and Caroline Pung** (2007), 'Driving Radical Change', The McKinsey Quarterly, 4, 1–12; and 'Organizing for successful change management: A McKinsey Global Survey', (2006), **www.mckinseyquarterly.com**.

Chapter Seven

[1] United States Patent Application 20080082565, Kind Code A1, **Chang, Kenneth N.** *et al.*, 3 April, 2008.

[2] See **http://www.rga.com/award/nikeplus.html**.

[3] **Reynolds, B.A.** and **S. Weiss** (1992), 'Generation of Neurons and Astocytes from isolated Cells of the Adult Mammalian Central Nervous System', *Science*, 255, 5052, 1701–1710.

[4] For example, see: **Hillary L. Burdette, MD, MS** and **Robert C. Whitaker, MD, MPH** (2005), 'Resurrecting Free Play in Young Children: Looking Beyond Fitness and Fatness to Attention, Affiliation, and Affect', *Archives of Pediatrics and Adolescent Medicine*, 159, 1, 46–50.

[5] **Horsnell Michael,** 'Why Texting Harms Your IQ', *The Times*, 22 April, 2005. **http://technology.timesonline.co.uk/tol/news/tech_and_web/personal_tech/article384212.ece**.

[6] See: **Lehrer, Jonah** (2006), 'The Reinvention of the Self' (interview with Elizabeth Gould), *Seed Magazine*, accessed at **http://seedmaga3ine.com/content/article/the_reinvention_of_the_self**.

[7] See: **Narasimhan, Kalyani** (2006), 'More Neurons May Not Make You Smarter', *Nature Neuroscience*, 9, 6, 722; Van Praag, Henriette, Gerd Kempermann and Fred H. Gage (1999), 'Running Increases Cell Proliferation and Neurogenesis In The Adult Mouse Dentate Gyrus', *Nature Neuroscience*, 2, 3, 266–270; Spedding, M.T., Jay, J. Costa e Silva, and L. Perret (2005), 'A Pathophysiological Paradigm For The Therapy of Psychiatric Disease', Nature Reviews. Drug Discovery, Vol. 4, No. 6, pp. 467–476; Optale, Gabriele, Salvatore Capodieci, Pietro

Pinelli, Daniela Zara, Luciano Gamberini, Giuseppe Riva (2001), 'Music-enhanced Immersive Virtual Reality in the Rehabilitation of Memory Related Cognitive Processes and Functional Abilities: A Case Report', *Teleoperators & Virtual Environments*, 10, 4, 450–462; Eichenbaum, Howard and Harris, Kristen (2000), 'Toying With Memory in the Hippocampus', *Nature Neuroscience*, 3, 3, 205–206; Rampon, Claire, Ya-Ping Tang, Joe Goodhouse, Eiji Shimizu, Maureen Kyin and Joe Z. Tsien, (2000), 'Enrichment Induces Structural Changes and Recovery From Nonspatial Memory Deficits in CA1 NMDAR1-Knockout Mice', *Nature Neuroscience*, 3, 3, 238–244; Fischer, Andre, Farahnaz Sananbenesi, Xinyu Wang, Matthew Dobbin and Li-Huei Tsai (2007), 'Recovery of Learning and Memory Is Associated With Chromatin Remodelling', *Nature*, 447, 7141, 178–183; Van Dellen, Blakemore Anton, Deacon Colin, York Robert, Denis and Anthony J. Hannan, (2000), 'Delaying the Onset of Huntington's in Mice', *Nature*, 404, 6779, 721–722; Rampon, Claire, Ya-Ping Tang, Joe Goodhouse, Eiji Shimizu, Maureen Kyin and Joe Z. Tsien, (2000), 'Enrichment Induces Structural Changes and Recovery From Nonspatial Memory Deficits in CA1 NMDAR1-Knockout Mice', *Nature Neuroscience*, 3, 3, 238–244.

[8] For an experimental example, see **Harburger Lauren L., Talley J. Lambert** and **Karyn M. Frick** (2007), 'Age-Dependent Effects of Environmental Enrichment on Spatial Reference Memory in Male Mice', *Behavioural Brain Research*, 185, 1, 43–48.

[9] For a more detailed explanation and further references, see: **Walvis, Tjaco H.** (2003), 'Avoiding advert Research Disaster: Advertising and the Uncertainty Principle', *Journal of Brand Management*, 10, 6, 403–409.

[10] **Tierney, Joan** (2006), 'Enriched Environment: Putting Evidence Into Practice – Why Bother?', Presentations from Traumatic Brain Injury Functional Rehabilitation Conference, New Zealand.

[11] See **Walvis, Tjaco H**. 'Three Laws of Branding: Neuroscientific Foundations of Effective Brand Building', *Journal of Brand Management*, 16, 3, 176–194.

[12] **Van der Vorst, Roland R.R.** (2007), *Nieuwsgierigheid: Hoe We Dagelijks Worden Verleid*, Amsterdam: Nieuw Amsterdam.

[13] **Johnson, Steven** (2005), *Everything Bad is Good For You: How Today's Popular Culture Is Actually Making Us Smarter*, New York: Riverhead Books.

[14] *Financial Times*, 11 April 2008, 'Beaten on Costs, Companies Seek To Burnish Their Brands', p.7; *Business Standard*, 18 March 2008, 'Emaar Plans To Build Residences Designed By Georgio Armani', **www.business-standard.com**.

[15] *The Wall Street Journal Europe*, 'When You Want Your Virtual Trainer', 14 May 2008.

[16] See: Trend briefing 'From Status Symbols To Status Stories' April 2008, **www.trendwatching.com**.

[17] **Wasik, Bill** (2006), 'My Crowd, or Phase 5: A Report from the Inventor of the Flash Mob', *Harper's Magazine*, 312, 1870, 56–66

[18] **Li, Charlene,** and **Josh Bernoff** (2008), *Groundswell: Winning In A World Transformed By Social Technologies*, Boston, MA: Harvard Business Press.

[19] **Walvis, Tjaco H.** (2001), *Expo 2000 Hanover in Numbers*, Amsterdam: Stardust New Ventures.

[20] **Schmitt, Eric** (2004), 'What Next For TV Advertising?', *Forrester Report* Cambridge, MA: Forrester Research Inc.

[21] *The Wall Street Journal Europe*, 'Unilever Steps Up Move To Interactive-TV Ads', 14 May 2008.

[22] **McLuhan, Marshall** (1964), *Understanding Media: The Extension of Man*, Cambridge, MA: MIT Press.

[23] **Prahalad, C.K.** and **M.S. Krishnan** (2008), *The New Age of Innovation: Driving Co-Created Value Through Global Networks*, New York: McGrawHill.

[24] **Eco, Umberto** (1962), 'The Poetics of The Open Work', in Participation: *Documents of Contemporary Art* (2006), ed. Claire Bishop, London: Whitechapel/Cambridge, MA: MIT Press, 20–40.

Chapter Eight

[1] See my colleague Roland van der Vorst's forthcoming book on Hope: *Hoop: Hoe We Door de Toekomst Worden Verleid*, Amsterdam: Nieuw Amsterdam.

[2] The term 'mobilising minds' is taken from a book on organisational alignment by Bryan, Lowell L. and Claudia I. Joyce (2007), *Mobilizing Minds: Creating Wealth from Talent in the 21st Century Organisation*, New York: McGraw-Hill.

[3] **Knutson, B., S. Rick, G. Elliott Wimmer, D. Prelec,** and **G. Loewenstein,** (2007), 'Neural Predictors of Purchases', *Neuron*, 53, 1, 147–156.

[4] See: **Bargh, John A.** and **Tanya L. Chartrand** (1999), 'The Unbearable Automaticity of Being,' *American Psychologist*, 54, 7, 462–479; Wallis, Jonathan D, (2006), 'Evaluating Apples and Oranges', *Nature Neuroscience*, 9, 5, 596–598; Pan Xiaochuan, Kosuke Sawa, Ichiro Tsuda, Minoru Tsukada and Masamichi Sakagami (2008), Reward Prediction Based On Stimulus Categorization In Primate Lateral Prefrontal Cortex, *Nature Neuroscience*, 11, 6, 703–712.

[5] See **Greg Andersen** (2008), 'Marketers, Don't Just Blindly Follow Latest Media Trends', *AdAge*, 2 June, accessed at www. Adage.com.

[6] **Coricelli, Giorgio, Hugo D. Critchley, Mateus Joffily, John P. O'Doherty, Angela Sirigu** and **Raymond J. Dolan** (2005), 'Regret And Its Avoidance: A Neuroimaging Study Of Choice Behaviour', *Nature Neuroscience*, 8, 9, 1255–1262.

[7] **Van der Vorst, Roland R.R.** (2007), *Nieuwsgierigheid: Hoe We Dagelijks Worden Verleid*, Amsterdam: Nieuw Amsterdam.

[8] **Nagourney, Adam** and **Jeff Zeleny** (2007), 'Obama Formally Enters Presidential Race', *The New York Times*, 11 February, accessed at www.nytimes.com.

[9] **Greenwood, Jesse** and **Will Sansom** (2007), 'Behind the Hype: The Dark Knight', *Contagious,* 4th Quarter, 36–37; The Dark Knight ARG Wiki, Timeline, http://batman.wikibruce.com/Timeline, accessed 25 July 2008.

[10] **Li, Charlene** and **Josh Bernoff** (2008), *Groundswell: Winning In A World Transformed By Social Technologies*, Boston, MA: Harvard Business Press.

[11] **Madge, Jamie** (2007), 'Sophisticated Launches', *Contagious*, 4th Quarter, MA 34–35.

Chapter Nine

[1] **Klein, Naomi** (2000), *No Logo: No Space, No Choice, No Jobs*, New York: Picador.

[2] **Carr, Nick,** 'Neuromarketing Could Make Mind Reading the Ad-Man's Ultimate Tool', the *Guardian*, 3 April, 2008.

[3] For an excellent discussion on ethics and child advertising see Nairn, Agnes and Cordelia Fine (2008), 'Who's Messing With My Mind? The Implications Of Dual-Process Models For The Ethics Of Advertising To Children', *International Journal of Advertising*, 27, 3, 447–470.

[4] **Bernays, Edward L.** (1928), *Propaganda*, New York: Horace Liverlight.

[5] Any comparison or similarity with an actual person is coincidental. The hypothetical consumer activist is what she is: hypothetical.

[6] **Carr, Nick,** 'Neuromarketing Could Make Mind Reading the Ad-Man's Ultimate Tool', the *Guardian*, 3 April, 2008.

[7] **Aristotle,** Nicomachean Ethics (1998), Oxford: Oxford University Press.

[8] **Collini, Stefan** (1991), *Public Moralists: Political Thought and Intellectual Life in Great Britain 1850–1930*, Oxford: Clarendon, 178.

[9] **Mill, John Stuart** *Utilitarianism* (1998), Chapter 2: 'On Liberty and Other Essays', Oxford: Oxford University Press.

[10] **Mill, John Stuart** *Utilitarianism* (1998), Chapter 2: 'On Liberty and Other Essays', Oxford: Oxford University Press.

[11] **Dijksterhuis, Ap, Maarten W. Bos, Loran F. Nordgren** and **Rick B. van Baaren** (2006), 'On Making the Right Choice: The Deliberation-Without-Attention Effect', *Science*, 311, 1005–1007.

Chapter Ten

[1] **Goleman, Daniel** (1995), *Emotional Intelligence: Why It Can Matter More Than IQ*, New York: Bantam Books.

Index

ABN-AMRO 123
accessibility in brand choice 43
action
  in AIDA model 24, 213
  in brand choice 34
  in subconscious rationality 31–2
activation in brand association 76
Adidas 12–13, 15, 158, 160
advertising
  and branding 15–16
  interactive 158
  investment in 215
  subliminal 39–41
affective tags 50
AIDA in conscious-choice model 24–7, 213
Amazon 148–9
American Express 128
Apple 142–3
  advertising 15
  as brand house 127, 128
  packaging 162
  and participation 152
application in needs cocktail 73
Aristotle
  branding with brains 199–202, 206
  ethics and character 199–200, 203
  moral checklist 200–2
Armani, Giorgio 151
Arthur Andersen 89
attention in AIDA model 24, 213
attributes in needs cocktail 73
authenticity trap 13, 14
automatic affective valuation 30
Avoriaz 123–4, 156
awareness
  of brand choice 34
  and relevance 53–4
  in subconscious rationality 31

Barclay's Capital 95
Batman 160
Beckham, David 12
Bedbury, Scott 60
Bentham, Jeremy 203
Bernays, Edward 40, 194
Bic 89
Big Brother 159–60
Bliss, Tim 90–1
BMW 128, 160
BNP Paribas 95
Booz-Allen Hamilton 132
bounded rationality 27
Bourdieu, Pierre 51
Bower, Marvin 87–9
brain imaging 70
brain scanning techniques 36–8, 70
brains
  branding with 10–15
    Aristotle on 199–202
    Kant on 195–9
    Mill on 203–6
  and coherence 90–2
  and participation 143–7, 170–3
    deep impressions 143–5
    enrichment factors 145–7
    linking to individual goals 145
    multiplying existing connections in 144–5
brain's search engine 34–5

brand battle in subconscious 30–1
brand building approach 15–19
  branding and advertising 15–16
brand choice 10–11
  and accesibility 43
  algorithm for 10–12
    traps 13–14
  awareness battle in 54
  rational 35
  and relevance 50, 53
  search engine for 34–5
  situation- and category-specific 53
  in subconscious 29, 211
brand coherence profiling 125–6
brand concepts in needs cocktail 82
brand dilution trap 13, 116–17
brand evaluation 32–4
brand-led organisational change 130–4
brand love 54–6
brand memory loss 8
  preventing 92
brand mix and needs cocktail 75–7
brand portfolio alignment 126–30
  as game 128–30
  naming structure 127–8
  and organisational change 130–4
  repositioning 126–7
brand positioning 9, 89
brand socialisation 51–2
brand strategy 16
  adherence to 87–8
  charting 79–80
  integrating 161–2
  open-ended 155–7
branding
  with brains 10–15
    Aristotle on 199–202
    Kant on 195–9
    Mill on 203–6
  coherent 91
  and communication 180
  consistent 8
  more effective 212–13
  as subconscious persuasion 41–4
branding research 18–19
branding triangle 12–14, 67
brands
  asset values 5
  field of meaning of 50
  and share values 5–6
  tipping point for 117–21
    brand power 120–1
    marshmallow test 117–19
    resisting short-term gains 119–20

Capa, Robert 54
Cartier-Bresson, Henri 54, 56
catalysts in participation journey 176
Categorical Imperative (Kant) 196
central idea in creative brand concept 121–2
character and ethics (Aristotle) 199–200, 203
chief marketing officers (CMOs) 9
choice overload 23
CitiBank 95
Clarkson, Jeremy 102
co-creation as marketing 159–61
Coca-Cola 123, 158
  coherence in branding 94, 95, 98
coherence 87–110
  and the brain 90–2
  in brand choice algorithm 12
  brand promise for
    accountability, forgetting 109
    inconsistencies, avoiding 108–9
    repetition 107–8
    specific yet broad 107
  in branding 93–9
  as harmony 93–4
  implementation 135–6
    meaningful concepts 135–6
    people 135

tools for 136
inconsistencies, banning 97–8
and leadership 215–17
marshmallow test 88–90
measurement of 125–6
in Obama's campaign 168
and organisational change 130–4
and price 103–4
and propositions 104–6
repetition for 90–2, 94–5
tipping point for brands 117–21
brand power 120–1
marshmallow test 117–19
resisting short-term gains 119–20
coherent branding 91
Commercial Alert 36
Commerzbank 95
communication planning
conventional 179–88
end of 187–8
competition for brand choice 34
connecting as reason for participation 154
conscious-choice
model 24–5
as oxymoron 25–7
conscious decisions, subconsciously prepared 26
conscious deliberation, liklihood of 34
conscious evaluation 34
conscious veto 32–4
consciousness, limits of 23–7
consequences and ethics (Mill) 204–6
consideration set 33–4
consistency and coherence 90–1
contributing as reason for participation 154–5
conventional communication planning 179–88
end of 187–8
Corbijn, Anton 54
core brands 128
core mentality in creative brand concept 122–3
costs in participation journey 175
creative brand concept 121–5
central idea 121–2
core mentality 122–3
in decision making 124–5
visual identity 123–4
creativity
objective judgments of 17–18
and participation 217–18
Credit Suisse 95
customer control
as enrichment factor 146
in participation 147–52
games in 151–2
potential for 150–2
rules of the game 149–50
customer goals in participation journey 174
customers
and brands 6
goal-driven 8
mobilising 169–70
participation 8
subconscious choices of 7
'thick' information 67
'thin' information 74–7

Darhma Initiative 172
The Dark Knight campaign 172, 177–9, 180, 185
Deitsche Bank 95
deliberation 32–4
and consideration set 33–4
high involvement in 32
joint decisions in 32
and maturity 32
Descartes, René 24
desire in AIDA model 24, 213
dialogues in participatory branding 181–2
diary-reporting information for 'thick' information 67
Dichter, Ernst 69

discounts and coherence 103–4
Disney 127, 130–1
Disneyland 148
distinctive relevance 80–2
  subconscious in 81–2
DLJ 89
dopamine system 51
Dove 104–6, 121–2

eBay 56
Eco, Umberto 160–1
The Economist 123
Eisenstadt, Alfred 54
emotional benefits in needs cocktail 73
emotional intelligence 215
engagement, levels of 183–5
enrichment factors of participation 145–7
Enron 89
Epicurus 204
ethics
  and character (Aristotle) 199–200, 203, 206
  and consequences (Mill) 204–5, 206
  and intentions (Kant) 196, 198–9, 206
ethnographic information for 'thick' information 67
evaluation in brand association 76
executives
  brands' meaning for 6
  remuneration strategy 17
experiential benefits in needs cocktail 73

Facebook 154
FedEx 149
Financial Times 128
Ford, Henry 159
Forrester Research 24, 183
Freud, Sigmund 40, 194
fun as reason for participation 154
functional magnetic resonance imaging (fMRI) 25, 36, 70

games in participation 151–2
Getronics 120, 124
goal activation
  and needs cocktail 71
  and participation 145
  and relevance 50
  in subconscious rationality 29–30
goal of brand choice 34
Goleman, Daniel 215
Google 15, 34–5, 215
Gould, Elizabeth 143
gratification postponed 171
greatest happiness principle (Mill) 204

Harley-Davidson 6
harmony in branding 93–4
Havaianas 5, 179
'have it your way' as reason for participation 153
Heineken 149
heuristics 50
Hewlett-Packard 119
high involvement in deliberation 32
HSBC 95–6, 135
Huxley, Aldous 36

IBM 126–7
identity as reason for participation 153–4
identity loss trap 13
IKEA 215
inconsistencies
  avoiding 108–9
  at Volkswagen 99–103
inconsistencies in coherence
  banning 97–8
  costs of 98–9
indirect questions, asking 68–70
indirect reach in participatory branding 183–6

ING Wholesale Banking 96–7
intentions and ethics (Kant) 196, 198–9
interactive advertising 158
interest in AIDA model 24, 213

Jeep 78–9
Jobs, Steve 142
Johnson, Steven 151
Johnston, Samuel 39
joint decisions in deliberation 32

Kahneman, Daniel 30
Kandel, Eric 91
Kant, Immanuel
- branding with brains 195–9, 206
- ethical tests 196–7
- ethics and intentions 196, 198–9
- moral formula 197–8

Kaufmann, Andreas 56
Kennedy, John F. 168
King, Martin Luther Jr. 168
Krishnan, M.S. 159

leadership and coherence 215–17
learning as enrichment factor 146
LEGO 146–7, 148–9
Leica cameras 54–8, 162
- boosting relevance 56–7
- brand love 54–6
- response, analysing 57–8

Lenovo 5
levels of engagement 183–5
Levi's 14
Libet, Benjamin 25–6
Lømo, Terje 90–1
Lomu, Jonah 12
long-term potentiation 91
Lost 172

McKinsey & Company 61, 70–1
- coherence logic 87–90

McLuhan, Marshall 159
Macy's 154
marketing, participation as 155–61
- brand strategy 155–7
- co-creation 159–61
- new media 158–9

marketing funnel 24–5
marshmallow test 117–19
maturity and deliberation 32
Meijden, Eric van der 120, 124
Mercer 17
Merck, George 119
Mexx 153–4
Mill, John Stuart
- branding with brains 203–5, 206
- ethics and consequences 204–5

Mischel, Walter 118–19
moral checklist (Aristotle) 200–2
moral formula (Kant) 197–8
Morelisse, Huib 16
Morgan Stanley 95
mutually exclusive and collectively exhaustive (MECE) portfolios 128
MVRDV 156–7
MySpace 158, 169

Nachtwey, James 54
Nader, Ralph 36
narrative information for 'thick' information 67
needs cocktail
- brand concepts in 82
- brand strategy, charting 79–80
- ingredients 71–3
- mapping 78–9
- and 'thin' customer information 77–80

network effects 169
neuroeconomics 6
neurogenesis 143
neuromarketing 35–41
- differences with traditional approaches 44
- limits of 193–5
- subconscious, swaying 36–41
- suspicion and concerns over 43

Newton's apples 14–15

Nike 13, 70, 142
Nike Plus *(Nike+iPod)* 142–3, 162
  enrichment 146, 154
  and participation strategy 169, 177, 187
    catalyst 176
    indirect reach 185
    proposition 175
    rewards 172
Nintendo 151–2
Nokia 152

Obama, President Barack 136
  and coherence 168
  and participation strategy 167–70, 174–5, 176
open-ended brand strategy 155–7
Orange 133
organise self-organisation 150
Orwell, George 36
outcome control 148–9

Packard, David 119
Packard, Vance 40
PageRank™ 35
pain minimisation as enrichment factor 146
Panasonic 56, 57
Parker, Mark 142
participation 141–62
  biases against 180–8
    dialogue 181–2
    indirect reach 183–6
    rewards 186–7
    target groups 182–3
  and the brain 143–7, 170–3
    deep impressions 143–5
    enrichment factors 145–7
    linking to individual goals 145
    multiplying existing connections in 144–5
  in brand choice algorithm 12, 14
  and creativity 217–18
  customer control in 147–52
    games in 151–2
    potential for 150–2
    rules of the game 149–50
  as game 177–9
  gratification postponed 171
  importance of 161
  levels of engagement 183–5
  as marketing 155–61
    brand strategy 155–7
    co-creation 159–61
    new media 158–9
  opening up 161–2
  reasons for 152–5
  rewards for 171–2
  strategy, creating 173–9
    journey 173–7
  value, assessing 172–3
  virtual and physical 162
PepsiCo 89
Philips 133
Piëch, Ferdinand 99
Pinker, Stephen 27
place of use in needs cocktail 72
Prada 155–6
Prahalad, C.K. 159
price and coherence 103–4
process flexibility in customer control 148–9
Procter & Gamble 15, 126, 149
product category in needs cocktail 72
proposition in participation journey 174–5
propositions and coherence 104–6
Puma 153

relevance 49–62
  awareness battle in 53–4
  in brand choice algorithm 12
  choosing 49–54
  distinctive 80–2
  embracing 58–61
    customer learning and changing 60–1
    on low-cost brands 59
    rigorous implementation 58

starting at bottom 59–60
emotions as indicators of 53
establishing in 'thin' customer information 74
field of meaning of brands 50
of Leica cameras 54–8
boosting relevance 56–7
brand love 54–6
response, analysing 57–8
and social learning 51–2
as strategy 214–15
and survival 50
Renault 149
research statements in 'thin' customer information 74
rewards
as enrichment factor 146
in participation journey 175–6
in participatory branding 186–7
risk management, branding as 6
Royal Dutch Shell 7
RWE 16

Sachs, Jeffrey 61
St Elmo Lewis, E . 24
Schultz, Howard 115–17, 118, 120
scoreboard in participation journey 177
Second Life 148–9, 158
Sidgwick, Henry 204
Smart car 13
social class 51
social learning 51–2
social stimulation as enrichment factor 146
socialisation and relevance 51
Sontag, Susan 55
Sony Bravia 158
specificity in branding 93
Spielberg, Steven 36
Starbucks 115–17, 120, 125, 215
status as reason for participation 153–4
strategy, relevance as 214–15
stress minimisation as enrichment factor 146
Strong, Edward 24
Stuff magazine 56
subconscious
and choices 170
in distinctive relevance 81–2
gaining 26–7
researching 81–2
swaying in neuromarketing 36–41
subconscious customer goals 68
subconscious persuasion 40
subconscious rationality 27, 28–35, 213–14
action in 31–2
awareness in 31
brand battle in 30
goal activation in 29–30
survival and relevance 50
sustainability 61
synapses 144

target groups in participatory branding 182–3
Tata 5
'thick' customer information 67
indirect question, asking 68–70
listening 70–1
needs cocktail
ingredients 71–3
'thin' customer information 74–7
brand mix 75–7
brand tracking tools, repairing 74
Tierney, Dr. Joan 146
time in participation journey 175
time of use in needs cocktail 72

UBS 95
Unilever 149, 158
coherence 104–6
repositioning 126–7
Utilitarianism (Mill) 203

Vicary, James 40
viral advertising 158
Virgin Atlantic 123

visual identity in creative brand
concept 123–4
Volkswagen 99–103
Vondruska, Jamie 103

Wal-Mart 119
Walton, Sam 119
Warner Brothers 179, 185
Wii 151
Wikipedia 14

YouTube 158

Zaltman Metaphor Elicitation
Technique (ZMet) 68